D0425730

You, _____ ,
have what it takes
to go Over the Top.

Over the Top

~

Zig Ziglar

THOMAS NELSON PUBLISHERS

Nashville • Atlanta • London • Vancouver

Published in Nashville, Tennessee, by Thomas Nelson, Inc.

Annual Inflation Data 1944 to 1992 from © *Stocks, Bonds, Bills,
and Inflation 1993 Yearbook*™, Ibbotson Associates, Chicago (annu-
ally updates work by Roger G. Ibbotson and Rex A. Sinquefield).
Used with permission. All rights reserved.

Unless otherwise noted, Scripture quotations are from THE NEW
KING JAMES VERSION. Copyright © 1979, 1980, 1982, Thomas
Nelson, Inc., Publishers. Scripture quotations noted KJV are from the
King James Version of the Bible.

Library of Congress Cataloging-in-Publication Data

Ziglar, Zig.
    Over the top / Zig Ziglar. — Rev. ed.
        p.   cm.
    Includes bibliographical references.
    ISBN 0-7852-7119-8
    1. Success.   2. Conduct of life.   I. Title.
    BJ1611.2.Z52   1997
    158.1—dc21   97-27090
                                                               CIP

Printed in the United States of America.

13 14 15 BVG 00 99

To my friend and mentor,
Fred Smith, who is fun and inspiring.
He is also the wisest and
most effective teacher I've ever had.

Contents

Objectives

Since a significant portion of *Over the Top* deals with establishing a goals program, I share with you my goals for this book in your life.

1. To give you legitimate hope and fuel it with encouragement, which is as vital to the soul as oxygen is to the body.

2. To share with you how you can acquire more of the things money will buy and all of the things money won't buy.

3. To show you how to have employment security in a world where job security no longer exists.

4. To persuade you that failure is an event, not a person.

5. To help you change the picture you have of yourself so you can change your perception of what life has to offer.

6. To encourage you to make decisions today that will enable you to live well *and* finish well.

7. To demonstrate why you've got to be before you can do and do before you can have.

8. To raise both your IQ and your EI (emotional intelligence).

9. To help you develop the right attitudes, combine them with the right skills, and develop a character foundation to ensure a balanced success.

10. To "sell" you on why you should make friends with your past so you can focus on the present and safeguard your future.

11. To show you how you can be happier, healthier, more prosperous, more secure, have more friends, greater peace of mind, better family relationships, and more hope.

12. To show you why you can have everything in life you want if you will just help enough other people get what they want.

This book covers one procedure that can double your income, improve family relationships, and make you happier and healthier.

Mystery Solved

*Ninety-five percent of the people who hear, under-
stand, and agree with a principle do not have the ability to apply it to their lives because they do not have
the necessary resources.*   Stanford University

When I acquired the Stan-
ford University information, I really got excited because it
solved for me some mysteries about life and motivation. Why
do so many people start on a project, get marvelous results for
a brief period of time, and then revert to their old humdrum
way of thinking and living? Why does motivation change some
people permanently and others only temporarily? Why do we
get roughly two hundred times as many letters, phone calls,
and personal statements from people who say my books and
tapes changed their lives as we do from people who say my
presentation changed their lives?

The answer is now clear. They hear me speak and get excited, then they encounter negative situations, problems, and
people. Little by little, over a period of time, they lose their
enthusiasm, and they are back on square one.

Wonderful news! You have in your hands the resource necessary to implement and apply the princples that will change
and enrich your life.

As you read *Over the Top* you will note that I never make a
promise or promises, as I did on the preceding page, without
giving you a plan to fulfill the promise. You will in each case
discover why you should use the plan and, even more important, how you can. *Over the Top* is the resource book that will

enable you to keep hope alive and give you the inspiration, conviction, and know-how to follow through.

Motivation, as I will say in the book, is not permanent—but then neither is bathing. However, if we bathe every day, we are ahead of the game. From a motivational point of view, if we deliberately seek encouragement (motivation) on a daily basis, it will become a habit and enable us to get ahead and stay ahead in life.

CHALLENGE: After you have thoroughly read and highlighted the parts of the book that are most meaningful to you, keep this book highly visible so that you can grab it at any time of the day or night. Then I challenge you to read a thought or page. I promise there will be some information on it that will reignite the sparks and get you excited again about what's really important in life. In short, you will receive the encouragement you need to continue your winning ways.

Preface

Somebody once said that truth could be denied, but it could not be avoided. I agree. The information presented in *Over the Top* is designed to give you hope based on some of the great truths of life. In the process of sharing this information, I will use many real-life stories, examples, illustrations, and parables to make a number of very important points. When combined, these points reveal a solid blueprint for life based on facts and principles, not theories. I assure you that I have researched and evaluated the information in *Over the Top* from psychological, theological, and physiological points of view and have secured endorsements from authorities in each of these disciplines.

Over the Top gives you the guidelines you need to exchange the fears, guilt, and anger of the past for a future built on a solid base and filled with hopeful expectancy. Since encouragement is the fuel of hope, encouraging thoughts and ideas are on every page to get you started and keep you going. As you read, you'll see that the people and companies that build their lives and businesses on an ethical base, and operate on the belief that their purpose in life is to serve others, are the ones that enjoy the greatest success. Most important, you will come to know that without God all things are permissible, but with God all things are possible. In the process you will understand why God's possibles will produce infinitely more over-the-top people than man's permissibles.

Thank You

Over the years many clients, friends, acquaintances, family, and staff have supplied me with information and inspiration that have enriched my life and made *Over the Top* possible. However, there are a few people whose contributions are so significant I want to give them special recognition.

I especially want to express my gratitude and love for the most significant person in my life, my wife, Jean Abernathy Ziglar, The Redhead, who has been my encourager since November 1946. Her ability to critique and make thoughtful suggestions has been invaluable. Her willingness to handle many of my "usual" responsibilities has enabled me to complete this project.

Second, I would like to thank my editor. Her ability to cut through the issues, pinpoint the objectives, and stay focused has helped me to be more concise and effective. Her availability to discuss thoughts, ideas, concepts, and philosophies has been extremely helpful. Her writing ability makes it easy for me to understand why the folks at *Guideposts* selected her as one of 15 people from over 4,400 contestants to receive their highly specialized training in their biannual *Guideposts* Writers Workshop. She's my youngest daughter, Julie Ziglar Norman.

I would also like to thank my late daughter Suzan, whose knowledge, ideas, intuition, and "feelings" vocabulary helped make this a better book. Her husband, Chad Witmeyer, along with Julie's husband, Jim Norman, stretched me with challenging thoughts and insights that will be helpful to many readers. And of considerable importance is my executive assistant, Laurie Magers. In addition to her regular responsibilities, her servant's heart attitude while working many extra hours on this manuscript was invaluable.

One constant source of information and inspiration has been my mentor, Fred Smith, whose thought-provoking observations and ideas added much to the message. As always, Bernie Lofchick (Brother Bern) dissected every word and made innumerable suggestions that made the message live and breathe in an even more usable manner.

Dr. J. Allan Petersen, through his monthly publication *Better Families,* contributed significantly to the *Over the Top* message and image. Psychologist Don Beck has given me some interesting ideas and challenged me to keep growing while validating some of the concepts I share with you. Forest Tennant, M.D., is an ongoing source of inspiration and encouragement and keeps me up-to-date on new research on everything from proper sleeping habits to the latest in the drug war.

I'd also like to thank Dr. Adrian Rogers, Rabbi Daniel Lapin, Leland Heller, M.D., Dr. John Maxwell, Dr. Ike Reighard, Dr. William Arthur Ward (posthumously), Dr. Ken Cooper, psychiatrist Louis Cady, and psychologists Robert Wubbolding and John Leddo for their ideas and encouragement.

And to the most famous, willing, and prolific contributor of all, the world-renowned Anonymous, a heartfelt expression of gratitude. To all authors, speakers, teachers, preachers, philosophers, friends, neighbors, clients, boosters, and people on the street, your contributions have been monumental, and I'm grateful for them. See you *Over the Top*.

ZIG ZIGLAR

A book of passion

The dictionary says that *passion* is "a strong emotion, an ardent love, zeal, eager desire, hope and joy." It has been my observation that in every field of endeavor the men and women who reach the mountaintops of life have a passion to give their all and be the best they can be. For example, the fathers of our country were passionate believers in freedom.

Maribeau said that "none but men of strong passions are capable of rising to greatness." Tennyson said, "The happiness of a man in his life does not consist in the absence but in the mastering of his passions." Franklin said that "he is a governor that governs his passions and he is a servant that serves them."

Misdirected passion ultimately becomes an obsession, and there is a substantial difference between having a "passion" for something and being "obsessed" with something. Passion is positive, controllable, and tremendously energizing. An obsession is negative and destructive. The person with a passion for what he or she does becomes a peak performer. Those who have an obsession with it become workaholics. People with a passion do what they are doing out of love for the people they're doing it for and for the results they expect to obtain. The person with an obsession, who becomes a workaholic, will work out of fear and/or greed or denial.

Directed passion founded on an ethical, moral base enables anyone to utilize his or her full potential. The results can be awesome. Throughout *Over the Top* you will read story after story of average people whose accomplishments have dramatically exceeded their abilities. Give passion the credit.

To be candid, I am a man of many passions. I have a passion to serve my God, my family, and my country. I have a passion to be and to do the best I'm capable of being and doing, regardless of what my mission of the moment happens to be.

I have a passion to positively impact your life by persuading you that you are endowed with the seeds of greatness and that when you use what you've got, you can do great things.

I say that because I have a conviction that passion—like courage—is transferable, so a major objective of mine is to transfer some of my passions, as well as the passions of the people you will meet in *Over the Top,* to you. To accomplish that objective, I will speak from my head and heart to your head and heart because the head is the gateway to the heart. When you are logically informed and emotionally inspired, you will be moved to recognize, develop, and use all that is within you and become the best you can be. That's all God or man can ask of you. Fortunately, that will be more than enough to take you over the top.

CHAPTER ONE

What or where is the top?

Men and women are limited not by the place of their birth, not by the color of their skin, but by the size of their hope.   John Johnson

John Johnson was fortunate enough to be raised in Arkansas City, Arkansas. That was a real break, because it is an established but little-known fact that Arkansas City, Arkansas, is the geographical center of the world. You can start there and go anywhere in the world you want to go—and the maximum distance is just twelve thousand miles. Mr. Johnson went less than two thousand miles from the tin-roofed shotgun house where he was born, but he did go far enough to live in a high-rise on Chicago's Gold Coast and next door to Bob Hope in Palm Springs, California, and he has been listed as one of the four hundred wealthiest men in America.

You, too, are fortunate because regardless of where you live you are in the geographical center of the world. You can go from where you are to anywhere you want to go, and I speak of far more than just a geographical location. To be fair, I must warn you that it is not an easy trip. There will be the inevitable hills and valleys before you can go over the top. However, if you will supply the want to, the information you have in your hands will supply the how to. Though the trip is demanding, it is also exhilarating. The good news is that the view from over the top is spectacular—and the rewards, including much of what money can buy and all of what money can't buy, make the trip far more than worthwhile. Best of all, you will discover that even though the rewards are great, what you become by reaching your destination is far more important than what you get by reaching your over-the-top destination.

THINK ABOUT IT

It is not who your parents are—it's who you are and what you do that count.

Fifty-two percent of the CEOs of the Fortune 500 companies are from lower-middle-class or poor families, and 80 percent of the millionaires in America are first-generation millionaires. Opportunity is alive and well.

Gerry Arrowood was baking cakes and taking in sewing but later became the vice president in charge of sales training for a multimillion-dollar cosmetics company.

Seventy-five percent of the three hundred world-class leaders in a recent study were raised in poverty, had been abused as children, or had some serious physical disability.

Charlie Wedemeyer can only move his mouth and blink his eyes, but he coached his football team to its only state high-school championship.

Pam Lontos was a depressed, overweight household executive who had been told by her psychologist that she could never get better, yet she became a published author and speaker.

John Foppe was born without arms, but the United States Junior Chamber of Commerce in 1993 named him one of the Top Ten Outstanding Young Americans.

John Johnson, the great-grandson of slaves, was shy, insecure, inarticulate, bowlegged, wore homemade clothes, and was subjected to ridicule, but he became one of the wealthiest people in America.

Jan McBarron-Liberatore had been a nurse for eight years, weighed over two hundred pounds, and was a heavy smoker. Today she's a slender nonsmoker and her colleagues call her Dr. (as in M.D.) McBarron.

NOTE: You just read nine success stories of individuals and groups who overcame adversity to achieve remarkable success. Surely, *hope* just reared its head for you to see it face-to-face. (If they can, you can, too.)

All of these people succeeded by following over-the-top principles. My conviction is strong that these same principles will work for you if you will work on them. Let's start the trip over the top by looking at some serious questions.

LOTS OF QUESTIONS AND SOME ANSWERS

Is there such a thing as the top? Is the top a destination, or is it really a journey, as I have repeatedly heard?

With the help of thousands of people, I've learned that everybody wants to be happy, healthy, reasonably prosperous, and secure, to have friends, peace of mind, good family relationships, and hope. Many, if not all of these things, are open to change—sometimes instantly and dramatically. You can have it all one day and lose all or most of it the next day. QUESTION: Were you ever at the top one day and at the bottom the next? Are life and success that fickle?

Is the top defined by your position and prestige in your community? Are you at the top when you have what you want—or are you there when you want what you have? Are you at the top when you know who you are—and whose you are—or are you there when you are rich, famous, envied, and idolized by millions?

Is the single mother with a limited education who demonstrates her love and accepts her responsibility by working two jobs to feed, clothe, educate, and give her children a chance in life at the top?

How old must you be when you get to the top? Can a teenager be at the top? Can you stay there, once you have arrived, for the rest of your life? Can you reach the top by yourself, or do you need help from others?

Can you be at the top and not be successful, or can you be successful and not be at the top? Can you be at the top and not really like what you do, or must your heart really sing because of what you do in order for you to be at the top?

If you are rich, well known, successful, and respected in your professional life but have a string of failures in your personal and family lives, are you at the top? If you have rich and satisfying personal and family lives but struggle in your business or professional life, are you at the top? If you haven't made it in your personal, family, or business life, can you reverse a lifetime of failure and frustration at your age and still make it to the top? Is it really true that failure is an event and not a person?

What is the top as God sees it versus the top as man sees it? How can you know when you have reached the top? Is the top a clearly defined place? Is it a state of mind? Is Madonna at the top, or is it Mother Teresa who is at the top?

There must be dozens—even hundreds—of questions concerning this matter. I'm going to answer enough of them to persuade you that you can make it to the top and then go over the top. However, I doubt that anyone can think of all of the questions, much less come up with all of the answers. Fortunately, many questions do not need answers, but this I promise: Within the pages of this book are all the answers you will need to reach whatever the top is for you in your life's journey. Your responsibility and opportunity are to locate the an-

> **Your first reading will produce realistic hope and encouragement. Your second and third readings will produce even better results.**

swers and take the necessary steps to get the desired results. You might even have to read *Over the Top* several times to get the answers you need and want.

Now let's turn back the clock, take a short stroll down memory lane, and explore the objectives of *Over the Top*.

SEE YOU AT THE TOP

More than twenty years have passed since I wrote my first book, *See You at the Top*. I have written this sequel to show how and where the foundational principles I taught in the first book have led me and countless others. *See You at the Top* was the result of thirty years of experience. *Over the Top* spans a half century and includes information I've gained by reading and researching an average of three hours daily for the last twenty-five years.

I view *See You at the Top* as somewhat of a basic or foundational book on motivation and positive living. The results have been so outstanding they speak for themselves. The fact that *People* magazine identified it as the eighth-best-selling hardback book of the decade—and it still sells approximately forty thousand copies each year—verifies the effectiveness and timelessness of its message. To use a baseball analogy, the concepts of *See You at the Top* enabled many people to move into the major leagues.

Over the Top will help you secure that position in the major leagues, and it will enable you to step up to the plate with even more confidence and hit the ball out of the park with more frequency. By the time you've finished reading *Over the Top,* which delves considerably deeper into the hows and whys of living life with values, character, honesty, integrity, and sensitivity than did *See You at the Top,* you'll be more at peace with yourself and be able to accomplish more with your skills and abilities. You'll be able to do more of the things you must do in a shorter period of time. This will give you more time to do the things you want to do with the people you love to be with. You'll be able to put more into life, which means you'll be able to get more out of life.

LET'S GROW *OVER THE TOP* TOGETHER

In the years since I wrote *See You at the Top,* according to my family, I have learned a few things—among them, to be more compassionate, more accepting, and more understanding. I have apologized to my children for being such a stickler in their growing-up years about not letting them express negative feelings of any kind. Ol' Zig has learned an awful lot about life in the last twenty years, primarily that much of life in-

> **❝** *Living has taught me the true application of the theories and concepts I once struggled to understand.* **❞**

volves moral absolutes and that truth is truth, and mistakes are minimized when you acknowledge them and take appropriate action.

I, like many of you, have read countless books, listened to hundreds of tapes, and quizzed every authority I have come in contact with. I have simplified the process of discerning how to, when to, and why to take steps toward a better tomorrow. My wife and children tell me how reassuring it is to have a reality-based husband and father. Twenty years ago, I would not have believed it possible to be too positive. Today, I know from personal experience that some of my positive thinking was actually denial of reality. I will go into detail on that one a little later in a section about what positive thinking will do and what it won't do.

The basis for *See You at the Top* is a stairway to the top. A picture of the stairs with the steps that lead to success is in the front part of the book. Each step has a word or words printed on it. The first step has *self-image* printed on it. The second has *relationships;* the third, *goals;* the fourth, *attitude;* the fifth, *willingness to work;* and the sixth, *desire.* At the top of the staircase is a door with several wonderful results of having taken the first six steps printed on it. *Over the Top* is about opening that door and claiming life's treasures.

Because I have long since opened and walked through that door, I will tell you what it is like to live over the top and how you can join me there.

Hope is the principal ingredient to do just that. As a matter of fact psychiatrist Alfred Adler says that hope is the foundational quality of all change. Think about it for a moment. Without hope there is no action. The unemployed individual with no hope of finding a job will not look for one. The couple whose marriage is in trouble will make no effort to mend the fences if they feel there is no hope in reconciling their differences. The student who has no hope of passing won't bother to study.

Industries have been built on hope. Cosmetics companies sell hope. Diet programs sell hope. Exercise programs sell hope. Education sells hope.

Life itself, from time to time, presents us with what we perceive as being "hopeless situations." However, I want to strongly reinforce the concept throughout this book that there are really very few hopeless situations—only people who lose hope in the face of those situations. That's the reason you will find "hope builders" as you turn each page, because when the going gets tough, that's when the hopeful keep going.

Getting started is, of course, the first step because, as

speaker Joe Sabah says, "You don't have to be great to start, but you have to start to be great."

To this thought I add, encouragement is the fuel of hope. It's true that people become what you encourage them to be, not what you nag them to be.

Planning also produces hope. Example: Lose one ounce each day (you can do that) and in one year you will lose nearly twenty-three pounds. If you need to lose weight, you probably just said to yourself, "I can do that." That's hope, my friends, and this book is loaded with hope-building examples. Read on.

With enough hope in your life you are going to have considerable enthusiasm and zest for what you are attempting to accomplish, and with each accomplishment that enthusiasm will build. The English word *enthusiasm* comes from two Greek words—*en,* which means "in," and *theos,* which literally means "God within."

I love what newspaper columnist Niki Scott said in her column "Working Woman":

Enthusiasm is hard to define, difficult to maintain, impossible to fake for long. It's a genuinely optimistic, energetic way of looking at almost everything, an attitude which allows us to tackle the most difficult, troublesome jobs with the cheerful certainty that we'll get them done and do them well. A positive attitude is no substitute for competence and hard, focused work. We all know people who "enthuse"—make a great show of scurrying busily around—but, in the end, don't deliver.

The truth is, we can be enthusiastic and professional at the same time. We can get the work out and still joke about it, tackle difficult situations and still look for their positive aspects. We can be the sort of people who are seldom self-absorbed and almost never gloomy, who have the knack of making the people around us feel better, who make the of-

fice bearable on dismal Monday mornings and sunny on Friday afternoons.

The neat thing about the book you are reading at this instant is that it is written with the idea in mind to help you achieve the objectives Niki Scott has so eloquently described.

> *Success is going from failure to failure without loss of enthusiasm.*
> Winston Churchill

LIFE *OVER THE TOP* STILL HAS ITS MOMENTS

Over the Top, as a practical matter, was signed, sealed, and sent to the publisher. Back it came with an interesting—and frustrating—challenge. I was told that I must clearly identify the *top* before the book could serve its intended purpose. In my own mind, I thought that would be a very simple process, but in reality it was anything but simple. I literally wrestled with it for three solid months. I wrote many pages; some of them contained germs of truth, but none of them specifically identified the top.

I did everything as a writer that I knew to do. I read every available piece of literature, talked with people I look to for advice and counsel, reread much of the manuscript, and took many long walks that almost always produce results. Still nothing came forth. Then, believing I had so saturated my thinking that a solution would surely come, I pushed it all aside and forgot about it. The breakthrough finally came at such an unexpected time I was left scrambling for a piece of paper. Here's what happened.

My wife (whom I lovingly refer to as "The Redhead"*) and

---

* In private conversation I call her Sugar Baby. Her name is Jean.

I were in Shreveport, Louisiana, visiting her sister, Eurie Aber-nathy. Because of multiple sclerosis, Eurie lives in Heritage Manor South Nursing Home. Each time we go there I feel like a fish out of water. I have devoted my life to finding solutions to problems, but many of the nursing home residents have problems that are beyond human solution. I see things that I have difficulty dealing with, and I stand around feeling help-less and confused.

In contrast, The Redhead feels right at home. I watch in ad-miration as she moves easily from one resident to the next, exclaiming with heartfelt sincerity how happy she is to see them again and inquiring with true interest about their health and their families as she affectionately hugs them. They re-spond to her with brightening eyes and widening smiles. Watching The Redhead naturally do what confounds me is one of the most beautiful sights I'm ever privileged to witness.

As I watched, I was eventually overcome by my feelings of inadequacy and left the room. As I did, I started praying, ask-ing God to give me compassion, understanding, and a spirit of helpfulness. Even as I prayed, my heart was touched, and I experienced a newfound peace. I walked back in and sat down at the table in the community room with my sister-in-law and The Redhead. Suddenly, ideas began to flow. Using the receipt from the motel we had just left, I started writing. Over 90 percent of what I wrote in the next twenty minutes is what appears on the next page under the heading "THE TOP." Some of it was obviously influenced by my surround-ings, but most of it came from my experiences, the experi-ences of others, and the research I've done in all areas of life. However, many of the thoughts and ideas were truly inspired by my prayer. I encourage you to *slowly* read each of the fif-teen points and think about the significance of each one in your own life. Then place each of the fifteen points on a 3″ × 5″ card and make it a focal point for one week.

THE TOP

You are at the top when . . .

1. You clearly understand that failure is an event, not a person; that yesterday ended last night, and today is *your* brand-new day.
2. You have made friends with your past, are focused on the present, and optimistic about your future.
3. You know that success (a win) doesn't make you, and failure (a loss) doesn't break you.
4. You are filled with faith, hope, and love; and live without anger, greed, guilt, envy, or thoughts of revenge.
5. You are mature enough to delay gratification and shift your focus from your *rights* to your *responsibilities*.
6. You know that failure to stand for what is morally right is the prelude to being the victim of what is criminally wrong.
7. You are secure in who you are, so you are at peace with God and in fellowship with man.
8. You have made friends of your adversaries, and have gained the love and respect of those who know you best.
9. You understand that others can give you pleasure, but genuine happiness comes when you do things *for* others.
10. You are pleasant to the grouch, courteous to the rude, and generous to the needy.
11. You love the unlovable, give hope to the hopeless, friendship to the friendless, and encouragement to the discouraged.
12. You can look back in forgiveness, forward in hope, down in compassion, and up with gratitude.
13. You know that "he who would be the greatest among you must become the servant of all."
14. You recognize, confess, develop, and use your God-given physical, mental, and spiritual abilities to the glory of God and for the benefit of mankind.
15. You stand in front of the Creator of the universe, and He says to you, "Well done, thou good and faithful servant."

What or where is the top? **11**

> **❝** *The solution to a problem I had wrestled with for three solid months came to me when I completely forgot about my needs and became engrossed in finding a way to meet the needs of others.* **❞**

Now that I have invested all this time in identifying the top, I'd like to make two apparently contradictory statements. I've identified more than success or the top. I've really identified *significance,* which is beyond success because it is spiritual. Ironically, as I've identified the top, I've far more clearly identified the foundation. By building on the top (everything of value has a foundation), you place yourself in position to achieve success and significance in the eyes of God and in the hearts of men. When that happens, you are not just at the top, you are over the top.

I understand that your objective at this moment might well be survival, so the first objective of *Over the Top* is to help you survive. The second objective is to move you from survival to stability, then from stability to success, and finally, from success to significance.

CHAPTER TWO

Right Attitude +
Specific Skills +
Golden Rule
Philosophy

Character
= Complete Success

Each of us will one day be judged by our standard of life, not by our standard of living; by our measure of giving, not by our measure of wealth; by our simple goodness, not by seeming greatness.

William Arthur Ward

The formula in the title of this chapter removes both fear and guilt because you will do the *right* thing in the *right* way because you are the *right* kind of person. With the burdens of fear and guilt removed you feel good about yourself and your climb over the top will be faster and easier.

THIS ASSUMPTION COULD BE WRONG

Let me assume, just for a moment, that your life has been one long series of disappointments, frustrations, and setbacks with the result that you really are not too optimistic about your future. Since the principal ingredient of *Over the Top* is hope fueled with encouragement, let me encourage you to remember the brief example I used in chapter 1 about three hundred world-class leaders. They clearly understood that what happens to you is not nearly as important as how you handle what happens to you. They also understood that failure is an event, not a person, and that yesterday really did end last night. They learned to respond to difficulties—and that's positive—instead of getting upset and reacting, which is negative.

I believe responding is a major key in accomplishing anything. *Over the Top* gives you solid teaching principles and motivational/inspirational techniques that will enable you to move from wherever you might be toward the top we all seek. With that in mind, let's look carefully at the content of this chapter as we explore the importance of the right attitude plus specific skills combined with the golden rule philosophy, all built on a solid character base.

ATTITUDE OR SKILL?

When I was in the seventh grade, I decided to go out for the boxing team. As a street fighter or, more appropriately, a playground gladiator, I was pretty handy with my dukes. However, when I got into the boxing ring, I very quickly learned there's a dramatic difference between having a nonstop slugfest on the school ground and fighting in a ring under the watchful eye of a referee. Certain rules and procedures were under strict observance in the ring, and more important, the fight moved from a freelance brawl to somewhat of a science.

I weighed in at 82½ pounds, so I was the second-smallest guy. The smallest was a classmate named Joe Stringer who weighed in at all of 62 pounds, so he and I were designated as sparring partners. Needless to say, I felt confident—and even a little guilty—being matched against such a little guy. However, he had been on the boxing team since the fifth grade and clearly understood the defensive aspects of boxing as well as the fact that a straight punch was the shortest distance to my nose.

I shall never forget the rude awakening I experienced about three and a half seconds after we started the first round and his left connected with the end of my nose. He apparently thought I had a short memory because about two seconds later, there it was again! I'm here to tell you that I never got so tired of stopping leather with the end of my nose in my life! Before the first round was over, I was somewhat embarrassed and hurt (and hurting), and I had about decided that I was really too busy to go out for the boxing team anyhow.

Fortunately, Coach Perminter, a man of real compassion, stopped the sparring (it was really more like pitch and catch and I wasn't doing any pitching) after one round. He took me aside and started instructing me on how to protect my nose and throw a few jabs of my own. The next day Joe gave me another lesson—though it was not quite as painful. By the end of the week, because of my extra twenty pounds, I was able to defend myself with a little more effectiveness. By the end of the second week, I was even able to get in a few licks of my own, and by year's end, the weight advantage, training, coaching, and experience really paid off.

Here's my point: When I first stepped into the ring, I was a confident, excited, positive thinker. All of those things disappeared in the flash of an eye (or maybe a fist!). All I'm saying is that in addition to having a positive attitude and enthusiasm for what you're doing, you have to learn the skills of your trade. Enthusiasm, by itself, is like running in the dark. You might get there, but you might also get killed on the way.

Enthusiasm and positive thinking are important, but they will take you only so far—and alone they will not keep you over the top. Example: For many years I was in the world of selling (still am), and many times I've seen men and women launch their sales careers with confidence and enthusiasm but with very little training. Unfortunately, in far too many cases, a constant series of rejections or refusals caused many of them to grow discouraged and quit because they did not understand the sales process. They simply did not have answers to the customers' legitimate questions and/or objections. That's the reason—whatever the field of endeavor—we need the qualities of excitement, persistence, confidence, and enthusiasm, but we also need the skills to go over the top and stay there.

Now let's take a close look at what happens when you have the necessary skills but not the right attitude.

In December of 1984, my son, Tom, and I were headed home from Phoenix, Arizona, after playing in a golf tournament. The weather had been beautiful during the tournament, but on the day we left Phoenix, it was hailing and traffic was heavy. When we reached the airport, there was such a traffic jam we couldn't get close to unload our bags. We got soaked! When we got inside the terminal building, there were 11,286 people (approximately), and most of them were upset!

We walked to the gate to catch our flight to Dallas, and there were 1,121 (roughly) irate passengers waiting to get their boarding passes for the flight to Dallas. All of them, or so it seemed, were more than just a little upset—mostly with the gate agent. They were blaming him for the weather, the delay, the computer foul-up, and even the general economic condition of the country. Each one proceeded to unload all his or her woes and anger on him.

INSTANT IMPROVEMENT

When we first got in line, the agent was a fair-skinned blond, but I noticed that as each person dumped on him, the red in his neck moved progressively upward. By the time we were face-to-face with him, he was a flaming red-head. He looked as if he had just gotten some junk mail, postage due. Somebody or in his case, everybody, had obviously licked all the red off his candy, or some similar tragedy had befallen him. At any rate, he was not a happy camper.

As my son and I stepped up to get our boarding passes, I enthusiastically greeted the gate agent, as I generally do, with the words "Good morning. How ya doin'?"

The young man looked at me and with a heavy dose of sarcasm replied, "Compared to who?"

I smilingly responded, "Compared to the individual who doesn't have a job, who doesn't have nice, warm clothes to wear or a comfortable building to work in, compared to those people who have no future they can call their own. And especially compared to those people who live in lands where there's no freedom of speech, travel, or worship. How ya doin'?"

Talk about a change in a human being! It was complete, total, and instantaneous. He grinned so widely he could have eaten a banana sideways. He replied, "I'm doing much, much better—and thank you very much for reminding me."

The young agent's change in attitude led to a dramatic

> **❝** *When you choose to be pleasant and positive in the way you treat others, you have also chosen, in most cases, how you are going to be treated by others.* **❞**

change in his actions. As a matter of fact, he got so excited he moved my son and me up to first class! And that excitement continued as he dealt with the passengers behind us. He was more cheerful, courteous, and patient in the face of complaints.

QUESTION: Do you believe that, as a direct result of a conversation that lasted less than thirty seconds, he instantaneously became a better gate agent and a more valued airline employee? Yes or no? Do you believe at that point that he even had a fair chance of keeping his job? Yes or no? Do you believe that if he was married with children, he was a better husband and father when he got home? Yes or no?

Yes is the most probable answer to each of these questions, so here's another: What did I teach him about being a better airline employee, a better husband, or a better father? Obviously, I taught him nothing—but he was better because he experienced a substantial change in attitude. I need to remind you that the weather was still bad, the planes were still running late, the computer was still down, and the passengers were still irate. However, things were substantially better for him because he had changed his attitude.

QUESTION: Why did he change?

ANSWER: It's true that as ye sow (or as somebody else sows), so shall ye reap.

COMPUTER VERSION: Garbage in, garbage out. All morning long he had been dealing with angry, frustrated, impatient, irrational people who had been dumping negative verbal garbage in his mind. He had been reaping that garbage, and instead of using his knowledge, expertise, and training, he was dumping it right back on them.

That's when my son and I entered the picture and introduced the gate agent to the Ziglarized version: Put the good stuff in, and you'll get the good stuff out. I took the same as-ye-sow principle and sowed thoughts in a friendly, enthusiastic, optimistic manner. He reaped those words, became motivated, and started sowing them in the minds of the next passengers with remarkable results. The message is simple—

but life-changing. What goes into your mind affects your thinking, your thinking affects your performance—and your performance affects your future.

I taught the gate agent nothing about the skills he needed to be an effective gate agent, nor did I teach him anything about being a better husband or parent. His performance, after my son and I departed, demonstrated conclusively that he already had the skills necessary to be an extremely effective gate agent. However, those skills were negated because he had an advanced case of "stinkin' thinkin'," which was well on its way to turning into "hardening of the attitudes." When his attitude changed, he was able to use his skills and, consequently, maximize his performance.

TWO POINTS: First, skill is critically important, but skill alone will not take you over the top—and keep you there. All companies, including our own, periodically employ people with superb technical skills but minimal people skills and a doom-and-gloom or barracuda attitude that makes them a liability because of their negative impact on the rest of the team. Second, attitude plus skills equals a dramatic improvement in performance.

CHARACTER COUNTS

There's yet another factor essential to success, and that's character. Vince Gill says, "Success is always temporary. When all is said and done, the only thing you have left is your character." When we combine attitude plus skill and build it on a solid character base, we maximize our ability.

HOW IMPORTANT IS CHARACTER?

A 1995 Harris poll dealt with adults who had spent five years in the Boy Scouts. The study did not include Girl Scouts, but since they teach essentially the same things, I'm convinced a study on them would produce similar results.

Ninety-eight percent of those who were in the Boy Scouts at

least five years finished high school; 40 percent finished college versus 16 percent of those who were not in Scouting. Thirty-three percent have incomes over $50,000 versus only 17 percent who were not Scouts. Seventy percent made "Who's Who in America." Other studies reveal that eleven of the twelve astronauts who walked on the moon are former Boy Scouts. Eighty-five percent of the graduates of our military academies are former Boy Scouts. In addition, 94 percent of those surveyed in the Harris poll said that the values they learned in Scouting had a substantial impact on their life values.

> **Character gets you out of bed; commitment moves you to action. Faith, hope, and discipline enable you to follow through to completion.**

The values taught by the Boy Scouts were—and are—significant. At each Scout meeting the Scout stands up, gives the Boy Scout salute, and quotes the Scout Oath: "On my honor, I will do my best to do my duty to God and my country and obey the Scout Law; to help other people at all times; to keep myself physically strong, mentally awake and morally straight." Following this the Scouts repeat the Scout Motto, which is, "Be prepared," and the Scout Law: "A Scout is trustworthy, loyal, helpful, friendly, courteous, kind, obedient, cheerful, thrifty, brave, clean and reverent." Scouts are constantly told to do a good deed every day.

The interesting thing is that all of these are character qualities, and they are taught in the form of self-talk, which has additional value. I encourage you to look at the character qualities we've just identified. I'm convinced you would love to have a child with all these qualities or, for that matter, a mate, parent, employer, neighbor, employee, government official, friend, or even president of our country. Wouldn't you enjoy being with and around people with these qualities?

To further support the benefit of these qualities I encourage you to pick up a copy of Daniel Goleman's runaway best-seller,

Emotional Intelligence, and you will discover that most of the qualities I identify in this book are ones he identifies as what "emotional intelligence" is all about. He contends, and his research proves, that these qualities have more to do with one's success in life than IQ does.

I'm often asked, Which is more important—attitude or skill? The answer is that it's somewhat like asking which leg of a three-legged stool is most important. It is my complete conviction, based on a considerable amount of research, that if you have the right attitude, combined with the right skills, and build your attitude and your skills on a solid character base, you can enjoy long-lasting success.

With character you will, to the best of your ability, say and do what is right. This approach eliminates both fear (of being "caught") and guilt (for breaking the laws of God and/or man). With the removal of these two weights your trip over the top will be much easier and faster. When you add the golden rule philosophy that you can have everything in life you want if you will just help enough other people get what they want, your chances for a balanced success go even higher.

EXAMPLE: Li Ka-shing, according to *Fortune* magazine, is one of the ten wealthiest people in the world. He is a Chinese businessman from Hong Kong, and he has made his fortune by financing small businesses that have good products, good management, and good ideas, but are underfinanced. An astute financial mind and the application of this philosophy are the keys to his success.

From the beginning of his entrepreneurship he believed— and still believes—that if the going rate for financing the business is 10 percent ownership but you can get 11 or 12 percent of the business, you should always take 9 percent. His reasoning is financially sound and eminently wise. First, he knows that the lower percentage gives the new business a much better chance of making it, and 9 percent of a thriving business is better than 12 percent of a struggling business. Second, Li Ka-shing knew that when the business world saw that he was not greedy, that he really did want the businesses he partnered with to succeed big time, all the good deals would come his way. He was right. NOTE: This approach is a philosophy, not a tactic. If you think you can do something for someone, expecting him or her to do something for you in return, it won't work.

OVERNIGHT SUCCESS?

On rare occasions we hear about people who seem to be overnight successes. Actually, the "overnight" success is rare, and it certainly didn't happen in my life.

My dream to become a speaker was born in 1952 after I heard speaker Bob Bale from Phoenix, Arizona. He had a lot of fun, did a tremendous amount of good and, I thought, made lots of money. All those things appealed to me.

For the next thirteen years I spoke for anyone who would permit me to speak. I spoke to people in service clubs, schools, churches, prisons, drug rehab centers, automobile dealerships, and more. I literally drove hundreds of miles, at my expense, to speak to small groups. My fee? The opportunity to speak and improve my presentation skills. Money seldom changed hands. I did it because I believed I had something of value to say. However, I understood that in order to be paid for saying it, I had to learn how to say it in such a way that the audience would be willing to hear the message and act on that message.

Fortunately, my job during those years enabled me to hone my speaking skills. As a salesman/sales manager, I was responsible for the motivation of myself and my associates. I spoke not only to my own sales team but to numerous other organizations throughout the company. By doing that, I was able to develop my presentation skills on the job as well as off the job.

By 1965, I was getting an occasional paid engagement, and in 1968, I was invited to move to Dallas to conduct a training school one week each month for a small company. They offered me enough money to take care of my family's needs and gave me the freedom to use the other three weeks to further my speaking career.

In 1970, after a series of marketing changes, some unfortunate investments, and unforeseen circumstances, the company filed for bankruptcy, and I was catapulted into the speaking business on a full-time basis.

In all candor, there were long stretches of time when, despite my best efforts, I could not get a speaking engagement of any kind. That was discouraging, but not once did I consider abandoning my dream of being a speaker. My commitment was strong, my attitude was optimistic, and I believed that if I persisted (that's a character quality) with a logical plan of action, ultimately, the reward would follow the effort.

One difference between those who make it and those who don't—regardless of their field of endeavor—is not the "talent" difference. Those who go over the top have a dream and the dream has them. They make the commitment and pursue that dream with dogged patience and persistence. Commitment produces consistent, enthusiastic effort that inevitably produces greater and greater rewards.

IT'S NOW YOUR TURN

If you're a football fan, you recognize the name of Jeff Hostetler. If you're a die-hard football fan, you know he played quarterback for the New York Giants before being picked up as a free agent by the L.A. Raiders (now the Oakland Raiders). The first four years he was in the league he had

> *A true commitment is a heartfelt promise to yourself from which you will not back down.*
> **David McNally**

thrown only sixty-eight passes in regular season NFL games. Going into the tail end of his seventh season, he had thrown less than two hundred passes, and none of them had any bearing on the outcome of a game. Then Phil Simms, the starting quarterback, went down with an injury, and Coach Bill Parcells looked to the bench and said, "Okay, Jeff, it's your turn."

Jeff Hostetler stood up, put his helmet on, ran out to the field, and led his team to victory not only in that game but in the remaining games of the season and into the Super Bowl. The Giants, with Jeff at quarterback, won the world championship that year.

Suppose when the coach called for him, Jeff had said, "Wait a minute, Coach, I've got to get ready"? Though I've never talked with Jeff personally, I'm confident that he felt he was ready to start after two or three years in the league. Based on media reports and his success since then, I know he was ready to start after four or five years in the league.

CONSIDER THIS: What you do off the job is the determining factor in how far you will go on the job. We begin with the assumption that while you're on the job, you're working and giving it your best shot. That's what you are paid to do, and your integrity demands that kind of performance.

However, if you're going to get ahead in that job, your activities and preparation off the job will be the determining factors. Every athlete, singer, dancer, or TV/movie star clearly understands that. Successful physicians, dentists, professors, public speakers, financial planners, or attorneys understand that what they do before they get to their client, patient, or customer determines how effective they will be when they arrive. In Jeff Hostetler's case, what was he doing during those nearly seven years before he was given a chance to start?

> **What you do off the job is the determining factor in how far you will go on the job.**

GET READY—THE OPPORTUNITY IS THERE

Jeff was completely loyal to his first-string quarterback, his coach, and his team. He was not constantly calling press conferences and proclaiming that he should be the starting quarterback. On the contrary, he roamed the sidelines, sending in the plays to Phil Simms, the starting quarterback. During time-outs and the halftime break, if he had spotted anything in the defense that Phil Simms might have missed, he would tell Phil what it was. In short, he was the consummate team player.

During those seven years, Jeff threw thousands of passes through a swinging tire. He worked with his wide receivers and running backs in countless practice sessions, sharpening and honing his skills. He lifted tons of weights, did hundreds of push-ups and sit-ups, jogged many, many miles, and did numerous wind sprints. He literally spent hundreds of hours poring over the playbook, studying not only his own offense and defense but the defenses of the opposing teams.

Jeff worked out all year long, including the off-season. During the season, he was at every practice session, and each week he was the scout quarterback, playing the role of the quarterback for that week's opponent. Each week he was under pressure from his own teammates as they tried to make the practice sessions as realistic as the games.

Then one day, nearly seven years after Jeff made the squad, Phil Simms was injured, and the coach said, "Okay, Jeff, it's your turn." I have a feeling that as Jeff slipped his helmet on and headed for the field, he thought to himself, *This is what it's all about. This is what I've been preparing for all these years. It's my turn.*

QUESTION: How do you prepare during your off-season (after work hours)? If, when you go to work tomorrow, your immediate superior were to call you in and say, "Okay, Sally (or Jim), it's your turn. We are moving you into the top spot," would you have to say, "Wait a minute; I've got to improve my attitude, hone my skills, and build my character"? Or would you jump up and say, "This is what I've been preparing for; I'm ready"?

❝ *Most people who fail in their dreams fail not from lack of ability but from lack of commitment.* **❞**

You develop the qualities of success we are identifying and bring them to full maturity in much the same way I brought my speaking career to a full-time occupation and Jeff Hostetler became a winning quarterback. We made the decision to "do." When you decide to "do" whatever it takes to acquire these qualities, you will end up like thousands of others and go over the top.

The heart of the message in *Over the Top* is that motivation gives you the "want to." Training and education give you the "how to," and the combination produces the necessary creative ideas to be more effective in realizing your dream. Character, commitment, discipline, and responsibility keep you going.

CHAPTER THREE

Having it all

There is a natural alliance between the creation of wealth and the cultivation of character. Economic success is built on moral foundations—on the rule of law, faith, discipline, contracts, savings, integrity, a work ethic. Sound families that elevate these beliefs are the source of much of our culture's strength and future.　　　　　　　　　　　　　　Jack Kemp

Several years ago I did something I normally don't do, primarily because I have neither the time nor the necessary training. I counseled a young man in my office in Dallas. Here's how it came about.

PUTTING LIFE IN PERSPECTIVE

I received a letter, with a substantial check enclosed, from a man in Toronto, Canada. He had written on behalf of a young friend who, as he put it, was literally working himself to death. He explained that the young man left for work every morning at six and generally did not get home until ten or eleven o'clock at night. That was his pattern six days a week. His family was falling apart, his health was suffering, and on several occasions he had run his car off the road because he kept falling asleep driving to and from work.

It seems the young man had chosen to model his life after his boss, whom he considered to be over the top. He wanted to be successful like him. My correspondent suggested to me that if I would spend an hour with him and his friend, he'd fly him to Dallas and I could keep the check. He explained that I was one of the few people his friend might be willing to listen to because of his friend's respect for me.

Well, as I say, I normally don't do counseling, but the man's sincerity convinced me that I had to make an exception. I returned the check and invited them to come to Dallas.

I began the interview by acknowledging that the young man had identified his boss, whom he considered to be over the top, as his hero and role model. Then I asked him to explain his definition of success. What would he have to be, do, or have in order to be over the top?

It took him about twenty minutes and he didn't list them in the same order I list them, but he identified the same eight factors I've discovered that people all over the world identify with success. He said that if he or any person is happy, healthy, reasonably prosperous, and secure, has friends, peace of mind, good family relationships, and the hope that things will either continue as they are or get better, he would consider that person to be successful.

QUESTION: If you had these eight things, would you consider yourself successful? The odds are good that you answered yes to that one.

USE A MEASURING STICK

I suggested to the young man, "Let's do something very few people do. Let's put a measuring stick on your boss to see how successful he is and if he really is over the top."

We had pinpointed what the young man considered to be the ingredients of success. We had identified his hero. So I went down the list, asking the young man where his boss stood. My first question was, "How happy is your boss?"

He reflected a moment and said, "Well, I don't think he's happy at all."

I responded, "Okay, I'll take your word for it and mark an *x* for failure on happiness. But why do you say he's not happy?"

The young man replied, "That's easy. I've seldom heard him laugh, he almost never smiles, and he has ulcers."

To that, I responded, "Well, since people get ulcers not because of what they eat, but because of what's eating them, that tells me we've also got to give him a failing grade on the health question and on peace of mind." Then I pointed out to the young man that I had asked him only one question, but his answer indicated that his boss failed on three of the eight things that everyone wants in life.

Then I asked him, "How prosperous is your boss?"

Smiling broadly, he said, "Man, he's very prosperous, and he's making more money by the day."

I said, "Okay, let's give him a big plus on that one. Then the next question is, How secure is your boss?"

Again he grinned and said, "Well, I believe he's very secure. He's got lots of money and is making more."

Since the young man equated security with money, I told him about a well-known Texas politician who, at one point, was worth an estimated $100 million but later filed for bankruptcy. Then I mentioned an industrialist who once was worth over a half billion dollars and was now bankrupt as well. I asked how his boss compared. Smiling, he acknowledged that his boss didn't have that kind of money.

So I said, "Let's put a question mark by how secure he is. Would that be fair?" The young man agreed that it would.

Next I asked, "How many friends does your boss have?"

The young man pondered the question for a moment, then replied, "Well, actually I don't think he has any friends. To be truthful, I'm not really his friend—I just happen to work for the man and I admire what he's done." Then he half smiled and said, "To be honest, the guy's somewhat of a jerk."

So I said, "Okay, we're going to give him a failing grade on friends." Then I said, "Tell me about his family."

Raising his eyebrows, the young man said, "Well, his wife's in the process of divorcing him."

I responded in the only way possible, "We have to give him a failing grade on good family relationships."

Now let's take another look at the things the young man identified as characteristic of the lives of successful individuals. They are happy—his boss wasn't. They are healthy—his boss wasn't. They are reasonably prosperous—so was his boss. They are secure—we gave the boss a question mark on that one. They have friends—his boss didn't. They have peace of mind—his boss failed that one. They have good family relationships—again, his boss failed.

When it came to the question of hope, the young man said he thought his boss had hope, but he personally felt it was a false hope. Based on the rest of his story, I had to agree. So we gave him a question mark on that one.

Of the eight measurements of success, the young man's boss received a plus on one, a question mark on two, and a failing grade on five!

Then I asked the crucial question: "Knowing what you now know and using this yardstick to measure your boss, would you swap places with him?"

For what seemed like forever, though it probably was no longer than a half minute, the young man carefully considered the question. Then he slowly rose to his feet and extended his hand as he said, "No, I sure wouldn't." The interview was over.

Let me pose the same question to you: Would you trade places with his boss? Or to put it another way, would you give up everything you hold dear to have a few more bucks in the bank? I think not.

The rest of the young man's story will take a lifetime to complete. But I am pleased to tell you that he changed to another, less-demanding job and two years later was doing better in all areas of his life, including his finances. Best of all the relationships at home had been healed, and a new member had been added to the family! That's an example of real growth.

DEALING WITH ALL OF LIFE

In many ways the story of the young man from Canada ties down one of the major objectives of *Over the Top.* To get all eight things life has to offer, we need to understand that we've got to deal with all aspects of life. This includes our personal, family, and business lives. We must also deal with the physical, mental, and spiritual. What you do in your personal life affects your performance on the job; what happens in your career affects your relationship with your family; what happens with your family affects every other phase of your life.

Your intellectual growth, your attitude, your physical and emotional health, and your approach to spiritual matters are all inseparable. That's the reason throughout *Over the Top* I will repeatedly mention balance in your life, because each part affects the financial life, which in turn affects all the others. ONE MORE TIME: They're all tied together.

CAN YOU REALLY HAVE IT ALL?

Your next question might be, "Zig, do you honestly believe that anyone (including me) can have all eight of the things you've identified?"

My answer is yes, with some qualification. I do not believe that everybody can become a multimillionaire or even a millionaire, but I do believe that everyone can be at the top, which is where you must be to go over the top.

I confess that I was once like the young man who equated security with money and money with success. I was able to help him see where his perspective was off because life had taught me that true contentment and total success come from the things money can't buy. Don't misunderstand. I like the things money can buy, and I'll bet you do, too. I like nice

> **❝** *Money will buy all kinds of things for my family, but it won't buy their love.* **❞**

clothes, a beautiful residence, big, comfortable cars, relaxing vacations, membership in a nice country club, and so on. However, I love the things money won't buy. It will buy me a house, but not a home; a bed, but not a good night's sleep; pleasure, but not happiness; a good time, but not peace of mind; and a companion, but not a friend.

If you go for standard of living (money) first, you will probably earn considerable sums of money, but you will have no guarantee that your quality of life will improve. However, if you go for quality of life first, your standard of living will inevitably go up. With this approach you will arrive at the end of life's road with more of the things money will buy and far more of the things that money can't buy.

I challenge you to carefully review the fifteen identifying points of the top in the first chapter and one by one ask yourself this question: If I'm at the top, will I be or have all eight of the things Zig has identified throughout the first part of chapter 3? A thoughtful analysis will convince you that with the possible exceptions of health and prosperity, your position at the top will guarantee you the other six, and you will probably be healthier and more prosperous. A major disease or disability may thwart your physical or financial health, but you can reach for and attain emotional and spiritual health. And your choice of vocation such as minister, teacher, or social worker may limit your income, but with patience, thrift, and good decisions, you can definitely be more prosperous. I know I'm promising a lot, but *Over the Top* is the instruction book that gives you the game plan that can make these promises a reality in your life.

I DID AND SO CAN YOU

I believe this because to a large degree I have achieved it. I can honestly say that I thought life was wonderful when I wrote *See You at the Top,* and it was, compared to what I had experienced up to that point. However, compared to where I am today, I must say I had just begun to live. The depth and width of every facet of my life today have far surpassed any concept I could imagine twenty-plus years ago.

See You at the Top was the springboard for the life I live today. My relationships are deeper, more personal and loving, and far more open.

" For years I was so wrapped up in learning and teaching that I was unable to sit back, relax, receive, and enjoy the love and attention I encouraged my readers to give to others. "

In *See You at the Top,* I promised that you can have everything in life you want if you will just help enough other people get what they want. Because I followed my own instructions (even subconsciously), I can candidly and gratefully say to you that the philosophy works. I do have the things that money can buy, and I also have the things that money can't buy.

SURPRISE, SURPRISE

I shouldn't have been surprised that the philosophy worked so well, but to a degree, I was. My emphasis was on helping those who hear me speak, read my books, or listen to my recordings, and I really didn't give much conscious thought to where "I" was in regard to that promise.

One by one my family members remarked on changes they saw in my life. Their comments were positive. They said I seemed more relaxed, more at ease, and more involved with them. I looked happier, healthier, and more content than they could remember me ever being. I was easier to talk to and with about family and social matters without steering the conversation back to business or the next project, as I had in the past.

As a result, I was participating in family gatherings to a much greater extent. I was available for chitchat, and it didn't take a crisis to get my attention. They noted that I had more real friends (not just acquaintances) than I had ever had. Because of in-depth discussions about topics I once would have discounted as negative, my children accused me of being real and thanked me for validating their feelings.

If I hadn't been real before, what had I been? The question led me to analyze where I started from to get to where I am today. What was the difference?

The difference? I got over the top. And it is wonderful. The constant striving is over, but best effort as always remains a permanent part of my life and my goals are more ambitious than ever.

The good news for you is this: I do not hold exclusive rights to this position, nor do the people I identify in *Over the Top*. There is plenty of room for you. As a matter of fact, the more of us who go to the top and then go over the top, the easier it will be for our friends, loved ones, and countless others to follow our example. The key to making it over the top is this: Help enough other people get what they want. This is one trip you can't make by yourself.

> **The key to making it over the top is this: Help enough other people get what they want.**

"But, Zig," you say, "I thought this book was going to be

different. You told me that in *See You at the Top* and every other book you've ever written. You verbalize that information every time you stand up to speak!"

I did and I do. It was truth then and it is truth now. What is different about *Over the Top* is that this book doesn't just state the truth; it dissects it, explains it, exposes it, validates it, verifies it, and proves it.

OH, YES, YOU CAN!

Now, just in case you question whether or not you really can have all these marvelous things I've already mentioned, I'm going to ask you some thought-provoking questions. Next, I'll challenge you with an example that will start the process of convincing you that you already have what it takes to make it to the top and be more successful.

FIRST, the question that only you can answer: Am I pleased with where I am on the eight wants of life (happiness, health, reasonable prosperity, security, friends, peace of mind, good family relationships, hope)? SECOND QUESTION: If I continue doing in the next five, ten, and twenty years what I've been doing the last five, ten, and twenty years, will I be pleased with who I am, where I am, and what I have?

If you answered no, relax. The answers on how to change, which you must do in order to be pleased with yourself, with where you are, and with what you have in the future, are in your hands right now.

As you read the rest of this chapter, I want you to consider this significant philosophical building block for your future growth and progress.

> **❝** *You've got to be before you can do, and do before you can have.* **❞**

JOB SECURITY? NO
EMPLOYMENT SECURITY? YES

One thing that became obvious to most careful observers in the late 1980s was the disappearance of job security. When you look at the number of old-line major companies that have had to lay off hundreds—even thousands—of workers, this fact comes through loud and clear.

However, there is employment security, and that's exciting. In today's climate of job uncertainty, if you take the approach I detail in the rest of this chapter, every employer I've talked with—and that's a large number—assures me that your employment security will substantially increase.

Dedicated people have employment security

My son-in-law, Richard Oates, is a superintendent for one of the nation's largest home builders. He has been with them for five years, and has never been late for work, regardless of weather, car trouble, traffic, accidents, or other delays. He is excited about his job, and has consistently given more than a full day's effort for a full day's pay. He has missed only four days of work during his tenure because of illness, and has left unused an average of three days of his vacation each year.

Those actions and attitudes build real job security as long as his company exists. Realistically, there are some things that people can't control despite their best efforts, but consider this: If his company should go under, what kind of recommendation do you think he would get from his employer? Remember now that Richard has demonstrated loyalty, dependability, promptness, excitement, a cooperative team player attitude, and many other qualities.

QUESTION: Does he sound like the kind of person you would enjoy working with or for or having as an employee? QUESTION: Doesn't that give him employment security? QUES-

TION: Won't taking those actions and developing those same qualities give you employment security?

UPDATE: On January 8, 1994, Richard accepted an even better opportunity with The Zig Ziglar Corporation and brought that same commitment and enthusiasm to his new company. RESULT: On July 23, 1996, he was made COO (chief operating officer) of the corporation.

Employment security = don't finish your education

A classic example of someone who hasn't finished her education is the woman who typed the very words you're reading. Laurie Magers has been my executive assistant since 1977. She came to work with less than a high-school education, but she clearly understood that she could continue her education as she had already been doing from the moment she left school and went to work. She's an avid reader and a good student of vocabulary. She attends lectures and seminars on a regular basis, and has been doing this for many years.

RESULTS: We recently conducted a comprehensive evaluation for the key people in our company, and Laurie scored slightly higher than the master's level of education average. To me, that says a great deal. Because Laurie continued her education on the job and off the job, she has not only job security at our company, but also employment security, should something happen to our company.

YOUR QUESTION: How can I achieve employment security in a no-job-security world? Before we get to the answer, consider some more questions:

QUESTIONS DEMANDING AN ANSWER

QUESTION: Are you *honest* and at least reasonably *intelligent*? If you didn't smile and think to yourself, *Absolutely!* was it the honesty or the intelligence part that caused you to hesitate?

NEXT QUESTION: As a general rule, on the day before you go on vacation, do you get two or three times as much work done as you normally get done in a day?

ANOTHER QUESTION: If you can learn *why* you are that much more productive on the day before vacation, and then repeat that process on a daily basis without working any longer or harder, does it make sense that you will be more valuable to yourself, your family, your company, and society in general?

NEXT QUESTION: On the night before the day before vacation, do you take a sheet of paper and say to yourself, "Now tomorrow I've got to do . . . ," and then make a list of things you must do? (I'll bet you said yes.) In its simplest form, that's *goal setting* and it's critical.

Next, you *organized* your must-do list in the order of importance and accepted *responsibility* for completing those tasks, knowing that if you did not finish your jobs someone else would have to take over, and you recognized the inherent unfairness of that.

As you accept responsibility, you immediately make the *commitment* to fulfill that responsibility. Unfortunately, many people make commitments with all the excitement of a kamikaze pilot on his thirty-ninth mission!

YOU REALLY ARE SELF-EMPLOYED

At this point something fascinating takes place because once you've set a goal, accepted responsibility for completing it, and made the commitment to do so, you are thinking as a self-employed person, and all of us fit that category. (If you don't believe that, just quit performing and you will become unemployed in reasonably short order.)

On the way to work the next day your self-talk was upbeat and centered on what you were going to get done. You arrived at work on time so you were *punctual*. You immediately *started* to work, making you a *self-starter*. You were highly *motivated* and *optimistic* that you were going to finish every task you had set for yourself. You were *enthusiastic* about your work and *decisively* moved from one task to the next, *making good choices* as you did so, even if the next job on the list was disagreeable.

An ol' boy down home said it best, "Friend, if you've got to swallow a frog, you just don't want to look at that sucker too long. He ain't gonna get no purtier! As a matter of fact, the longer you look, the uglier he gets." That's the way unpleasant tasks are.

As you moved from task to task, if someone tried to interrupt and talk about last night's television program or last night's game, you *disciplined* yourself to stay on task and not be distracted from your job. (You have surely noticed that people with nothing to do—as a general rule—want to do it with you!) Since there was no "tomorrow" for you on each job, you *persisted* until you completed each one. At that point, your *positive thinking* kicked into high gear, and momentum built with the completion of each task.

My daughter Cindy pointed out that when she applied this day-before-vacation attitude to her job, as she checked off each completed task on her list of goals for the day, she felt better and better about herself *(self-image)* and her ability to *manage herself well,* which also increased her *confidence* and level of *competence.* As she performed, she noticed that her *energy* level was increasing. You have probably noticed the same thing on your day before vacation.

THIS INCREASES PRODUCTIVITY

Interestingly enough, as you hit the inevitable snags or road bumps in the course of your activities, your *resourcefulness, creativity,* and *knowledge* were more fully utilized because you were on a roll and in a can-do attitude. That had a dramatic impact on overall productivity and an even bigger impact on the bottom line. You combined all of these factors, and you were literally *focusing* on each task at hand until you completed it.

The importance of focus was brought home to me in a recent conversation with Roger Staubach of Heisman trophy and Dallas Cowboy fame. He stated that he always had better grades at Annapolis during football season than at any other time. His time was so limited, he had to organize, focus, and do it now. That was exactly what you did on the day before vacation.

As you finished each task, you found yourself believing that you could get even more done than you had planned. *Believing* is one of the strongest words in our language because it demonstrates that your heart is in the objective. We can measure speed, strength, intelligence, and a host of other things, but we cannot measure the "heart," which is "drive," "desire," "want to," and so on. A high jumper who broke a world's record was asked how he did it. He responded, "I threw my heart over the bar and the rest of me followed."

MORE THAN POSITIVE THINKING

Positive believing is something that goes beyond positive thinking, which gives you the freedom and confidence to use your ability. Positive believing involves a new dimension that brings your heart into the picture and gives you a "feeling" and passion that move you from having a "job" to the job's having you. That's critical because we can measure a person's IQ, but we cannot measure the EI *(emotional intelligence).* According to extensive research done by Harvard psychologist Daniel Goleman, EI is even more important because it brings energy, *self-control,* discipline, and a host of other intangibles to the individual's list of "success" qualities, which will move that individual to a much higher level of accomplishment. More on this later, but it definitely will help ensure employment security in a no-job-security world and more—much more.

Perhaps the most exciting part of this vacation scenario is the fact that your coworkers instinctively picked up the pace, so your value to the company as an *extra-miler* went beyond your personal productivity. That also improved your employment security because it identified you as a *team player* stimulating *momentum* among other members. "Team," according to Mary Lou Retton, the gymnastics gold medal winner from the 1984 Olympics, forms an acrostic: "Together Everyone Achieves More." How true this is because it reminds us that individuals score runs but teams win games.

Interestingly enough, despite the fact that you did two or three times as much as you normally do, when the day was finished, your energy level was extremely high. By contrast, the days that exhaust you are the days when you have to "make work" in order to "fool" the boss. When those days finally come to an end, you think to yourself, *I don't know if I can handle much more of this!* In addition, you start finding fault with everything and become a supercritic. That's when your employment security plummets to zero.

As a result of your increased productivity on that day before vacation, you felt really good about yourself. Your self-image and confidence soared, and you truly had an over-the-top attitude. You knew you'd done a great job, and you wanted to tell the family what you'd done. You talked to yourself all the way home, "Boy, oh, boy! What a marvelous day!" You started painting pictures in your mind about the warm reception you were going to receive, how excited everybody was going to be, how packing and loading for the trip were going to be fun instead of a chore. Yes, you were an excited, productive human being.

PAUSE AND THINK WITH ME

Dear Reader, please slow down and *think* carefully about my next observations and questions. Notice I talked about working smarter, not longer and/or harder.

QUESTION: If this approach works so well on the day before vacation, won't it work just as well *every* day?

QUESTION: You do understand that what you did off the job

(planned your schedule the night before) played a major role in improving your performance on the job, don't you?

QUESTION: Do you believe an employer would fire anyone who adopted the day-before-vacation attitude every day of his or her life? The answer is obvious, isn't it?

QUESTION: If planning your work the night before and giving it your best shot the next day work so well in your career, doesn't it make sense that if you plan family time, recreation time, and exercise time, you will get more of these things done? After all, the reason you're going on this specific vacation is the fact that you've planned it. When you plan things, the odds of their happening go up substantially.

QUESTION: As you reread the above, doesn't it spell "balance" in your life, and won't this give you a better chance to get more of the things money will buy and all of the things money won't buy?

What I'm really talking about is running your day by the clock and your life with a vision. On that day before vacation you managed yourself, which you must consistently do before you can manage or lead others. Managing yourself includes having a vision—not just to go on vacation, but to be more, do more, and have more. The significance of having a vision was expressed by Helen Keller when she stated that it would be much worse to have perfect sight and no vision than the other way around. Solomon, the wisest man who ever lived, said, "Where there is no vision, the people perish" (Prov. 29:18 KJV). Jesse Stoner-Zemel said, "A vision is a clearly articulated, results-oriented picture of a future you intend to create." It is a dream with direction.

NOW IS THE TIME TO ACT

The next step I'm going to suggest could be the most significant personal growth step you will ever take. It's a "must do." Turn back to pages 37–41. Carefully reread them. Pay special attention to the words that are italicized—the words (qualities) that you used on your day before vacation. Obviously, if you used them, you have them. TWO THOUGHTS: First, you knew little, if any more, about your job on the day before you went on vacation than you did twenty-four hours earlier, yet you were dramatically more productive. Second, if you recognize, confess, develop, and use these qualities that you already have on a daily basis, doesn't it make sense that you can achieve employment security in a no-job-security world and live a more balanced life by acquiring more of the things money will buy and all of the things money won't buy?

THIS CAN'T HAPPEN

At this point you are probably thinking to yourself, *Yes, Zig, but suppose my company does what hundreds—even thousands—of other companies have done? It downsizes, goes bankrupt, merges, or a relative comes in and takes my job. Then what do I do?*

That's a good question. Let me answer with a hypothetical example. Suppose the impossible happens and the Dallas Cowboys go bankrupt. We know that's impossible because the league simply would not permit it. But if it should, you can just imagine owner Jerry Jones calling the players together, giving them the sad news, they are now officially unemployed. Do you believe there is a better-than-good chance that Emmitt Smith, Troy Aikman, Nate Newton, Larry Allen, Chad Hennings, Darren Woodson, and a number of the other players would be able to get jobs elsewhere? NEXT QUESTION: Would they get other jobs because they had played for the Cowboys or because they had *performed* for the Cowboys? The answer is obvious, isn't it?

ONE MORE QUESTION: Suppose your company, for whatever reason, folds, or you are downsized or replaced. Would you be able to get another job because you were employed by XYZ Company, or would you get another job because you performed for XYZ Company? Think about it. ONE MORE QUESTION: Whose responsibility is it to perform?

ONE FURTHER THOUGHT: If you performed every day on your job as you do on the day before you leave on vacation, in your own heart and mind what kind of reference do you think you would get? All of this simply points to one fact: We are far less victims than we realize. There *is* something we can do to give ourselves employment security in a no-job-security world.

ONE FINAL THOUGHT ON THIS SUBJECT: While it's true that many people who have found themselves unemployed as a result of the shifting economy have been unable to get jobs as good as the ones they formerly had, it is also true that tens of thousands of people have gotten even better jobs, and many of them started their own businesses and are thriving, primarily because they *responded* to the situation instead of *reacting* to the situation.

BACK TO EMPLOYMENT SECURITY

Remember the words you looked at on pages 37–41? If you looked at them carefully, you *know* that you are honest, intelligent, goal-directed, organized, responsible, committed, punctual, a self-starter, motivated, optimistic, enthusiastic, decisive; make good choices; are disciplined, persistent, positive; have a good self-image; manage yourself well; are confident, competent, energized, resourceful, creative, knowledgeable, focused, a believer, emotionally intelligent, self-controlled, an extra-miler, and a team player. The exciting thing is that these qualities are skills that you have acquired. Even more exciting is the fact that you also know that consistent use of these qualities will enable you to maintain your day-before-vacation momentum.

These are qualities that winners have *and* use. Now, just in case you're wondering why such an outstanding person as you—with these great qualities—isn't even farther down the road, let me explain with a simple analogy. If you are honest and someone told you she had put $1 million in your checking account, you would never write a check on that $1 million until you were sure it was in your account. However, once you learned it was there and had come from a legitimate source, you know you would use that bonanza, don't you? QUESTION: Doesn't it make even more sense to capitalize on your "qualities" bonanza, which will ultimately produce more money and more of all the things money could never buy?

More than forty years of personal growth and development and teaching experience have convinced me that the overwhelming majority of the people in the world don't have any idea they already possess the basic qualities necessary for outstanding success. QUESTIONS: Did you ever sit down and think through all the qualities you brought to the table on your day-before-vacation performance? Did you even realize you had and were already instinctively using those qualities?

Now, heaven forbid you should even hint at having a negative thought such as doubting whether you really do have all these skills that you used on your day before vacation. Read what Earl Loomis said:

> **"We deny our talents and abilities because to acknowledge or to confess them would commit us to use them."**

Unfortunately, when you deny your talents and abilities, you deny yourself, your family, your company, and your community the benefits of your talents and abilities.

With that in mind, let's now look at taking a significant step. I can personally testify that this has worked and is working for me—and literally thousands of other people.

ACTION NOW = BENEFITS NOW

Do yourself a favor. Stop reading here and now. Make a photocopy of the self-talk procedure in the next paragraph, or print it on a 3″ × 5″ card. Long before you finish this book you will realize the critical importance of taking this action now. For the moment, let me assure you that research conclusively proves that your self-talk has a direct bearing on your performance. For this procedure, we put the identification of your qualities in the first-person, present-tense form. Several times each day—but especially before you start your day and the last thing you do at the end of each day—take the card and read:

I, _____, am an honest, intelligent, goal-directed, organized, responsible, committed, punctual individual. I am a highly motivated, optimistic, enthusiastic, positive, focused self-starter. I am a decisive, competent, disciplined, persistent, knowledgeable, creative, resourceful team player who makes good choices. I am an emotionally intelligent, confident believer and an extra-miler. I am energized, have great self-control and a healthy self-image, and manage myself well. These are the qualities of the winner I was born to be, and by using them every day, I will maintain my momentum and have employment security in a no-job-security world. They will also enable me to get more of the things money will buy and more of the things money won't buy.

P.S. Remember: You've got to be before you can do and do before you can have. The self-talk procedure is an integral part of being.

CHAPTER FOUR

The responsibility is yours

Taking responsibility for your behavior, your expenditures and your actions and not forever supposing that society must forgive you because it's "not your fault" is the quality most needed in the next century.

Two-time Pulitzer prize winner Barbara Tuchman

According to Blanche Brick, Ph.D., "We demand corporate responsibility for a shoddy product or a polluted beach, however, we refuse to require individuals to accept responsibility for their acts of irresponsible behavior. Perhaps it is easier to legislate and regulate spoiled meat than it is to legislate or regulate spoiled people— whether they are from the west side of Chicago or the president of a savings and loan."

CHOICES ARE THE KEY

Taking a page from psychologist Bob Wubbolding, I have a surprising question: Do you believe there is something you can specifically do in the next two weeks that will make your personal, family, and business lives worse? SECOND

QUESTION: Do you believe there is something you can specifically do in the next two weeks that will make your personal, family, and business lives better? THIRD QUESTION: Do you believe the choice is yours? FOURTH QUESTION: Do you believe every choice you make has an end result?

If you answered yes to each of these four questions, let me tell you what you just agreed to, whether you realize it or not. You just said, "I don't care how bad or good my past has been, I don't care how bad or good my circumstances are at the moment, there is something I can specifically do *now* that will make my future either better or worse—and the choice is mine."

That is profound because it says, "I am not a victim. I can do many things that will make my future either better or worse, and it's up to me to make the right choices." Acknowledging this fact takes you out of the "blame game" and puts you squarely on the road to be more, do more, and have more.

So, if you were sincere in agreeing and really do accept responsibility for your future, you are within one step of some monumental changes and some serious progress in your life. When you decided to accept responsibility for your actions, you accepted responsibility for your future. That's almost earth-shattering in significance, because until you accept responsibility for your future, your future is left to chance, and chance is a cruel seductress.

PLAN—PREPARE—EXPECT

To go over the top, you have to plan to win, and the plan must be a good one. The good news is, you were off to a great start even before you were old enough to make choices. Your arrival was well planned eons ago. Your mother and father may not have specifically planned on having you, and they may have thought your timing wasn't quite right, but friend, I assure you, you are the winner you were meant to be. The next example says it well.

Listen to speaker James Parker: "Your birth, which obviously happened despite the odds of millions to one, means you became a winner before you were born. One sperm 'saw' one egg, took off in hot pursuit, made the connection, and you were on your way."

Think about it—never again will you face such apparently insurmountable odds. You've already won the big one, you are already the right person, and throughout *Over the Top,* you will learn how to develop the right plan and win scores of little victories that, cumulatively speaking, will assure you victory in the big game of life.

Bobby Knight, head basketball coach and winner of three national championships at Indiana University, accurately states that "the will to win is nothing without the will to prepare to win." He is right.

THOUGHT: Now is the time to take note of the game plan. These three words—*plan, prepare,* and *expect*—when put into action, determine your today and your tomorrow. If you are not happy with the level of success you have experienced thus far, you must change your plans and preparations for the future as well as your expectations of the future. To excel, you must expel false assumptions and avoid destructive behaviors.

DOES THE CITY MAKE THE DIFFERENCE?

Some of the answer could well be wrapped up in a report published in a 1987 issue of *Forbes.* A study of entrepreneurs revealed that invariably those who made money did so after they moved to a new city. Now before you start packing

> **❝** *You can plan, prepare, expect, and make the commitment right where you are, doing exactly what you're doing.* **❞**

your bags, let me point out that some of them made their money when they moved from Boston to Chicago. However, others made their money when they moved from Chicago to Boston. Some made their money when they moved from Dallas to Denver, and others made their money when they moved from Denver to Dallas.

The point is that in most cases the city was not the determining factor. "But wait a minute, Ziglar," you might say, "you just said they made their money after they moved." That's right. They did that because they planned to make money in their new city. They prepared to make money, and therefore, legitimately, expected to make money. Not only that, but they made the commitment to do so. FACT: You don't have to leave your seat to plan, prepare, expect, and commit.

When you spend time planning and preparing for your future, unconsciously you are outlining your mission in life. Since you are responsible for your future, and you don't want to leave it to chance, let me encourage you to be mindful of the mission your plans represent. You can do this by purposefully writing your own mission statement.

The next example and parable will help you understand why developing your own mission statement is important to your success and is a characteristic of over-the-top people.

MISSION POSSIBLE

The mission statement of The Zig Ziglar Corporation is:

> *To be the Difference Maker in the personal, family, and business lives of enough people to make a positive difference in America and the world.*

Now I recognize that is an extraordinary mission statement, and for a company our size, that might sound somewhat grandiose. However, I'm convinced that by the time you close the pages on the last chapter of this book, you will be enthusiastically endorsing and participating in our mission statement while developing one of your own.

The story is told of the grandfather walking with his grandson on the beach. The grandfather frequently reached down and picked up a sand dollar and threw it out to sea. After a period of time, the grandson said to his grandfather, "Granddaddy, what're you doing?"

And the grandfather smiled and said, "Well, Son, these sand dollars are living organisms, and if I don't throw them back out to sea, they will die in the sun."

The grandson replied, "But, Granddaddy, there are thousands and thousands of them! What possible difference can it make?"

The grandfather quietly reached down, picked up another sand dollar, threw it out to sea, and said, "To this one, it makes all the difference in the world."

> **When you change your world for the better, you have positioned yourself perfectly to change the world of those around you.**

MESSAGE: You might not be able to change the world, but when you change *your* world, you will have taken a major step in changing the world of others, many of whom you will never know, by the words you use and the deeds you do. Dr. John Maxwell says the average person impacts more than ten thousand people in his or her lifetime. That's significant.

YOU ARE A DIFFERENCE MAKER

Somebody once said that no raindrop takes any responsibility for the flood, nor does a snowflake blame itself for the blizzard, yet the reality is that each one played a part. Unfortunately, too many people throw up their hands and say, "What can I do?" Figuratively speaking, you can throw the sand dollar back out to sea so that it can live. You can reach down and extend a helping hand to people in need. You can speak out and be an encouragement, not only to those around you, but through them influence countless other people. The life you live makes quite a statement.

A REMARKABLE SPEAKER—A MORE REMARKABLE MAN

One of the most remarkable men I've ever known is Charlie Wedemeyer from Los Gatos, California. Charlie coached the Los Gatos high-school football team to the only state championship they've ever won. I remember the day I attended a practice session with Charlie and his team. He and I were carrying on an extended conversation from the sidelines when periodically an assistant coach would run up and ask questions about an offensive or defensive assignment. It might be, "How do you keep them from trap-blocking on that play?" Without hesitation, Charlie, who had been watching intently during our entire conversation, would spell out the specifics he should follow. A few moments later yet another coach would come by with a question, and again, Charlie had an answer ready for him.

The amazing thing is that the only parts of his body he can move are his eyes and mouth. Charlie Wedemeyer suffers from Lou Gehrig's disease. The disease has physically affected him so dramatically that no sound comes from his mouth. His wife, Lucy, is his interpreter. She reads his lips and effectively delivers the message.

Charlie has the most remarkable attitude and the greatest sense of humor I believe I have ever seen. Though travel arrangements are difficult, he regularly speaks to people in schools, businesses, prisons, and churches. He has something to say, and Lucy verbalizes it to the audience. He might be the only speaker in America who can't speak. Needless to say, his life and wife communicate a powerful message of hope, love, and a never-give-up spirit. They both have a passion to make a difference.

CHARLIE'S VICTORY

On May 29, 1992, Charlie was honored as the Disabled American of the Year. President Bush was scheduled to attend, but at the last minute had to cancel his appearance. In his acceptance speech, Charlie expressed regret that the president was not there because he was going to specifically say to him, "Read my lips." I don't need to tell you that when Lucy verbalized Charlie's message, it brought down the house! What an inspiring team they make!

Charlie's example of commitment and courage while maintaining his upbeat attitude toward life is an inspiration to literally millions of people. His book, *Charlie's Victory*, will lift anyone who has ever been the least bit discouraged. I can assure you that when you read his story, your PLOM (poor little old me) disease, if by chance you are afflicted with it, will improve dramatically.

When you look at Charlie and know he was Hawaii's Athlete of the Decade for the 1960s, you realize that this man, who was once so athletically gifted and is now reduced to moving his lips, truly is a man who fully uses what he has and doesn't dwell on what he lost. He has many outstanding qualities, but heading the list are faith, courage, a positive mental attitude, and a great sense of humor. Charlie is also an amazing communicator, team player extraordinaire, and a host of other things. When you see Charlie and talk with him, you realize that his very life is an inspiration, and it makes you want to do more with what you have. Wherever he goes, people from all walks of life agree that Charlie Wedemeyer's life makes a profound statement.

ZIG, YOU JUST DON'T UNDERSTAND

Just in case you have even a small trace of PLOM disease and are saying, "But, Zig, you don't understand about my past. I'm not like Charlie Wedemeyer. Let me tell you what's happened to me and why my life probably will never make a statement of any kind," I've got a better idea for you. Instead of explaining why it won't work for you, let me tell you how it has worked for others.

A study of three hundred world-class leaders, including Franklin D. Roosevelt, Sir Winston Churchill, Clara Barton, Helen Keller, Mahatma Gandhi, Mother Teresa, Dr. Albert Schweitzer, and Martin Luther King, Jr., revealed that 25 percent of them had serious physical disabilities and an additional 50 percent had been abused as children or were raised in poverty.

The world-class leaders responded (positive) instead of reacted (negative) to what happened to them. Remember, it's not what happens to you; it's how you handle what happens to you that's going to make the difference in your life.

Neil Rudenstine's father was a prison guard and his mother a part-time waitress. Today, Dr. Neil Rudenstine is president of Harvard University. He says he learned very early in life that there is a direct correlation between performance and reward. Rudenstine and the three hundred world-class leaders personally learned that it's not where you start—it's where you finish that counts.

> **It's not where you start—it's where you finish that counts.**

It's not who your mother and/or your father were that's important—it's who you are and what you do that matter.

THE PLOM CURE

In 1990, I spoke for the National Quality and Business Development Foundation in Colorado Springs. Another speaker on the platform was a young college student named John Foppe. I was very much impressed that the young man, only twenty years old, could speak so forthrightly and enthusiastically to the heads of the largest companies in the world. Even with admirals, generals, and the secretary of defense in attendance, he did a marvelous job.

I determined to get better acquainted with him, and over the last few years I have learned that he is one of eight boys in his family, that he worked as a speaker while in college and graduated cum laude in three and a half years. He speaks to high school, church, and business audiences all over the world. Today he's one of the most capable, self-sufficient young men I've ever seen, and he has a great sense of humor.

John is an inspiration to know and watch. He was born with no arms. To see him drive a car is an impressive sight. He shaves, makes coffee, cooks eggs and bacon, and does virtually everything else you and I do on a daily basis.

Something most of us can't do on a daily basis is draw well. John is also a talented artist. One of my proudest possessions is a portrait of me that John patiently drew and beautifully shaded. It occupies a prominent place in my private office. Here's a young man who has learned to adapt and excel to a remarkable degree.

Like most people, there was a point in John's life when an incident had a dramatic impact on him. When he was ten years old, John's mother, realizing that he was someday going to leave home and be on his own, put a stop to all the help he'd been getting from his brothers. John was pouting and "raising sand" as a result of the sudden change. His mother, without saying a word, put a newspaper column in front of him. It was a story of a little girl who also did not have arms, but neither did she have feet. John says that was the day he started looking at what he had instead of what he did not have.

At that moment John Foppe started growing and maturing. Today, he assures audiences everywhere that all of us are disabled in some way, but over-the-top people develop and use what they have to become the winners they were born to be.

CONDITION OR PROBLEM?

The remarkable story of John Foppe is made possible by the fact that his parents, and particularly his mother, truly an amazing woman, chose not to make his physical condition a problem. EXAMPLE: A broken arm is a problem that can be solved. Missing arms are a condition. Later, John himself adopted this attitude, which is one of the reasons he was selected by the U.S. Junior Chamber of Commerce as one of the Top Ten Outstanding Young Americans for 1993.

John and his parents had an option on how they handled his condition. They could react to it, which is negative, or they could respond to it, which is positive. Fortunately, they elected to respond to the condition, working with and around it. Many people would believe there could be nothing positive about being born without arms, but real winners in life look at a problem and understand that there is an equivalent or perhaps even greater benefit in that problem. So they look for the solutions, the alternative.

Your question might well be, What possible benefit could there be in having no arms? Well, let's examine it from a realistic point of view. If John had been born with the biggest, longest, strongest arms ever attached to a human body, there still would have been only so much he could have done with them. Since there is a limit to what we can do with arms, there is a limit to what John has missed by not having them.

As a small child, John sensed his loss when he realized he could not play ball with the other children and could not climb trees with his brothers. The one incident that had the greatest impact on John occurred when he was in Haiti on a church mission trip. He saw extreme poverty and children starving— not only for food but for affection as well. A little guy, four or five years old, very friendly and open, ran up and threw his arms around John's legs. John looked down and wanted so badly to hug the child back, but he obviously could not. Yes, there are instances when John would particularly love to have arms, but he has accepted their absence, and he is using what he does have with conviction, confidence, and gratitude.

John's story is the classic example that validates Dr. Nathaniel Branden's statement that "the more solid our self-esteem, the better equipped we are to cope with the troubles that arise in our careers and personal lives."

USE WHAT YOU'VE GOT

In order for John to function in today's society, he's had to be extraordinarily creative and extremely patient. On many occasions he has had to display an incredible amount of courage and wisdom. There is a limit to what we can physically do; mentally, the ceilings are infinitely higher. The fact that John was forced into all of these creative efforts has made him more compassionate, brighter, wiser, and more productive. He has to use his creative imagination more in a day than most people have to use theirs in a month. Because John wisely capitalizes on the creative opportunities his condition creates, he is able to compete and excel on the playing fields of life.

John has several qualities that everyone admires: his courage, positive attitude, sense of humor, intelligence, willingness to adjust, ability to improvise, creativity, and adaptability to virtually any situation. He's truly an inspiration to those of us who work with him and to all who are fortunate enough to know him or hear him speak.

Most of us have arms and legs as well as the qualities John Foppe has, so Fred Smith challenges us with the question, "Why is it that people do not use their talent?" He points out that we're stewards of our talents and we have a responsibility to develop and use them. We should accept God's talent gifts to us and say thank you. The only way we can really express our thanks is to develop and use the talents.

QUESTION: Why would people not develop and use their

talents? According to Fred Smith, one reason is *denial.* Many people find it comfortable to deny a talent. They use the excuse "poor little me," "I'm only a housewife," or "I'm only a high-school graduate." (NOTE: Fourteen of the CEOs of the Fortune 500 companies only finished high school.) After all, if they deny their talents, then perhaps they can persuade others that they really don't have anything to offer. Consequently, they will not be criticized or condemned for not doing anything because they have nothing to do anything with.

Then Fred offers the second reason for people not using their talents, and it's called *procrastination.* They're going to use them in the nonexistent future on Someday Isle ("someday I'll"), which is a nonexistent island. Someday Isle is one of the greatest excuses ever given. Tomorrow is the greatest laborsaving device ever brought to light.

I believe *fear* (which is faith in reverse) is a major reason for not using our talents. Many people don't understand that failure is an event and not a person, so they decide to play it safe and not do anything at all. Then they will not have failed because they never tried.

The fourth reason people do not use their talents is *irresponsibility.* They find it more comfortable to blame other things and other people for their failures. They accept no responsibility for failure and are comfortable in blaming the system. In their minds, being irresponsible is not a failure, but accepting responsibility and not succeeding represents failure.

Some of the saddest words you'll ever hear are "what might have been." Speaker Vicki Hitzges puts it in a unique and dif-

> **"** *These ten little two-letter words—* If it is to be it is up to me—*are absolutely valid. The solution is to do it now.* **"**

ferent way when she asks, "Will you look back on life and say, 'I wish I had' or 'I'm glad I did'?" *Over the Top* is going to make it possible for you to look back one day and say, "I'm glad I did." You do have a choice.

"LET ME REINTRODUCE MYSELF"

Several years ago after I had spoken in Atlanta, Georgia, a woman and her husband patiently waited while I autographed books. When everyone else had departed, she and her husband came forward. She introduced herself, saying, "I'm Jan McBarron. I'm the one who wrote you the letter, and this is my husband, Duke Liberatore. I wanted to identify myself and elaborate on what I said in the letter. Like you, I, too, weighed well over two hundred pounds and as you can see, I am no longer overweight"—and she wasn't. "Unlike you, I smoked two to three packs of cigarettes a day, and I no longer smoke. Unlike you, I drank, and I'm embarrassed to say there were occasions when I probably drank too much. I no longer drink."

She continued by saying, "I was a nurse for eight years, and I loved being a nurse because I knew I was performing a vital service. But to be honest, my self-image was down to zero. Then I started listening to your How to Stay Motivated tape series, and I heard some things that were tremendously encouraging to me. Among my favorites were,

> ❛*If you don't like who you are and where you are, don't worry about it because you're not stuck either with who you are or where you are. You can grow. You can change. You can be more than you are.* ❜ ❜❜

She said, "I loved it when you quoted Dr. Joyce Brothers who says that you cannot consistently perform in a manner that is inconsistent with the way you see yourself."

Jan continued, "I particularly appreciated the fact that you emphasized that life is tough, but that when you are tough on yourself, life will be infinitely easier on you. That if you discipline yourself to do the things you need to do when you need to do them, the day will come when you can do the things you want to do when you want to do them. But," she said, "I think the thing I appreciated the most was that you really hit hard on the fact that to do the things we really want to do requires a considerable amount of effort, but that the effort is worth it. It is tough, but the rewards are great."

Then she paused and said, "I would like to reintroduce myself, Mr. Ziglar. I'm Jan McBarron, M.D. I'm one of six women in America who specializes in bariatrics, the area of medicine that deals with weight management or weight control."

She went ahead to say that she worked her way through medical school. Now, that's like climbing Mt. Everest backward. Most doctors will tell you that the toughest thing they ever did in their lives was to get through medical school, and for Jan to have worked her way through as a full-time nurse is almost beyond belief. NOTE: What she did off the job (medical school) not only determined how far she went on the job but expanded every area of her life.

JAN AND DUKE HAVE IT ALL—
AND SO CAN YOU

Jan and Duke are now good friends of ours. I frequently see them when I'm in their area, and they've been to Dallas to visit with The Redhead and me. I can tell you they are a happy couple. They're healthy, reasonably prosperous, and secure. They have friends, great peace of mind, good family relationships, and that priceless ingredient called *hope* that the future is going to be even better than the past and present.

> *Jan and Duke enjoy "total" success because they balance their physical, mental, and spiritual as well as their personal, family, and business lives.*

Today, Jan McBarron has a nationally syndicated radio and television show called *Duke and the Doctor.* You can hear her on the radio five times a week and look her up at NBC on television. She also has three clinics and travels the country giving lectures. Even with all of these activities, she takes time—one-on-one—to teach functionally illiterate people how to read. Not surprisingly, this unselfish task gives Jan her greatest satisfaction.

She explains that having a senior citizen express gratitude because he no longer has to ask a complete stranger the name of the street he is on is truly a unique experience. What moves her most, however, is when a grandparent tells her that she can now read Bible stories to her grandchildren.

Yes, Jan McBarron touches a lot of lives, many of whom she will never know. She was Georgia's Author of the Year in 1995, and her books have sold more than 500,000 copies. Put all these things together and you can rest assured that the difference she makes in many lives is substantial!

The rest of this exciting story is that Duke Liberatore has not only been tremendously encouraging and supportive of Jan, but he "bought" the ideas and philosophy himself. In January of 1992, he opened a natural foods store, PeachTree Natural Foods, which was chosen as the Health Foods Business Store of the Year for 1993 in the Best New Store category. By 1996, he had expanded his business considerably and now owns six thriving health food stores.

The Jan McBarron and Duke Liberatore story is a classic example of the philosophy on which we've built our business and run our personal and family lives: You can have everything in life you want if you will just help enough other people get what they want.

WHAT IT TAKES TO GET WHAT YOU WANT

Obviously, there are many facets and qualities of a person like Jan McBarron-Liberatore who makes such dramatic changes in her professional, personal, business, and community lives. She is a very caring individual, as evidenced by her desire to be a physician and the role she plays in educating functionally illiterate people. She is also an intelligent, hardworking person and a self-starter who displays enormous amounts of character. When Jan decided to become a physician, she went back to school to get that part of her education. It required vision and persistence for her to see down the road and spend those years working as a full-time nurse and being a full-time medical student.

I'm certain there were many times when Jan was stressed out, needing sleep, relaxation, and personal time. Because she had made her plans, prepared, and committed to become a physician, she knew if she continued in the pursuit of her dream, the day would come when the rewards would compensate her far more than the price she was paying at the moment (actually, you don't pay the price—you enjoy the benefits—better picture isn't it?).

Speaking of pictures, chapter 5 deals extensively with changing your picture so you can begin to see yourself as someone whose life can make the kind of statement that John Foppe's, Charlie Wedemeyer's, Jan McBarron's, and Duke Liberatore's lives do. That's exciting and necessary to go over the top.

CHAPTER FIVE

Changing the picture

The most important opinion you have is the one you have of yourself, and the most significant things you say all day are those things you say to yourself.

Anonymous

U nlike so many of the movie and television mysteries, in the case of your life and the progress you have or have not made, it probably was not the butler who did it or caused you not to do it. There's a pretty good probability it was the architect. HYPOTHETICAL SITUATION: Suppose, at long last, you had the resources to build your dream home. You found a marvelous architect with an excellent reputation, you explained what you wanted, and he drew the architectural plans for your home. He made some innovative suggestions that substantially enhanced your original ideas while giving you everything you had ever dreamed of, plus some exciting extras.

MAYBE IT REALLY ISN'T ALL YOUR FAULT

W hen the plans were finally complete down to the minutest detail, you sought and found a builder who had an

63

impeccable reputation and had been in the business for years. You turned the plans over to him with instructions that they were to be followed to the letter. He was to use the materials the architect had recommended and follow that plan exactly.

True to his charge, the builder did exactly as the architect had prescribed. He used exactly the same materials; he acquired the finest carpenters, masons, plumbers, electricians, and every craftsman required to build your beautiful home.

Finally, after what seemed like forever, the home was ready, and it truly was a magnificent structure, beautifully designed and built. With great fanfare you and your family moved in, and once everything was settled, you had an open house, inviting all your friends, family, and business associates. The occasion was a success; the compliments flowed. Like any proud new-home owner, you were completely happy. When the party was over and the cleanup job was finished, you and your mate sat around talking excitedly about the years ahead in your new dream home.

The first few months were all up to your expectations, but then things started to happen. Cracks appeared in the walls and ceilings. The floors started to sag. In a few more weeks the home became unsafe to live in. Some of the supporting beams were at the point of collapse, and the home was a disaster. The question is, Who is to blame?

Now remember, the architect had drawn the plans and the builder followed them to the nth detail. Do you blame the builder or the architect? A moment's reflection will obviously reveal that the architect was the culprit. The materials were of superb quality, and the workmen were the best available. The builder had followed the plan exactly. The problem was very simple: The plan was faulty.

CHANGE IS A CHOICE

Here are my questions, which are primarily designed to give you comfort and encouragement: Is there a possibility that you're not as far along in life as you would like to be? Is it because you don't have the ability, or is it far more likely that you have everything it takes, but you have been following the wrong plan of action for your life? Reality says that regardless of how many wonderful qualities you have, if you make the wrong choices and follow the wrong game plan, you won't make it over the top.

> **66** *One definition of insanity is to believe that you can keep on doing what you've been doing and get different results.* **99**

Now you're faced with a choice. You can choose to keep on doing what you've been doing (following the same blueprint), which means you'll keep on getting what you've been getting, or you can choose to accept that you do have what it takes (you do), but you've been following the wrong blueprint.

THE BLUEPRINT IS A PICTURE IN YOUR MIND

Psychologists will tell you in a New York minute (which, for your information, is thirty-two seconds) that you invariably, inevitably, move toward the strongest impression in your mind. For example, a law enforcement officer who stops a lawbreaker on the side of the road has seven times as good a chance of having his patrol car hit by a passing motorist if he leaves his flashing light on as he does if he turns the light off.

We are attracted to the strongest impression in our minds. The picture we paint in our minds is likely to be fulfilled. The parent who says to the child who wants to help with the dishes, "Okay, but be careful. This is our best china; don't break it," could not have given better instructions had he or she sat up all night praying, "Lord, what can I do to help this child break more dishes?" The picture painted in the mind is clear—break the dishes.

The field goal kicker who says to himself, "If I miss, we lose the game," has just painted a clear picture—miss. Therefore, he is far less likely to make the field goal than is the kicker who says, "I'll split the uprights [a better picture] and we will win the game." (I'm assuming that both kickers have the leg strength and expertise to kick the field goals.) The picture concept works or influences performance in the family, school, business, team, church, and community.

VERBAL COACH? YES
FOOTBALL COACH? NO

I am a football fan, not an expert. The only thing I really know about football is that when the official calls a foul on my home team, the Dallas Cowboys, he is wrong. I also know that over 20 percent of all the points scored in the National Football League are scored in the last two minutes of the first and second halves of the game.

There are two reasons for this. One reason is that all week long the teams practice their two-minute offense; they plan to score, they prepare to score, and as a result they expect to score. I might add that in life when we plan to win and prepare to win, we have every legitimate reason to expect to win.

The second reason for the increased scoring is that, incredibly enough, the defense cooperates with the offense to help them score. Now I'm confident you football experts will take serious issue with that last statement. I can almost hear you say, "That's ridiculous! Why, they even set up a special 'prevent' defense. They bring in their best pass rushers, pull their linebackers, and send in their fast nickel backs. They get into a bend-but-don't-break mode, they are willing to concede a few yards but not the bomb, and everything is all set to prevent the touchdown that the offense is planning, preparing, and expecting to score." QUESTION: Does the prevent defense work? ANSWER: The offense scores three times as fast against the prevent defense as it does against the regular defense.

MAJOR POINT: The offense is playing to win; the defense is playing not to lose. That is a major difference between success and failure. When you play not to lose, the most vivid picture in your mind is painted by the word *lose.* A few thousand years ago, a man named Job said, "The thing I greatly feared has come upon me" (Job 3:25).

Now, back to that football game. As the prevent defense rushes onto the field, you can hear the fans screaming, "Don't let 'em score!" "Hold 'em!" "Keep 'em away from the side-lines!" The defensive coaches say to their players as they send them in, "Heads up fellows—watch your man, check him, don't let him get behind you." The fans, the coaches, and many times the players are afraid the offense is going to score.

YOUR QUESTION: What kind of defense should they play? Since I'm not a football coach, I will leave the choice of the players and the formation they use up to the football coaches. However, I am a verbal coach, so I would saturate my description of the defense and the defenders with positive word pictures. I'd call it our control defense, take-away defense, or takeover defense (think about those pictures).

Instead of calling them nickel backs (In your mind, how valuable is a nickel?), I would call them the intimidators, the takeover guys, or the turnover specialists. I'd use words like *the power team, the wall,* or *the dominators.*

RIGHT PICTURES HELP— WRONG PICTURES HURT

In the business world the sales manager who says to the salesperson as he goes out to make a call, "This is our number one client. Be careful. Don't foul up the deal," is obviously painting the wrong picture and shakes the confidence of the salesperson. RIGHT PICTURE: "This is our number one client.

That's the reason I'm sending you out to make the call. I know you can handle it very professionally and effectively."

Right pictures and wrong pictures can be painted with one sentence. The person who says, "I hope I don't forget," or "Don't let me forget," has just given himself the wrong instructions. It's far better for him to say, "I'm going to remember that I placed the keys in my top desk drawer."

The list can be endless. I encourage you to take a notepad and each time you catch yourself saying something that paints a negative picture, write down what you've just said and then rephrase it to paint a positive picture. Repeat that positive statement until it becomes a part of you. The March 1990 issue of *USAir Magazine* clearly states that scientific evidence is conclusive that your self-talk has a direct bearing on your performance. In reality, the most influential person who will talk to you all day is you, so you should be very careful about what you say to you.

> Scientific evidence is conclusive that your self-talk has a direct bearing on your performance.

Thus far I've primarily talked, as far as pictures are concerned, about reaching objectives in life like kicking field goals, remembering, or saving on dishes. Now I'll get into considerable detail on changing the picture you have of yourself, because until that picture is changed, you will continue to follow the wrong blueprint.

NEEDED—GLAREPROOF GLASSES

One evening, The Redhead and I walked into an optical company in the Prestonwood Shopping Mall in Dallas, Texas. A young man approached us with the standard question, "May I help you?"

I responded that yes, I wanted a pair of glareproof glasses. He asked if I was a photographer, and I explained that no, I planned to use them for a videotaping for satellite transmission. He then asked if I was a producer.

I replied, "No, I'm a speaker." So he wanted to know what I spoke about. I said, "Primarily on leadership, motivation, sales training, goal setting, attitude control, and family-type seminars on *Courtship After Marriage* and *Raising Positive Kids in a Negative World.*"

With that he brightened up considerably, saying, "Oh, kind of like Zig Ziglar!"

And I responded, "Well, sort of."

"This *is* Zig Ziglar," The Redhead said, pointing toward me.

He was a very cool young man. He took a step backward, looked me over for several seconds, then started shaking his head as he said, "Oh, no! This is not Zig Ziglar. I've seen videotapes of him and he's always jumping up and down."

At that I smiled and said, "You see, Sweetheart, I told you we were not going to be able to fool this young man. He's probably looking for some forty- or fifty-year-old codger, and he sees two youngsters instead. He's looked me over pretty good, and he knows I could never be Zig Ziglar."

The young man smiled and said, "That's right."

So we went ahead with our transaction. When he was ready to do the paperwork, he picked up his pen and asked, "Now, what is your name?"

I smiled and said, "Well, I spell it Z-I-G-L-A-R."

The young man literally dropped his pen on the counter, and he exclaimed, "You *are* Zig Ziglar!"

So I laughed and said, "Yeah, I have been for a long time."

THE PICTURE WAS NARROW AND SHALLOW

I relate this story because the young man had a picture of me, and as far as the picture went, it was accurate. On occasion I do jump up and down. But realistically, his picture of me was so narrow and shallow that it bore little resemblance to who I am or what I am capable of doing.

Over the years in all the reading and research I've done, I've become completely convinced that the overwhelming majority of the people in our great country—and for that matter, around the world—have a picture of themselves that is so narrow and shallow that it bears little or no resemblance to who they are or what they can do.

> *Far too many people have no idea of what they can do because all they have been told is what they can't do. They don't know what they want because they don't know what's available* for them.

Unfortunately, too many people see how success and the good life would be available for everybody else, but they protest, "For me? No way!"

My goal is to work with you to change that picture to a more realistic one that will enable you to recognize your true abilities. Just having ability and intelligence is not the key—it's recognizing that ability, confessing it, appreciating it, developing it, and then using it. That's the key.

DO YOU KNOW WHO HIS DADDY IS?

In his beautiful book *Rising Above the Crowd,* Brian Harbour tells the story of Ben Hooper. When Ben Hooper was born many years ago in the foothills of East Tennessee, little boys and girls like Ben who were born to unwed mothers were ostracized and treated terribly. By the time he was three years old, the other children would scarcely play with him. Parents were saying idiotic things like, "What's a boy like that doing playing with our children?" as if the child had anything at all to do with his own birth.

Saturday was the toughest day of all. Ben's mom would take

him down to the little general store to buy their supplies for the week. Invariably, the other parents in the store would make caustic comments just loudly enough for both mother and child to hear, comments like, "Did you ever figure out who his daddy is?" What a tough, tough childhood.

In those days there was no kindergarten. So, at age six, little Ben entered the first grade. He was given his own desk, as were all the children. At recess, he stayed at that little desk and studied because by then none of the children would play with him. At noon, little Ben could be found eating his sack lunch all alone. The happy chatter of the children who shunned him was barely audible from where he sat.

It was a big event when anything changed in the foothills of East Tennessee, and when little Ben was twelve years old, a new preacher came to pastor the little church in Ben's town.

Almost immediately, little Ben started hearing exciting things about him—about how loving and nonjudgmental he was. How he accepted people just as they were, and when he was with them, he made them feel like the most important people in the world. Reportedly, the preacher had charisma. When he walked into a group of any size, anywhere, the entire complexion of that group changed. Their smiles broadened, their laughter increased, and their spirits rose.

THE FIRST STEP IN GROWTH IS ACTION

One Sunday, though he had never been to church a day in his life, little Ben Hooper decided he was going to go and hear the preacher. He got there late and he left early because he did not want to attract any attention, but he liked what he heard. For the first time in that young boy's life, he caught just a glimmer of hope.

Ben was back in church the next Sunday—and the next and the next. He always got there late and always left early, but his hope was building each Sunday.

On about the sixth or seventh Sunday the message was so

moving and exciting that Ben became absolutely enthralled with it. It was almost as if there were a sign behind the preacher's head that read, "For you, little Ben Hooper of unknown parentage, there is hope!" Ben got so wrapped up in the message, he forgot about the time and didn't notice that a number of people had come in after he had taken his seat.

Suddenly, the services were over; Ben very quickly stood up to leave as he had in all the Sundays past, but the aisles were clogged with people and he could not run out. As he was working his way through the crowd, he felt a hand on his shoulder. He turned around and looked up, right into the eyes of the young preacher who asked him a question that had been on the mind of every person there for the last twelve years: "Whose boy are you?"

Instantly, the church grew deathly quiet. Slowly, a smile started to spread across the face of the young preacher until it broke into a huge grin, and he exclaimed, "Oh! I know whose boy you are! Why, the family resemblance is unmistakable. You are a child of God!"

And with that the young preacher swatted him across the rear and said, "That's quite an inheritance you've got there, boy! Now, go and see to it that you live up to it."

Many, many years later, Ben Hooper said that was the day he was elected and later reelected governor of the state of Tennessee. The picture had changed, and when the picture changed, everything in little Ben's life changed. He had gone from being the child of an unknown father to being the child of the King.

To be candid, I do not remember my earthly father, who died when I was five years old. On July 4, 1972, I met my heavenly Father, whom I can never forget. When I, like Ben, became a child of the King, every facet of my life changed for the better.

It's true that what one person says to another can dramatically change the latter's performance. The same is true of you and the woman in the next story. Change the picture, and you will change your life.

FROM CAKE BAKER/SEAMSTRESS TO VICE PRESIDENT/SALES

My first professional career start was selling heavy-duty waterless cookware. When I had been in the cookware business for a period of time, I realized I needed some help. I ran an ad in the Columbia, South Carolina, newspaper, and a woman named Gerry Arrowood responded. Prior to our interview, Gerry's work experience included baking cakes and taking in sewing to earn money for her family. The interview went well. She was quiet but pleasant. She explained to me when the interview was over that the job certainly sounded interesting and that she loved to cook. She even assured me that she did not mind washing dishes or cleaning the kitchen; however, she was shy and did not relate to people. Therefore, I must never call on her to participate in the demonstration. As she put it, "Zig, I'll do all the work—you do all the talking."

Well, I could immediately tell that Gerry and I were going to get along real good—and we did for the next three months. Then one night my mouth overloaded my back, and I made more promises than time would let me keep. As a salesman in the cookware business, I conducted dinner demonstrations where we prepared meals for six or eight couples whom the hostess had invited into her home. The demonstrations enabled us to sell cookware to the hostess and guests. We then delivered the cookware to the purchasers and taught them how to use it on their own stoves.

One night, as I said, my mouth made promises I couldn't keep; I made too many appointments. When I realized I would be unable to keep them, I asked Gerry to help. She naturally asked me what I wanted her to do. I explained I wanted her to deliver the cookware to the six couples I had sold that evening and teach them how to use it on their own stoves.

Chances are good that you will be unable to relate to the next statement. Terror appeared in Gerry's eyes. Her hands shook as she said, "I can't do it! I can't do it!" However, on the way home, she gave it some more thought, and as she started to get out of the car, she said to me, "Okay, I'll do it. You stuck your neck out, and I don't want to see it cut off. However, let me be honest, Zig, and tell you that I won't sleep a wink tonight; I'll be absolutely miserable." Then she did something that she denies doing, but it is clear in my mind. She shook her finger in my face (well, almost) and said, "Zig, I'm going to tell you that if you ever do this again, it's your neck that will be cut off, not mine."

She was not exactly happy. To be candid, I don't know if she slept that night or not. I sure didn't.

THEY BRAGGED ON ME

My fears, as most fears are, were groundless. The next night I got one of the most exciting telephone calls I've ever received. Gerry was wound up tighter than a nine-day clock. With enormous enthusiasm, she said, "Zig, you cannot believe how much fun I've had today! The first family I delivered cookware to had the coffeepot on and a piece of cake waiting for me. They really bragged on me and told me how professional I was, what a nice personality I had, and how much they enjoyed having me in their home. They even invited me to come back with my girls and have dinner and said they would do the cooking! Three of the six couples had the coffee and dessert ready, and all of them told me what a good job I had done. They really made me feel good!"

She concluded our phone conversation by saying, "I don't ever remember having this much fun or feeling so good about myself. I'll be glad to do this for you anytime." Her "picture" (self-image) had just undergone a dramatic change.

SUMMATION: It didn't happen that week, that month, or that year, but less than five years later, Gerry Arrowood was the international vice president in charge of sales training for a multimillion-dollar cosmetics company. I had no idea what an exciting future she had when I asked Gerry Arrowood to deliver those six sets of cookware.

How I wish I had retained the names of the customers Gerry met with that day, especially the first one. I have an idea that after the warm reception the first couple gave her, Gerry headed for that second home with considerably more excitement, enthusiasm, and confidence. That first couple turned out to be catalysts, didn't they? By seeing Gerry's good qualities and telling her about them, they started a growth process for Gerry that continues to this day.

Today, she and her husband, Bob Volberding, live in San Rafael, California, where they manufacture cosmetics for a number of private label, quality-conscious cosmetics companies. When the picture Gerry Arrowood had of herself changed, her life changed. That will also be true in your life.

LOOKING AT GERRY'S STORY FROM YOUR PERSPECTIVE

What is exciting about Gerry's story is that it is so applicable to you and your life. First, it required enormous courage on Gerry's part to take that step and deliver that cookware. Actually, courage is the base upon which all of our good qualities are built. Without the courage to take the first step, we are going to remain right where we are.

One reason she took that step was because of the compassion

Caring is more than compromise and more than mutual agreement not to hurt each other. It is a tacit agreement to help each other.

Anonymous

she felt for me. She knew that I was in a jam and that if she didn't deliver the merchandise for me, it would affect my credibility, and she did not want to see that happen. She really cared.

Gerry is a very humble, gentle person, which makes her very teachable because she starts with the advantage of not knowing it all. She also has pride in her performance and neatness of appearance. Gerry is, and always has been, very conscientious and completely dependable in what she does. She does everything required of her and then some. That kind of commitment produces over-the-top results.

After taking that first step, she became highly motivated, and her self-image improved dramatically. Her confidence started to soar, her personality blossomed, and she became more assertive. She started setting bigger goals; she developed a keen sense of humor; her optimism rose; she became more positive and extremely grateful for the opportunity life offered her. The results speak for themselves.

Let me point out that Gerry started with only seven of those qualities, which she had developed to any degree. She had courage, compassion, pride, and humility; she was conscientious, absolutely dependable, and a very hard worker. The other qualities were developed as a direct result of using what she already had. That's a tremendous lesson for you to learn about motivation!

> **Don't wait until you feel like taking a positive action. Take the action and then you will feel like doing it.**

Don't miss a major, major point. The motivation came after she took action. LESSON: Don't wait until you feel like taking a positive action. Take the action and then you will feel like doing it. That's taking responsibility, and when Gerry did that, the picture she had of herself changed, and her life changed.

ANOTHER MAJOR POINT

I am absolutely certain that when Gerry Arrowood agreed to deliver those sets of cookware and teach our customers how to use them, she was not thinking, *I'm going to do this because I really want to be the vice president in charge of sales training for a large cosmetics company, and Zig told me that I can have everything in life I want if I will just help enough other people get what they want.*

Obviously, that would be ludicrous. That's the reason you must clearly understand that I'm talking about a philosophy and not a tactic. Gerry did what she did for me because she genuinely wanted to help by bailing me out of the predicament I was in. There was no profit motive in it for her. It's a classic example of what happens when you are the right kind of person and go the extra mile.

> *It's not what you know or who you know—it's what you are that finally counts.*
>
> Anonymous

THE PICTURE AFFECTS THE GRADES

The February 1992 issue of *Scientific American* had a fascinating article concerning educational results when certain procedures are followed and genuine pride is developed. The article focused on immigrants from Indonesia who came into America after having been held in detention camps for two or three years. They settled into the inner cities of America, and what they accomplished academically was outstanding.

A number of factors were involved. First, the parents frequently read to their children, and whether they read in their native tongue or in English made little difference, academically speaking. Second, the children were taught to be proud of their heritage and to be both proud and grateful that they were privileged to be Americans. Third, the parents cooperated and worked with the educators so that together they could give the children the best possible education.

Similar results were recorded for Japanese-American students after World War II when prejudice and animosity toward the Japanese were at an all-time high. Those students who were read to and encouraged to study by their parents and taught to be proud of their culture, while also being proud to be Americans, did extremely well in school.

A history of the Jewish people who came into America and followed the same procedures produced the same results. The article also noted that African-Americans in inner-city America who took the same steps produced the same academic results.

On December 15, 1992, an interview with Senator-elect (now Senator) Ben Nighthorse Campbell from Colorado appeared in *USA Today.* He revealed some interesting data about results in tribal colleges in America. He stated that nine out of ten Native American students who go directly from high school to a mainstream college fail. However, nine out of ten who go to tribal colleges succeed.

Moreover, many tribal college graduates return to their reservations as doctors, nurses, teachers, artists, engineers, counselors, and role models for the next generation of Native Americans. The pride they develop and continue as they maintain their own culture, while getting a quality education to enable them to compete in modern America, is exciting.

As we look at these academic examples, the same picture emerges from each group. The students all had a healthy picture of themselves. The picture was developed and repeatedly reinforced by the love, attention, and time devoted to them by their parents. It was strengthened by the cooperation between parents and educators and undergirded by the development of pride in their culture and heritage.

THINK ABOUT IT

If you will carefully evaluate what you just read, you will realize that I have just spoken of many races, colors, and creeds that encompass a variety of religious beliefs from all over the world. All of them achieved almost identical results when they were given the same treatment that I am covering throughout *Over the Top*. Think of the incredible opportunities and possibilities that concept offers.

> **❝** *To eliminate prejudice (self-prejudice included) in our land would enable us to use our greatest resource, which is our people—all of them.* **❞**

NOTE: In the event you did not receive love, time, attention, and encouragement to develop cultural pride from your parents and educators, let me remind you that most of the three hundred world-class leaders discussed earlier did not have these advantages, either. What has happened to you or where you started is not what makes the difference. What you do now with this information will make a difference.

THE MIKE IS OPEN AND THE CAMERA IS ON

We regularly hear about some politician, athlete, movie star, or other public figure who makes an intemperate (to be kind) statement and gets roasted by the media. The personality then offers a lame excuse about not knowing that the mike was open or that the camera was on. The next incident makes a point and teaches a valuable lesson.

Several years ago I was speaking at a trade school in Tulsa, Oklahoma, with several hundred students in attendance. Early on, approximately one-third of the students were attentively listening. About one-third were reading newspapers, magazines, or something that appealed to them, and the other third of the students had their eyes closed, pretending to be asleep.

The local television station had gotten word that I was to be speaking at the school and sent a camera crew to get some shots. They walked in the back of the auditorium with camera in hand and spotlight glaring, so they could film the students listening to the presentation. They walked down the left-hand aisle, came up on stage, got behind me, and started filming the entire student body as they listened to the presentation.

An interesting phenomenon took place. One hundred percent of the students suddenly became alert, sat up straight, rearranged their clothing, combed their hair, and became enormously attentive. The spotlight was on them.

In many ways the spotlight is always on all of us as far as our morals, ethics, and responsibilities are concerned. For instance, if we knew that a permanent picture was being made of us and our behavior at this very moment, we would instinctively rush about trying to change and improve the image that permanent picture will portray. Multitudes of ever-present mirrors in portrait studios are evidence of this undeniable fact. Let's don't get caught unaware. By conducting our lives as if the camera is on and the mike is open, we will be living with integrity, and the picture we have of ourselves will be character based and nonhypocritical, which means we won't have to apologize for or explain tomorrow what we did today. This really is a character issue.

And on trust you can build friendships, a marriage, a career, and a high quality of life. Over-the-top people have character.

> *Men of genius are admired. Men of wealth are envied. Men of power are feared, but only men of character are trusted.*
> Arthur Friedman

CHAPTER SIX

The immigrant's attitude

Real optimism is aware of problems but recognizes the solutions, knows about difficulties but believes they can be overcome, sees the negatives but accentuates the positives, is exposed to the worst but expects the best, has reason to complain but chooses to smile.

William Arthur Ward

s an American citizen, I am deeply concerned that in 1990 the top-selling T-shirt in Japan was,

We're Number One!

while the top-selling T-shirt in America carried the message

Underachiever—And Proud of It!

Unfortunately, some people think that's funny, but when you consider the picture it paints, the humor quickly evaporates. I'm convinced that it's tragic, or that it certainly indicates an unfortunate attitude. Why? In my opinion, any individual who would wear a T-shirt like that probably just became unemployable. Furthermore, if an employer thought that prospective employees held that attitude, whether they wore such a shirt or not, the employer probably would not hire them.

It would be difficult to overestimate the importance of your attitude. One of the most fascinating bits of data I've acquired recently came from author and speaker Walter Hailey, an outstanding, successful former insurance executive. He tells me that legal immigrants are four times more likely to become millionaires than people born in America. That's true whether the immigrant is from the Orient, Central or South America, Africa, the Middle East, or Europe. The reason for that was made clear to me one day by a little four-year-old girl.

GOSH

It was Friday, July 10, 1992, 12:48 P.M. I departed Dallas on American Airlines flight #874 to Norfolk, Virginia, seated in seat *2C*. I was the first passenger to board the aircraft. I had just taken my seat when a mother and three little girls came aboard. I suspected it was their first flight. The mother led the way, carrying an infant and leading a toddler. They passed me quickly and headed toward the rear of the aircraft.

The four-year-old was several steps behind. As she boarded, she noticed that directly in front of her the caterers were loading the food for the in-flight lunch. Stopping in the middle of the aisle, she bent her little legs, placed her hands just above her knees, and looked intently for a few seconds at the two caterers who were quickly moving containers of food aboard. Then she slowly turned her head to the left to look into the cockpit. I'm certain she was absolutely enthralled with what she saw—three very impressive figures dressed in uniforms with a bunch of bars across their shoulders. Before her were the dual control levers, the two flight wheels, the dozens and dozens of lights, and probably more electronic gadgetry than she had seen in her entire lifetime.

For a number of seconds she stood there, utterly fascinated. When she slowly turned around, her blue eyes were as big as saucers. The sight before her was a long—and I do mean long—fuselage, made up entirely of empty seats—she could see all the way to the rear of the plane. As she looked down that long aisle, she uttered one word that said it all: "Gosh!"

NOW THEY TELL ME

That's what legal immigrants say when they come to America. They can't believe what's before them. In most cases, they see beauty, luxury, and opportunity beyond their wildest imaginations. They view it all every day with the "Gosh!" attitude. They look in astonishment at the number of jobs advertised in the paper, then busily set about acquiring one of them. They recognize that they are earning minimum wage, but minimum wage in America is maximum wage compared to that of many other countries. Typical immigrants are willing to live as cheaply as possible and, if need be, get a second job. They work incredibly hard, are thrifty, and save their money.

Before they discover all the problems and difficulties we have in America, it's too late—they have already become successful. They are hooked on the idea that their future is bright, and they accept the responsibility that it is going to be as bright or as dull as they choose to make it. They have been given a dream beyond all their childhood expectations. Their hopes are unbelievably high.

Before them lies the opportunity to live, to work, to grow, to succeed in the greatest country in the world. And almost without exception, their gratitude for America and the opportunity it represents is deep and heartfelt.

Think about it. When you claim the qualities we cover throughout *Over the Top,* you are expressing gratitude for what you have. That's the key to having more to express gratitude for

The immigrant's attitude 83

QUALITIES MAKE IT HAPPEN

A few weeks after the incident with the four-year-old girl, I traveled to New Orleans, Louisiana, to speak at a national convention. After I finished speaking, I caught a cab back to the airport, and when I spoke with the driver, I recognized that he was not a citizen of the South. So I asked him where he was from, and he told me he was from Nigeria. His name was Pious Obioha. He told me a great deal about his background and his family. He had come to America twelve years before with his wife, and they now had four children, ages four, six, eight, and ten.

When I asked him if he'd been getting more education since he'd come to America, he replied with a big smile: Oh, yes, he had. As a matter of fact, he was to receive his Ph.D. in October of 1992. He also pointed out that his wife had already earned her master's degree. So I commented that I figured his children must be doing quite well in school, also. He proudly responded that yes, the three who were in school were all honor students.

Then I asked him about his parents, and he told me that both of them were illiterate. He explained that he did not know that until his first day of kindergarten, when he came home needing help with his homework. They couldn't give it to him because they could neither read nor write. He said it was then he decided to get a good education.

When I observed that insight like that was most unusual for a five-year-old, he replied yes, perhaps it was. But he well remembered the hurt and pain on his parents' faces when they had to tell him they could not help him with his homework. That day he promised himself it would never happen to him.

Then I asked him how he had provided for his family during his years in America. He pointed out that, as I could see, he was driving a cab at the moment; he had also been a grave digger and a security guard; he had loaded and unloaded trucks; and he had served as a tutor. In short, he had done whatever it took to accomplish his objectives. He made certain I understood that his wife had worked just as hard as he had.

He also shared with me that he had secured a job with a major Wall Street firm, and that he was moving to New York as soon as he received his doctorate in business and finance. He planned to work two years on Wall Street, then return to Nigeria where he had been assured a prominent position in his government.

TEMPORARY PAIN—LIFETIME GAIN

Let's take a look at the qualities that enabled Pious Obioha to achieve his dream of a good education. It took great *faith* to leave his native land and his extended family and come to America. It took faith in his ability to accomplish his objective and faith that this new country really was the land of opportunity. He made a tremendous commitment, accepted the responsibility for his future, focused on exactly what he wanted, and displayed an enormous amount of persistence. He was a very *patient* man and, of necessity, very *thrifty* since he had provided for his family with menial jobs.

He was obviously a *student,* and he exhibited a willingness to delay gratification by working hard and denying himself in the present so he could be assured of better things in the future. All of these are sure signs of *sound judgment* and *maturity.* They are qualities anyone can take to any marketplace in the world and know that they are highly marketable. These qualities ensure employment security and all the other benefits that go with being an over-the-top person.

CONVICTION PRECEDES COMMITMENT

Pious Obioha had a tremendous desire fueled from childhood by the illiteracy of his parents. When he saw their hurt because of their inability to help him with his homework, a desire was born, and it grew steadily all of his life. That strong *desire* caused him to focus intently on getting his *education.* Consequently, he became quite creative in his thinking and proceeded to accomplish his objective. He had a deep *conviction* that education was the key to everything he wanted in life.

Perhaps the most significant part of this story is the realization that *discipline* had to be a major part of that family's life for twelve years. *Can we even imagine the number of times he came in from work, dead tired, needing to get some sleep, but family responsibility and tomorrow's assignments demanded his time and energy?* To do what he needed to do instead of what he wanted to do required discipline to an incredible degree. Since the word *discipline* has a tendency, because of a total misunderstanding of the word, to evoke those here's-something-else-I-have-to-do pictures, I'll delve into its positive aspects a little later.

Just in case you think the Pious Obioha story is unique, let me remind you that legal immigrants are four times as likely to become millionaires as are native-born Americans. They do this despite the additional *obstacles of language, lack of contacts, culture shock,* or *separation from family.* Or do they become millionaires because they become stronger and more creative as they work through the obstacles?

Other legal immigrants and children of immigrants who have done well include General John Shalikashvili (to simplify it for all of us President Clinton calls him General Shalik), who immigrated from Poland to America and is now our chairman of the Joint Chiefs of Staff; Bob Maynard, owner of the *Oakland Tribune,* the son of immigrants from Jamaica and the first African-American to own a major daily newspaper; and also the son of immigrants from Jamaica, General Colin Powell, who grew up in the Bronx and is our former chairman of the Joint Chiefs of Staff. Sam Moore, the publisher of this book, is an immigrant who still has the "Gosh!" attitude, as are the CEOs of four of the top ten corporations identified by

Fortune magazine as the most desirable places in America to work.

I frequently encounter immigrants from all over the globe at my seminars. The one comment I hear the most is, "If disgruntled Americans would go to my country and live as I did for one week, they would be just as grateful for America as I am."

On a personal note, Krish Dhanam, a friend and a key member of our staff at The Zig Ziglar Corporation, is a native of India, and he verifies everything I'm talking about. He's one of our top people because he is bright, hardworking, perceptive, and committed. As a young lad, he made his decision to come to America, made his plans, and arrived in America with lots of dreams and nine dollars to finance his start. He patiently sacrificed many things in the beginning. Today, Krish is doing quite well for himself and doing a marvelous job for us. I'd say his future is bright.

The immigration attitude embraces honesty, faith, discipline, conviction, focus, direction, desire, hope, personal growth, patience, thrift, persistence, flexibility, and gratitude with a capital *G.* And let's not forget about the tendency to say, "Gosh!"

THOSE HAMBURGER FLIPPERS

QUESTION: How many of us who were born in America would be willing to dig graves, drive a taxi, or load trucks to accomplish our long-term objectives? What would our friends and family think if we started "flipping hamburgers"? False pride keeps many people at the bottom because they are unwilling to do today what needs to be done so they can be, do, and have what tomorrow has to offer.

I'm disappointed and upset when I hear some of our highly paid athletes, as well as television and movie personalities or politicians, make disparaging remarks about "hamburger flippers." They frequently say, "If you don't get an education, you'll end up flippin' hamburgers."

QUESTION: Is that really bad? First, it is honest work, and it's infinitely better to make the minimum wage "flipping hamburgers" than it is to make maximum wage dealing drugs or accepting welfare because such a job is beneath your dignity and ability.

Second, our company does a lot of work in the fast-food industry (chicken, pizza, hamburgers, submarine sandwiches, etc.) and family-type restaurants. I personally know many young people who earn important money in the fast-food industry and have won college scholarships for their performance.

Third, because of the expansion of the fast-food industry and the need for highly motivated, enthusiastic younger (or older) people, the opportunities for advancement are great, and these people can move up quickly in that industry.

Opportunity does not lie in the job; it lies in the individual who looks at the possibilities instead of the problems. Many of these people move up into management positions before they are twenty-five years old, receive bonuses of really nice automobiles to drive as their own, and earn fifty thousand dollars a year and more. That's good. Not only that, but they can even become franchise owners.

If more of us had the immigrant's attitude and were willing to "flip hamburgers" to get ahead in life, this country would be a better place to live.

THERE'S ONE MORE THING

Hamburger flippers" and immigrants have one more thing in common. Both of them frequently accept these jobs because of great financial need or the fact that these are the only opportunities available to them at the moment.

These circumstances encourage them to follow directions and do what they are told in order to keep their jobs. In short, be obedient, which incidentally is part of the Scout Law and "obey" is part of the Scout Oath.

OBEDIENT! YOU'VE GOT TO BE KIDDING

Unfortunately, lack of obedience is one of our most difficult problems in America. Many people erroneously believe that being obedient means being subservient to someone else. In reality, it indicates respect for the authority of an authority figure. Realistically speaking, you must respect authority before you can legitimately expect others to respect your authority. A classic example of this was brought to my attention when I had the privilege of speaking to the Notre Dame football team.

The night before the big game, my wife and I were guests of Lou Holtz and the team. Three assistant coaches were at the table as were three student managers. About every three minutes one of the assistant coaches addressed one of the student managers and said, "I need to know . . . ," or "Get me this," or "Do this for me." In each case the student manager instantly jumped up from the table and rushed to fill the request.

During the course of the evening, Lou explained to us that approximately 250 freshmen become student managers but because the job is very demanding and apparently thankless, by the end of the senior year only 50 of the original 250 are still serving. Lou then told me that when he is on the road and some young man or woman tells him that he or she was a student manager at Notre Dame for four years, Lou asks the question, "What is the name of the company you are now running?" Lou said that in the overwhelming majority of the cases they will identify the company. In many other cases, they will say, "Well, actually, I don't run the company, but my department has 175 [or whatever number] in it."

Lou believes, as do I, that one of the reasons this happens is that these young people really have learned to serve, and as the Good Book says, "He who would be the greatest among you must become the servant of all." Also, because they have demonstrated such respect for authority and have learned to be obedient, it is a part of them; consequently, they expect others to respect their authority. The results speak for themselves.

The immigrant's attitude 89

WEALTH IS AN ATTITUDE—
MILLIONAIRES ARE BORING

Right now you might be mildly confused about success, fame, and riches. Erma Bombeck said it well: "Don't confuse success and fame. Madonna has one, Mother Teresa the other." Let's take a look at some other successful people who might not fit the picture of the media's idea of success. (Notice the qualities wealthy people have in common with immigrants.)

The Louis Harris poll of people who earned more than $142,000 a year and had a net worth of over a half million dollars, not including their homes, described these successful people as being unexciting, middle-aged, and cautious. They emphasized family values and the work ethic. Eighty-three percent of them were married. Ninety-six percent of them acquired their net worth through hard work, which means they had the attitude of denial. (They denied themselves immediate gratification so they could have what they really wanted later.) Eighty percent are politically conservative or middle-of-the-road, and they are relatively nonmaterialistic.

In other words, their goals went beyond money. *Eighty-five percent said that their major objective was to provide for their family (that's an attitude of responsibility). Only 11 percent rated owning an expensive car as being very high on their want list. Prestige and the badge of success don't matter to them nearly so much as family, education, and their business or job. Not much excitement but lots of happiness. They have a good standard of living, but infinitely more important, they have an excellent quality of life.* Persistence, consistency, discipline, and hard work (all of which are learned skills) make the difference. Their lives seem to be in balance.

Another study by Thomas J. Stanley (*Medical Economics,* July 20, 1992) showed almost the same thing and identified a few additional qualities that I want to emphasize by setting them apart.

Dr. Stanley's research is consistent with what Solomon said in Proverbs 21:5, "The plans of the diligent lead surely to plenty." Attitude, the greatest difference between millionaires and the rest of us, makes diligence possible.

It's my contention that immigrants are four times more likely to become millionaires than nonimmigrants because they arrive in America with an attitude of hope, excitement, gratitude, and a dream.

Unfortunately, too many native-born Americans get up every morning, look around and instead of saying, "Gosh!" say with sarcasm, "Big deal," and start looking for a fast buck or a free lunch. Well, friend, I'm here to tell you that it really is a big deal to live in this great land.

QUESTION: When was the last time you awakened, looked around at your surroundings, and said, "Gosh!"? When was the last time you counted your freedoms (travel, education, worship, and so forth) and said, "Gosh!"?

I challenge you to immediately start looking through the eyes of that little four-year-old girl and the thousands of legal immigrants who regularly come to our shores and say, "Gosh!" Adopt the "Gosh!" attitude about life, and it will enrich your life immeasurably.

The profile of a wealthy person is this: hard work, perseverance, and most of all, self-discipline. The average wealthy person has lived all his adult life in the same town. He's been married once and is still married. He lives in a middle-class neighborhood next to people with a fraction of his wealth. He's a compulsive saver and investor, and he's made his money on his own. Eighty percent of America's millionaires are first-generation rich. (Doesn't sound to me like opportunity is dead.)

CHAMPIONS ARE DISCIPLINED

Discipline, according to the dictionary, means "to instruct or educate, to inform the mind, to prepare by instructing in correct principles and habits; to advance and prepare by instruction." Author Sybil Stanton says true discipline isn't on your back, needling you with imperatives. It is at your side, nudging you with incentives. These are better pictures because they are true and because they truly build hope for the future.

The great violinist Isaac Stern, who was instrumental in preserving Carnegie Hall, was asked, "Is talent born?" The question was in reference to an outstanding performance by Isaac Stern himself. He responded yes, talent is born, but musicians are made. It takes an incredible amount of discipline, hard work, and talent to become a great musician. No matter how great the talent or the field of endeavor, unless the individual is personally disciplined much of the potential will remain just that—potential.

Roy L. Smith says that "discipline is the refining fire by which talent becomes ability."

Former Secretary of Defense Donald Laird says, "You will get much more done if you will only crack the whip at yourself."

Tie discipline to commitment and it becomes an irreversible decision that you will do today what most people won't so you can have tomorrow what most people can't.

Let's assume that you are one of the millions of people in this world who have been unable, try as they might, to discipline themselves. Let me encourage you to accept the fact that it is not necessarily a weakness. However, it definitely is a weakness not to recognize and acknowledge that you have that problem. Recognizing a problem or weakness is the first step in remedying it.

To paraphrase James Baldwin, confronting a problem doesn't always produce a solution, but until you confront it there can be no solution. Think about it like this.

THE STRONG AND WISE ADMIT THEY ARE WEAK

There's strength in admitting a weakness. Most of us are vulnerable in certain areas of our lives, and those who are wise and ambitious will admit their weaknesses and vulnerability. For example, I have a friend who became addicted to pornography and has broken the habit. Recognizing that weakness, he is careful not to have even the slightest exposure to anything of a pornographic nature. If he's in a place where the television set is on and there's suggestive language or behavior that is of a lustful or seductive nature, he immediately leaves the scene. That's smart.

Recovering alcohol and drug abusers are repeatedly cautioned to avoid at all costs any scene, association, or circumstance having anything to do with drinking or drugs.

One of our former employees who was a most attractive, morally sound young woman was approached by a nice-looking young man whose interests obviously exceeded hand holding. When she refused to see him under any circumstances, he accused her of not trusting herself. She smilingly said, "You've got that right," and moved on. Good strategy.

Of an entirely different nature, many of us need help in some of the discipline areas of our lives, and it is a strength to recognize and compensate for that weakness. My son, Tom, needed to lose some weight, and his wife, Chachis, wanted to gain some weight and strength. In both cases, proper eating habits and exercise routines were of vital importance. Realizing they had started and stopped a health program on previous occasions, they signed up for an organized program and engaged a professional trainer and dietitian who would direct, encourage, and hold them accountable. They made the commitment to follow a disciplined schedule and to work regularly with him. Initially, they felt a fair amount of discomfort and there was a considerable amount of moaning and groaning, but they had made the commitment so they stayed with it.

Results in both cases were substantial. Tom lost the weight, increased his strength considerably, and gained additional energy and confidence (not that he was very short on them!). His effectiveness and productivity increased on the job, and the new picture he has of himself affects every area of his life.

Chachis, whom I call Bonita—which is Spanish for "pretty woman"—gained some weight, her strength and energy level increased dramatically, and her overall health and enthusiasm for life improved. MESSAGE: If you have a weakness, be strong enough to admit it and get some help in whatever area that might be.

DISCIPLINE—THE CHAMPIONSHIP INGREDIENT

M any athletes, musicians, and politicians are enormously disciplined in their quest for success in their profession, but they are undisciplined in their personal lives and ultimately suffer for it in every area of their lives.

One of the significant factors about discipline is that it involves more than just the drive to personally control your actions to accomplish your objectives. I'm speaking of the physical, mental, emotional, and spiritual aspects of discipline.

> **Check the records. There has never been an undisciplined person who was a champion. Regardless of the field of endeavor, you'll find this to be true.**

Many people are hurting in life, and pain involves many facets. It's difficult to stay focused when a member of the family is in a self-destruct mode of life, or when there are personality conflicts with someone on the job. It's also tough to persist when it appears we are not making progress despite our best efforts. We frequently feel hurt and cry out against the unfairness of life itself when we or our loved ones have been treated unfairly and are in pain through no fault of our own.

That's why personal growth as a lifetime commitment is so important. When we're growing and making progress in our lives, it's easier to handle the physical and/or emotional pain that serve as distractions for people who are not disciplined and who do not have their lives focused toward specific objectives. I'm confident that Pious Obioha was able to maintain his discipline because the steady progress he was making toward his goal of getting a superior education gave him the hope that he would ultimately reach his objective.

Over the Top is not intended to give you a view of life through either rose-colored or *woes*-colored glasses; it is intended to provide a very clearly focused view of reality. Reality can be a beautiful picture if you accept it, and that is what you're in the process of doing, even as you read these words. When you undergo pain in your personal, family, or business life, when you're hurting physically, mentally, and spiritually, you can handle that pain infinitely better as you review much of what we've already said. As psychologist John Leddo says, "Discipline itself frequently brings pain, but the pain is temporary while the growth is permanent."

HANDLING THE PAIN

Former Olympic champion Bob Richards, in interviews with Olympic champions, frequently asked, "How do you handle pain?" Someone asked him why he asked that question, and he responded, "You will never be a champion in the world of athletics without some hurting, and you've got to have a plan to handle that hurt." The plan must be specific, well thought out, and perfected before the need for it arises.

One champion was asked how he handled pain, and he said, "I pray through it. I say to the Lord, 'You pick 'em up, and I'll put 'em down.'" When we get that foot up, it's relatively easy to put it down and take that next step.

Champions start and keep going. Edwin Moses, former

world record-holder in the 400-meter hurdles and winner of 122 consecutive races, said he won over and over because he had a better capacity for pain.

I hasten to add that champions in raising well-balanced children, champions in business, academia, government, and other fields, also have to work through the pain peculiar to their field of endeavor. They start and keep going. They don't procrastinate, and they don't quit.

IT TAKES PRIDE

When you have an honest evaluation of yourself, recognizing all of your positive qualities, you will have pride in who you are and what you're capable of doing.

A number of years ago a friend of mine offered me an investment in a business venture. At that time I did not have the money to engage in a speculative investment. He acknowledged that it was high risk, but he was putting his own money

> 66 *False pride or vanity is a very negative quality and one that gets people into a great deal of trouble.* 99

into it and felt the risk was justified. My vanity—and that's all it was—would not permit me to candidly say that I did not have the money or that the timing was wrong. My friend labored under the illusion that I was flush, and I didn't want to disillusion him. That's ridiculous and is even somewhat like the bull standing on the railroad tracks. You admire his courage, but you certainly question his judgment! (I lost the money.) Now let's look at the results of genuine pride, and evaluate how we can develop that pride.

THE MILITARY INSTILLS WINNING QUALITIES

Many years ago when I learned that a military commander had retired and was given an outstanding executive position with a major corporation, I wondered, "What does that person know about running a big business?" That thinking quickly and dramatically changed when our company started doing some training with the military. It was an eye-opening experience. The military is made up of a superb group of people, and their training and experience prepare them exceptionally well for a second career in the business, academic, religious, or political world.

What qualities do they develop in the military that make them so successful in the business community? The first two we've already discovered are discipline and commitment. Now let's consider pride and precision. President Carter said he quickly learned in the navy that when they said 08:00, they did not mean 08:01. The preciseness of the drill, the crease in the trousers or the shirt, the shine on the shoes, the sharpness of the way the beds are made and the living quarters are kept—all scream pride and precision. There's a certain feeling that goes with a close-order drill, a snappy salute, and the beauty of watching hundreds of our military people marching in precise order.

The best way to develop pride and many other positive qualities is taught in the acrostic PRIDE, which is *personal responsibility in daily endeavors*. Two of the missing ingredients in much of our society today are pride in personal appearance and pride in performance on the job. Not to mention the carelessness with which we clutter our schools, streets, highways, airports, and other public buildings with trash. In the military, pride—pride in excelling in personal performance, pride in getting a job done, pride in maintaining the honor and integrity of the service—is an important part of the training.

Unfortunately, many casual readers of the Bible believe that pride was the cause of man's fall and view it as sinful. A careful reading of the Bible, however, and an evaluation of how words sometimes change meaning over time reveal that the Bible speaks to vanity. Vanity is false pride, and it truly is one of the most negative, destructive qualities a person can have. SIMPLE TEST: Is it wrong for me to say to a staff member, "I am proud of the work you're doing," or to one of my children, "I'm proud of the values you have in life"? Actually, healthy pride is an "honest evaluation of that which is good."

A classic example of how words change in their meaning is the word *silly*. Most of us would be upset if somebody were to accuse us of being silly, but the word *silly* comes from the Old English word *selig,* and its literal definition is "to be blessed, happy, healthy, and prosperous." Now that you understand, you would be delighted if someone were to call you silly. If that does happen, you should smile and quietly respond, "How right you are!"

FROM AUTHORITARIAN TO AUTHORITATIVE

Another important quality the military teaches is obedience. When an individual's life is at stake, obedience is vital. That's why military personnel are taught through discipline that commands are to be obeyed and not questioned. This is clearly ingrained from the beginning so that in the heat of battle, when there's no time for explanations and the sergeant says, "Move it out!" the troops will do so with confidence and without hesitation.

One of the more enduring truths is that "the huge door of

> **66** *All of us perform better and more willingly when we know why we're doing what we have been told or asked to do.* **99**

opportunity often swings open on the tiny hinges of obedience." You must learn to obey in order to learn to command. In the process, respect is established. First you give it, then you get it—because you've earned it. You expect to obey orders, and you pass that expectancy to those you are leading.

Initially, the approach is authoritarian, but as you move up the ranks in the military and in life, the style changes from authoritarian to authoritative. You've learned the rules of the game; your commander or boss knows the rules, and he or she also knows that intelligent people respond more to an authoritative person than they do to an authoritarian one. The authoritarian person says, "You do it because I said to do it." The authoritative person says, "We are going to take this step because . . . ," or "We're going to move in this direction because . . ." I saw a classic example of the authoritative approach in a family setting, but the principle and procedure work in any environment. Here's the story.

THE KEYS ARE RESPECT AND COURTESY

On December 16, 1992, I was met in the Cleveland, Ohio, airport by David Mezey and his two sons, Brian, a sixth grader, and Gregory, a first grader. On the way to my hotel, we stopped to pick up David's wife, Jane, and have a quick lunch. I was immediately impressed by many things about the family. Number one, the boys were dressed sharply in coats and ties, but more important, they were dressed with beautiful spirits, manners, and attitudes.

I spotted the reason for that as we drove from one location to another. Brian, who is very articulate and whose vocabulary would probably fit into the ninth- to tenth-grade range, suggested to his dad that they should turn left at a particular spot because it would save time getting to the next destination. David very pleasantly said, "Well, you know, Brian, I thought about that, but by going straight we will be able to travel in a more direct route and I believe get there even sooner. But you had a good idea. Thank you for mentioning it."

David's answer explained it all. He treated his son with respect, explained why he had chosen the route he was taking, demonstrated that he had listened carefully to Brian, and then thanked him for his offer of help. That is an important key to building winning relationships, whether in the family, in the military, or in business. FACT: You will never be rude to someone you respect, which brings us to the quality of courtesy.

Leaders in the home, school, or business are invariably courteous. David and Jane Mezey are courteous to their children and vice versa. Successful career military people are courteous. They are also tough—but fair.

The dictionary defines *manners* (another word for *courteousness*) as "deportment, conduct, and civility." Manners include far more than what happens at the dinner table, and individuals who do not possess them suffer a great disadvantage.

Dr. Smiley Blanton says, "Eighty percent of the problem patients that come to me come because good manners were never taught them as children. As adults they made mistakes and were rejected. They couldn't play the game of life because they didn't know the rules."

Parents teach their children self-discipline when they teach them manners. My favorite philosopher, Dennis the Menace, all dressed up in his magician's suit, said he could do only two magic tricks because he knew only two magic words, *please* and *thank you*.

The child who is not taught to say "thank you" is not taught one of our most important qualities—gratitude. The term *thank you* is the foundation stone upon which gratitude is built. The little boy or girl who is taught to always say "thank you" when someone says or does something nice for him or her is building a marvelous foundation for winning friends, influencing people, and being a genuinely happy child. I challenge you to show me one happy person who is not a grateful one.

DECISIVE ACTION IS CRITICAL

One of the classic examples of the importance of the total person approach that generates trust and respect was demonstrated by General Norman Schwarzkopf in Desert Storm. He was in constant contact with his commanders. Before the land movement started, he called them in for the final briefing and strategy session. He got their input, and they discussed a number of options. He made a basic strategy decision, which was contrary to what many of them thought. He carefully explained why his plan would work, made the decision, and got their agreement for total and complete cooperation. The rest is history.

He was authoritative. He had confidence in himself, and as a result of the success he had enjoyed in the military, combined with the way he treated them, his troops had confidence in him. He had a tough decision to make involving the lives of thousands of troops, so he gathered all the information from his commanders, carefully evaluated it, factored in what he instinctively felt, and quickly made the tough decision to take action. That's another quality that is learned in the military—decisiveness.

Military personnel also learn to be versatile. During their encampment in Saudi Arabia, they were in an entirely different climate and culture. They had to live by a different set of rules. Circumstances also are different from one military base to the next, Fargo, North Dakota, versus Pensacola, Florida, for instance. The climate and environment of Japan and Hawaii differ greatly. The cultures and the local population have to be adapted to. That gives military personnel very valuable experience in versatility that, in today's changing world environment, is important. We need to be versatile, to see things from others' points of view, to successfully communicate with them.

Integrity is a key ingredient to success in the military, and as in civilian life, without integrity no one listens and without

> **Once trust is betrayed, moving to the top of the ladder is out of the question.**

trust no one follows. In the military it's an established fact that if an officer lies to a fellow officer, his military career, as a practical matter, is ended. The same is true in civilian life (except in politics, the movies, and TV, where personality and glibness at least temporarily win out over character and conviction).

In the business world it's acceptable to make mistakes, to lay eggs—big ones—but the Center for Creative Research, in a significant study, learned that one thing that sounds the death knell for those who aspire to the top rung on the ladder is betraying a trust. Virtually anything else can be overcome over a period of time, but once trust is betrayed, moving to the top of the ladder is out of the question.

Among other things, trust is the key to communication. When trust is high, we communicate easily, effortlessly, instantaneously. We can make mistakes, and others will still capture our meaning. But when trust is low, communication is exhausting, time consuming, ineffective, and inordinately difficult.

COMPETENCE—CHARACTER—COMPASSION— LOVE AND SYMPATHY

When General Schwarzkopf was interviewed by Barbara Walters, she asked him for his definition of leadership. He reflected for a moment and said, "It's *competence.* More important, it's *character.* It's taking *action.* It's *doing the right* [ethical] *thing.*" These four qualities are critical for success in the business world.

Later Barbara asked him what he wanted on his tombstone. For a moment he grew very quiet. Then, with just the hint of a tear in his eye, he said, "I want it to say, 'He loved his family and he loved his troops—and they loved him.'" Compassion, love, and sympathy are very definitely part of the success formula. Having the ability to walk in the shoes of another is of paramount importance. When you truly know how the other person feels, you can communicate with him or her more easily and lead more effectively.

The idea that military leaders are essentially rigid, do-it-my-way, noncaring people is the farthest thing from the truth. As a practical matter, commanders realize that their very survival depends on what they communicate to their troops in word and deed. You cannot demand love and loyalty; they must be earned. You can require the troops or your employees to efficiently handle their responsibilities, but unless you can inspire a genuine feeling of love and respect for you, your people are far less likely to go that extra mile for you. This caring-for-people approach will cause your associates to think in terms of *our* company instead of *the* company. The difference in performance is measurable.

Personal growth is an earmark of military personnel and anyone who is serious about moving up in life. For example, most of the time, the troops are not engaged in combat, but they need to be busy doing something constructive to be happy and prepared to answer the call when combat is inevitable.

To fill this need, the military offers many educational opportunities through extension courses, universities, technical schools, and other specialized training opportunities. As a result, according to *U.S. News & World Report,* of the fifty thousand army officers who were discharged by 1995, 98 percent of them had their college degrees, 83 percent at the rank of major and above had at least a master's degree, and many of them had their Ph.D.'s.

BECOME IRREPLACEABLE AND YOU BECOME UNPROMOTABLE

A person's future in the military is to a very large degree determined by the number of people he or she develops for a higher rank. The same is true in the business world. Your ability to develop others is the way you get ahead. Donald K. David says the best way to get ahead is to teach the person below you how to get ahead. You never get promoted when no one else knows your current job. The best basis for being advanced is to organize yourself out of every job you're put into. Most people are advanced because they're pushed up by the people underneath rather than pulled up from the top.

LESSON: When you encourage, develop, or train the people under you so that they are promoted, you help them get what they want. RESULT: You are promoted, which is what you wanted. The philosophy works.

QUESTION: Do you have to join the military to learn the qualities taught in the military? No. They're all skills, and you already have some of every one of the qualities inherent to military success and can develop the rest of them.

As we look at all of the qualities exhibited by immigrants and military personnel, the question undoubtedly comes to mind, "If I develop the 'Gosh!' attitude and the qualities that go with it, how do I go about using them so that instead of being where I am, I really can accomplish the things we're talking about?" Well, I'm convinced the starting point is motivation, and that's what the next chapter is about.

CHAPTER SEVEN

Motivation is the key

Motivation is the spark that lights the fire of knowledge and fuels the engine of accomplishment. It maximizes and maintains momentum.   Zig Ziglar

The question is: Do we handle life or do we drift with the current and subject ourselves to whatever happens? Your answer is important because

LIFE HAS ITS UPS AND DOWNS

The trip to the top is seldom, if ever, in a straight line. All of us have our ups and downs. That's why motivation is critical and often is the key to getting up when life has knocked us down. In fact, our down times can be our most profitable if we handle those times by responding (positive) instead of reacting (negative).

EXAMPLE: You probably have been caught in more than one horrendous traffic jam at exactly "the wrong time." If you're honest, you will have to admit that on occasion you were not excited or grateful for that roadblock in your life. You might even have slapped the steering wheel, stomped your foot, shook your fist, sat on your horn, and to no one in particular demanded to know when "they" were going to do something about it.

This probably will surprise you, but I encourage you to do exactly that because I'm certain you noticed the louder you honked that horn, the more rapidly the traffic in front of you opened up so you could go through. Seriously, if you follow that procedure enough times, you're courting heart trouble, high blood pressure, a stroke, a nervous breakdown, a shorter life span, and other health problems.

The typical American spends more than four hundred hours and some spend as much as one thousand hours a year in an automobile. You can choose to react and follow the fist-shaking, foot-stomping, horn-blowing routine above, or you can respond and take a giant step forward.

SUGGESTION: Smile when you encounter the next traffic jam, estimate how long it will take you to get through, and say, "In thirty minutes, right here I can learn several new words for my vocabulary or something about financial management, leadership skills, sales technique, communication skills, etc., by plugging in a tape."

The choice is yours. You can choose to respond and educate yourself, or you can choose to react and endanger your health.

Stephen Payne from Bartlesville, Oklahoma, responded and learned both Spanish and French so well that he is now translating for his company. He is also now conversant in Italian and German with Japanese, Latin, and his native Cherokee language on his goals chart. (Beats pounding the steering wheel and honking the horn, doesn't it?) That's exciting, but the next story identifies another benefit motivation gives us.

MOTIVATION + INFORMATION = INSPIRATION

During a break at one of the sessions we recorded at the Meyerson Symphony Hall in Dallas, Mary Ellen Caldwell approached me with considerable enthusiasm. She showed me a list of things she had prepared for her father to get involved in when he and her mother moved to Dallas.

She explained that her dad at age sixty-two had been forced to retire, and he was very unhappy as a result. He felt that he had no real purpose in life and nothing worthwhile to contribute. She stated that she had been concerned about him, but thanks to the seminar, she had an exciting list of things for him—and them—to do.

A few weeks later at another seminar at the Meyerson, she introduced her father to me. They were both excited, but her dad especially was beaming. He gave no hint that he was a man without a purpose.

FACT: The seminar Mary Ellen had attended where she got those ideas and developed those plans was not a planning or goal-setting seminar. As a matter of fact, I did not discuss or even identify a single one of the ideas or plans she had listed and was so excited about.

QUESTION: What happened?

ANSWER: She got motivated. To be motivated, as stated earlier, means to pull out or draw out what is inside. However, as newscaster Paul Harvey would say, "Here's the rest of the story," as well as an expansion of what happens when motivation enters the picture.

READ VERY CAREFULLY—IT WILL AFFECT YOUR LIFE

Not only does motivation enable you to effectively use what is fresh on your mind, but it also helps you pull out and make use of things that had long ago been buried and, you thought, forgotten.

It has been scientifically proven that inspirational information related in an enthusiastic way causes the pituitary gland to release neurotransmitters that enhance our energy, creativity, and endurance. My message that day was exciting, and I was excited about delivering it.

RESULT: Mary Ellen's brain was flooded with those creative neurotransmitters, and many of the ideas and information that she had been storing in her memory bank all of her life were activated and went on parade. The new, completely unrelated information and ideas I gave her were also placed on parade.

At that point a marriage took place. The accumulated information, wisdom, and ideas of her lifetime joined forces with those ideas and information that I provided, and new concepts and ideas were born. Those new ideas were what she had listed on her notepad.

MAJOR POINT #1: If she had not been acquiring information and ideas during her lifetime and if she had not had that love and concern for her dad and if she had not been involved in personal growth that brought her to the seminar in the first place, her ideas would undoubtedly not have seen the light of day.

MAJOR POINT #2: Motivation really is the spark that lights the fire of knowledge and produces creative ideas.

MAJOR POINT #3: The more valid information you have in a broad range of subjects, the more benefits you will reap from new ideas and information enthusiastically presented to you on a regular basis. This permits or causes the marriage of the old and new ideas. Information that causes the birth of ideas and concepts will set you apart and move you forward in many areas of life.

The same thing that happened to Mary Ellen at the seminar happens to me when I visit with Fred Smith. He teaches me many things, but even more important, he makes me think by giving me little nuggets that motivate me to be and do more.

For example, just last week while The Redhead and I were having dinner with Fred and his wife, Mary Alice, he told me that "great learners are not necessarily great thinkers." He emphasized that all of us need to take more quiet time to think about what we know, and he explained why that's important and how we can use it for the benefit of others as well as ourselves.

MAJOR POINT #4: Spend that quiet time to do some serious thinking so you can use what you know. There are very few things that will generate as much joy and excitement as the creation of a usable idea or solution to a problem.

To be very specific, all the thoughts in this "Motivation + Information = Inspiration" section jelled in my mind during a forty-minute thinking walk in Tampa, Florida, and the very quiet dinner that followed it. My thoughts came together because of (a) previous information and experiences, (b) the motivation that came from Fred Smith's thought-provoking statement, and (c) the quiet time I devoted to some intense thinking on the subject. That's why I never listen to tapes of any kind when I take my walks.

While working on this book, I hit a wall at least twenty times and did not know which way to turn. When that happened, I stopped writing and took my walk. Invariably, I came back physically refreshed and with a creative idea that was the solution to going through, around, or over that wall. A major exception was my experience in defining the top as described in chapter 1, and even that breakthrough came during some quiet prayer time.

MOTIVATION + INFORMATION ALSO = BETTER BUSINESS

At age twenty-five, I became the youngest divisional supervisor in the sixty-six-year history of a major direct sales company that distributed heavy-duty waterless cookware. When the divisional supervisor for our area resigned to take another position, I was promoted to that position over two other candidates, both of whom were over fifty years old.

With that promotion I had four field managers in my division. In direct selling the field managers are the key to the organization's success. They hold weekly sales meetings and regular training sessions, make frequent telephone contacts, and do a lot of follow-up work. They're the heart and soul of the business.

I was on top of the world, but very quickly, my world started to collapse and come tumbling down. One of my field managers suffered a heart attack and was unable to work. His organization deteriorated rapidly. Almost immediately, a second field manager cut the big toe on his right foot almost completely off with a lawn mower. He was in the hospital twenty days and on crutches for over two months; his field organization collapsed. A third field manager had some integrity problems. His people lost confidence in him, and his organization shrank substantially. The fourth one had been promoted prematurely to fill the slot I left when I was promoted. That manager simply was not ready for that type of assignment, and the organization took a nosedive.

Here's the picture: One month we were a high-producing, gung ho, enthusiastic organization. Two months later the organization was producing less than half as much business, and rumors started flying that the company was going to "can" me because I could not handle the job. Needless to say, I was dismayed that such rumors would even start. In my mind, I was the good guy, the fair-haired boy, the heir apparent to even bigger things. I had nothing to do with the heart attack, the toe getting cut, and so on. At that point I was hit with an advanced case of stinkin' thinkin', and I was rapidly heading for the dreaded PLOM disease.

FROM DR. PEALE TO ZIG

Then one day, I was walking down the street in Knoxville, Tennessee, and spotted a book written by the late Dr. Norman Vincent Peale, prominently displayed in the window. The title was *The Power of Positive Thinking*. I was badly in need of that book, so I went into the store, bought the book, and headed to the airport to catch a flight to Nashville, Tennessee, where I was to speak at a meeting. Dr. Peale had written his book specifically for me and to me.

I could almost hear him say, "You're absolutely right, Zig. You had nothing to do with the heart attack, the integrity problem, the toe severance, etc. Those things really were not your fault or even your responsibility. But, Zig, you are totally responsible for how you handle that problem, and yes, there is something you can do to turn the business around."

Now I hasten to add that the toe problem still existed, as did the integrity problem, the heart problem, and the lack-of-experience problem with one manager.

Suddenly, despite the fact that nothing had changed "out there," everything changed in my own mind and thinking. Once more I became a highly motivated, enthusiastic, gung ho divisional supervisor. Instead of weeping, wailing, and gnashing my teeth, I turned the creative juices on, renewed my commitment and enthusiasm, set some specific objectives, drew up a plan of action, and went to work with a passion.

> **It's not what happens to you but how you handle what happens that makes the difference.**

I took my lifetime of knowledge and experience and combined all of it with the new information and motivation from Dr. Peale. New ideas and a totally different attitude were the result.

Here's what happened: Though I had been promoted in May, by the end of the year our division was twenty-second in the nation out of sixty-six divisions. The following year we were number five. In 1954, which was my last year with the company, we were number three with only New York and Kansas beating us by less than $7,000 in sales.

It's amazing how everything changed in my division when my thinking changed. When things change inside you, things change around you. You get along better with other people; your business improves; your health improves; everything improves. Do I believe that motivation and right attitudes are important? You bet!

REMINDER: Dr. Peale taught me nothing about the cookware business, but he changed my thinking with some new information and inspired me to use the information, experience, and ability that I already had. That's a real benefit of motivation.

THOUGHT: If this book teaches you nothing about life or business but inspires you to use what you already know and have, it will make a dramatic difference in your life.

THE STRANGE THING ABOUT MOTIVATION

People in the media frequently ask me before I do a public seminar if I'm going to get the crowd excited. I always respond that, generally speaking, the people who come to the seminars are already excited. My objective is to get them more excited and to give them directions on how they can maintain a higher level of excitement and competence. Almost without exception, they ask, How long will that excitement last? Where will those motivated people be a month from now or a year from now? What they really want to know: Is motivation permanent?

I've already indicated via the gate agent story that motivation is not permanent—but neither is eating nor bathing, yet most of us do not really expect these physical activities to be permanent. One of my favorite observations is that it's too bad our minds and emotions don't growl when they need nourishment like the stomach does when it needs food. If they did, we would feed them daily and in the process produce a permanent cure for the PLOM disease.

Since motivation is the key to using our abilities to reach worthwhile objectives, we need to explore the subject thoroughly.

HOPE IS "A CONFIDENT EXPECTATION"

People who smell success are highly charged, and they pursue their objective with enthusiasm. They are motivated and heading in the right direction. In athletics and in life, we know that momentum is a tremendous factor and that momentum is fueled by hope, which is a "confident expectation." We also know that momentum can change in the twinkling of an eye in athletics and very quickly in our fast-changing business world.

One football team is dominating another when a big break suddenly occurs for the losing team—a turnover, an interception, a fumble recovery, a long punt or kickoff return—and every athlete on the team instantly feels a sense of excitement, fueled by hope that turns to belief that they can—and will—win the game. They feel victory, and that feeling is reinforced by the look in the eyes of the opposing players, many of whom are thinking, *Uh-oh, here we go again!*

Life is that way. When we sense that something positive is going to happen, we're energized dramatically. When we feel or fear we're going to lose, we are deenergized and tighten up with negative results. That's why motivation is important for good times and bad. That's the reason a person who wants to maximize life will deliberately schedule regular motivational input just as surely as he will schedule putting food into his stomach.

The infusion or injection of a new idea, a confidence-building thought, or a concept that makes sense will energize that person, and momentum builds within him. You perform better and learn more when you're up, so that's the time to take out some motivation insurance. You need it to get back up when circumstances have given you some tough blows. For example, every salesperson with any longevity will tell you that you can be struggling for survival when a breakthrough occurs and you're off to the races. You make that big sale, then another one comes your way, and suddenly, expectancy gives momentum another boost.

Unfortunately, it works the other way as well. You miss several sales in a row, and you start doubting yourself and expecting people to say no. Many salespeople, and I speak from more than forty-five years of sales and sales management experience, reach the point where they almost literally start daring their prospects to buy. Others throw in the towel early on and never learn whether they've got what it takes to succeed in selling (or for that matter any other job or profession that offers more challenges than expected).

> **"** *Motivation fuels the attitude that builds the confidence necessary to sustain the persistence.* **"**

FAILURE CAN BE, SHOULD BE, A MOTIVATOR

Dr. J. Allan Petersen, in his monthly publication *Better Families,* said it best:

> *Everyone, at one time or another, has felt like a complete failure. Many have allowed the fear of failure to destroy them. Actually, fear is far more destructive than failure and in any area of life fear of failure can defeat you before you get started.*

What makes us so afraid of failure? It's worry about what people think. "What will they say?" we ask, as if it were the ultimate scandal to fail. We assume that because we've made one or several mistakes, we're failures and therefore forever disgraced. What a ridiculous assumption! How many people are completely successful in every department of life? Not one. The most successful people are the ones who learn from their mistakes and turn their failures into opportunities. Every scientific invention, every business enterprise, and every happy marriage has resulted from a series of failures. No one succeeds without them.

A failure means you've put forth some effort. That's good. Failure gives you an opportunity to learn a better way to do it. That's positive. A failure teaches you something and adds to your experience. That's very helpful. Failure is an event, never a person; an attitude, not an outcome; a temporary inconvenience; a stepping-stone. Our response to it determines just how helpful it can be.

OUR PICTURE DETERMINES HOW WE HANDLE FAILURE

Cal Ripken, the shortstop for the Baltimore Orioles who broke Ty Cobb's "unbreakable" record of playing in 2,130 consecutive games, signed a five-year contract for more than $30 million. However, last year Cal got only about one hit for every four times at bat. Think about it. If you had failed three times out of four in your job, how would you feel about it? What would your self-image or picture of yourself be?

QUESTION: What do you think Cal Ripken's picture of himself is when he steps up to the plate? Do you really think that he's thinking, *Boy, what a waste of time! Chances are only one out of four I'm going to get a hit! I don't know why I bother with this anyhow. Sure, they pay me a lot of money, but this is embarrassing and terribly discouraging to get only one hit for every four trips to the plate. There has to be another way to make a living! I'm just a loser. I'm no good, and I don't know why I put myself through this torture so everybody else can see what I already know!* Do you think that's his self-talk? Then what is his self-talk?

I believe as he steps to the plate with considerable eagerness to face the pitcher, Cal is thinking to himself, *Okay, you got me the last time, but I've got your number this time. I've been thinking it through, watching you, and I happen to know I'm one of the best athletes in the world. I've hit that ball under every circumstance known to man. I've gotten hits off tall pitchers and short pitchers, winning pitchers and losing pitchers. I've hit in close games and runaway games, and this time you better watch out because I'm coming after you. This is my turn!*

Cal Ripken sees himself as a winner, and he is elated that he now has a chance to step back up to the plate.

MESSAGE: Regardless of what happened to you the last time you stepped up to the plate, this time it's a brand-new day, and at this very moment you are preparing to make it a winning one. That is motivation.

ONE FAILED—ONE SUCCEEDED, THEIR MOTIVATION WAS DIFFERENT

I love the story the late Dr. Ken McFarland delighted in telling.

It seems a gentleman worked on the 4:00 P.M. to midnight shift, and he always walked home after work. One night the moon was shining so brightly he decided to take a shortcut through the cemetery, which would save him roughly a half-mile walk. There were no incidents involved so he repeated the process on a regular basis, always following the same path. One night as he was walking his route through the cemetery, he did not realize that during the day a grave had been dug in the very center of his path. He stepped right into that grave and immediately started desperately trying to get out. His best efforts failed him, and after a few minutes, he decided to relax and wait until morning when someone would help him out.

He sat down in the corner and was half asleep when a drunk stumbled into the grave. His arrival roused the shift worker since the drunk was desperately trying to climb out, clawing frantically at the sides. Our hero reached out his hand, touched the drunk on the leg, and said, "Friend, you can't get out of here . . ."—but he did! Now that's motivation!

PERSONAL GROWTH VS. SELF-FULFILLMENT

The motivation of self-fulfillment creates the Dead Sea Syndrome. It's the pond without an outlet that becomes stagnant, toxic, and unfit for human use. Self-fulfillment is a self-centered approach to life that ultimately prevents us from reaching our full potential.

When our thoughts are primarily upon ourselves, our motivation is self-fulfillment. That's looking out for number one. That's a thought pattern that leads to difficulty, hampers our effectiveness, restricts our productivity on the job, and destroys a major portion of our future. This attitude also seriously limits the number of friends and long-term relationships we can build. Very few people are interested in being friends with or establishing long-term relationships with those who are motivated by self-fulfillment.

Yes, self-fulfillment is a dead-end street, whereas the motivation of personal growth is the flowing river that gets its water from one source and delivers it to another, watering crops or generating electricity on the way. Self-fulfillment is the perennial student who acquires knowledge primarily for the sake of knowledge so he or she will have the answers. Motivation for personal growth is the teacher who acquires the knowledge so he or she will have the answers to share with others.

Self-fulfillment is the bodybuilder who develops a sculptured physique so he can parade in front of the mirror and hope that others will oooh and aaah. Personal growth is the athlete who gets in marvelous physical condition to make a contribution to the team that benefits him personally as well—another win-win situation.

Now let's look at some scientific evidence followed by a

story that puts personal growth, motivation, and the philosophy of you can have everything in life you want if you will just help enough other people get what they want to work for your benefit and the benefit of mankind.

THE EVIDENCE IS SCIENTIFIC

There is validation of the importance of optimism, motivation, and positive thinking. In a copyrighted article published in the *New York Times* (February 3, 1987) by Daniel Goleman, we read that optimism—at least reasonable optimism—can pay dividends as wide-ranging as health, longevity, job success, and higher scores on achievement tests.

The January 1992 edition of the *American Institute for Preventive Medicine* said in its New Year's resolution list that an attitude adjustment (such as one from pessimism to optimism) is more important in preventing disease than changes in diet and exercise habits.

Princeton University psychologist Edward E. Jones reviewed the research on expectancy in a recent issue of *Science* magazine and said, "Our expectancies not only affect how we see reality, but also affect the reality itself."

This is evidenced by the fact that virtually every medical student, at some stage of training, will acquire the symptoms of one or more of the diseases being studied.

CLASSIC EXAMPLE: Dr. Harvey Cushings, unquestionably the greatest neurosurgeon who ever lived, early in his career made the prediction that he would undoubtedly die of a brain tumor. That is exactly what happened to him. His expectancies became a reality.

A speech therapist in Houston, Texas, told me that when she was preparing for her career, she and every other member of her class became stutterers while they were studying stuttering. When people get intensely involved in a matter, study it carefully, and concentrate on it daily, they often become emotionally and empathetically involved. Dr. Cushings and the students in the speech therapist class certainly did.

Michael E. Scheier, a psychologist at Carnegie-Mellon University in Pittsburgh, has found that optimists tend to respond to disappointment, like being turned down for a job, by formulating a plan of action and asking other people for help and advice. Pessimists more often react to such difficulties by trying to forget the whole thing or assuming there is nothing they can do to change things. That attitude is adopted by optimists only when there is objectively nothing more that can be done.

Dr. Martin Seligman of the University of Pennsylvania said, "It is the combination of reasonable talent and the ability to keep going in the face of defeat that leads to success."

That combination equals optimism. Dr. Seligman also said that people who think they have more control over their lives than they actually do usually end up doing better than the so-called realists (that is the pessimists) who pride themselves on having a clearer vision of how things truly are.

The *New York Times* article mentioned earlier also pointed out that some people are negative and pessimistic for good reasons. The next story is about a woman who had many reasons to be in that depressing condition. Her story should convince you, and just about anyone else, that where there is life, there is hope. And that the way you see and plan your future is the determining factor in how bright your future is going to be.

TEN STEPS FROM OVERWEIGHT HOUSEWIFE TO VP/SALES, DISNEY RADIO

Pam Lontos's depression was so severe she didn't want to get out of bed. Her energy bucket was empty. She had gained fifty pounds and was sleeping sixteen to eighteen hours each day. That's when she heard an ad on the radio that interested her. Since Pam's therapist had told her she couldn't get better, it's amazing that the advertisement for the health club sounded fun (something Pam hadn't had for a very long time) to her. What's even more amazing is that she struggled down to the health club to see what was going on. That was step number one, and had she not taken that first step you would not be reading her story now.

POINT: It takes action for you to go over the top.

The salespeople and members were friendly, energetic, and happy. She joined the club and started a limited exercise program (step number two). Over a period of time, her feelings and energy level changed considerably, and she persuaded the health club to give her a job as a salesperson (step number three). She had previously sold at the retail level in a shoe store with substantial success, but she had taken a detour, at her family's insistence, and become a teacher.

Pam was very unhappy as a teacher. She became depressed and started eating lots of chocolate cake, which explains the weight gain and energy loss. Selling brought back fond memories, but she had her ups and downs, so her manager gave her a set of our motivational tapes for daily listening (step number four). Almost immediately, her sales consistency and personal life improved considerably.

Pam had always been fascinated with radio sales and decided to move into that field, but her favorite station had no openings and would not even give her an interview. By then she had learned the importance of persistence and literally sat in front of the general manager's office (step number five) until he granted her the interview. Her conviction, enthusiasm, persistence, and determination persuaded him to give her a job. She got off to a marvelous start and was soon leading the pack.

Then her big break came. She broke her leg, and no pun is intended (step number six, and no, you don't have to follow suit!). She was to be in a cast and on crutches for many months, but that didn't stop her. Twelve days later she was back at the radio station. She hired a driver to drive her around to her appointments (step number seven). Since she had considerable difficulty getting in and out of the car and offices, she started using the telephone to make sales and solid appointments, and her sales took a substantial leap forward.

MAYBE WE SHOULD ALL PRAY FOR PROBLEMS

Pam's sales were greater than those of the other four salespeople combined, so they started asking her questions. Pam loved to share information, so she started teaching (step number eight) the other salespeople what she was doing. Shortly after that, the sales manager quit, and the salespeople petitioned management to give Pam the job. She took her new job seriously and prepared short daily sales meetings while maintaining her own sales volume. Though the station had less than a 2 percent share of the listeners market, billings increased from $40,000 to over $100,000 each month, and a year later the figure was over $270,000.

> When you combine confidence-building motivation with effective client-centered sales techniques, business improves.

MANAGEMENT IS LOOKING

The general manager of the Disney chain of radio stations got excited about those results because the station, which had the lowest listener ratings, was doing the most business. He invited Pam to go to their other cities and do seminars for them (step number nine). In each case the results were dramatic because when you combine confidence-building motivation with effective client-centered sales techniques, business improves.

Results were so consistently good the Disney radio chain made Pam the vice president of sales for the entire chain (step number ten). The National Association of Broadcasters invited her to speak at their national convention with over two thousand people in attendance. Outside of small groups, Pam had never made a speech before, but the confidence level she had in herself and in the techniques she had learned was high.

She carefully prepared her presentation. She started visualizing herself making that talk, seeing in her own mind the people responding with enormous excitement and enthusiasm and embracing what she was selling. At the end of each dry run she literally gave herself a standing ovation (a powerful picture-painting process).

The big day arrived. She had made a considerable number of notes and was well prepared to do her thing. However, when she got onstage, the glare of the lights made it difficult to follow the notes so she stepped out from behind the lectern and spoke from her heart. The response was fabulous. They interrupted her with applause and gave her the standing ovation she had already painted in her mind. Immediately thereafter, she was booked on an eighteen-city tour to do seminars all over the country.

IT WORKS

Today, Pam Lontos is a nationally known speaker, a published author, and president of her own company, Lontos Sales and Motivation, Inc., in Orlando, Florida. She is happier, healthier, more prosperous, and more secure; she has more friends, more peace of mind, marvelous family relationships, and genuine hope that the future is going to be even better.

Pam Lontos's story in many ways exemplifies much of what we believe and have been teaching for a number of years.

MAJOR POINT #1: Pam came to believe that you can have what you want if you'll just help enough other people get what they want. Initially, when she was sharing information with other salespeople at the radio station, her financial rewards were zero; she did it because she enjoyed doing it, she knew they needed help, and she felt everyone would benefit. That's the reason she became the sales manager. (It's still true that when you do more than you're paid to do, you'll eventually be paid more for what you do.)

MAJOR POINT #2: Had she not broken her leg, she would not have been forced to be more creative in the utilization of her time and to become adept at using the telephone. Nor would she have been around to encourage and teach the other salespeople. She took a negative (her broken leg) and made a big positive (the sales manager's job) out of it.

MAJOR POINT #3: She took the first step. That's the big one. She realized that if she was really going to overcome her advanced case of stinkin' thinkin', lack of energy, and weight problem (all of which had driven her to the brink of suicide), she had to accept responsibility for her future. At that moment her PLOM disease started to beat a hasty retreat.

MESSAGE: You take the first step, and doors all over the place will begin to open. Pam heard the radio ad for the health club, took action, and joined. When she started working on her physical health, her emotional health improved, her attitude changed, and more energy, excitement, and enthusiasm followed right behind. Her personality completely changed, and she outwardly manifested the kind of person she inwardly was. As a result, other people as well as other opportunities were attracted to her. As a matter of fact, that's what caught the attention of Rick Dudnick, and a beautiful courtship followed. They recently celebrated their eleventh wedding anniversary.

The Pam Lontos story says many things, but a major message is that her success can be duplicated in your life with the blueprint we will keep unfolding. Another significant message is that motivation, combined with training, produces significant change, growth, and results. Motivation is basically action, but it's like fire and needs to have fuel added to it regularly. Negative thinking is gravity and tends to hold you down, but once it's overcome, it takes dramatically less effort to keep going.

Motivation—hearing the promises or incentives offered in that commercial—got Pam Lontos into action. Her sales manager motivated her with his training and through the set of tapes. It's accurate to say that motivation gets you going—but habit gets you there. Make motivation your habit, and you'll get there faster and have more fun on the trip.

Motivation Creates Energy

For years I've had many people say to me that when they felt a little down, they would pop in one of my tapes, and it would give them a lift. I assumed they were talking about a psychological or encouragement lift, perhaps getting an idea that made their attitude a more positive one. That was true, but it goes farther than that. As I wrote about in an earlier book, there is now scientific evidence that a success message, enthusiastically delivered, can literally generate energy. Here's the story that I shared in *Ziglar on Selling*.

Dr. Forest Tennant, arguably the number one drug authority in America, attended a four-hour seminar I conducted in Anaheim, California. I spoke from 6:30 until 10:30 P.M. to more than 2,500 people.

Dr. Tennant ran blood tests on five volunteers from the audience before I started speaking. When the session was over, he repeated the process. The endorphin and cortisol levels were up as much as 300 percent. His conclusions were published in the May 1989 issue of *Meetings and Conventions* magazine: "There is a biochemical basis for why people feel good after these talks. Something in hearing about success gives people an emotional charge that releases chemicals into the bloodstream and makes the body function better."

These effects last no more than a few hours, but Tennant believes that regular doses of motivation will lead to better health, happiness, and achievement: "I put it in the same category of helping your health as aerobic exercise, sleep, and three meals a day."

That's exciting. Dr. Tennant is saying that inspiration can literally create the energy to do the job better and with more enthusiasm. Later tests conducted by Dr. Tennant not only verified the initial one but expanded his information base. He feels the message of hope and success, enthusiastically delivered, creates excitement and that floods the brain with endorphins, dopamine, serotonin, norepinephrine, and the other neurotransmitters.

He has proven scientifically that with positive input, you can literally create energy, endurance, and creativity. That's very significant (as you shall see in the next example). That's the prime reason that, unless I have a short studio insert, all of my recordings are done in front of live audiences. That way the listener picks up not only the information but the inspiration coming from the sheer excitement of an enthusiastic delivery and the response of the audience.

I hope you agree that when we need energy, it is far better to pop a motivational tape in the tape deck and listen to something inspiring on the way to and from work than it is to pop a pill in our mouths. The results from the tapes are all positive, and there's no hangover.

At this point it is important that you understand the difference between motivation and manipulation.

My friend and mentor, Fred Smith, says, "Motivation is getting people to do something out of mutual advantage. Manipulation is getting people to do what you want them to do primarily for your advantage."

Fred tells how one night a psychiatrist friend chided him by saying, "You businessmen mistake manipulation for motivation. The difference is you can substitute the word *thirst* for *motivation,* but not *manipulation.*" He was saying that unless you are satisfying someone's thirst, you are probably manipulating rather than motivating. I've found that to be a good principle for distinguishing the two. I can motivate with integrity when I bring into consciousness a genuine thirst;

otherwise, in most cases, manipulation is the prostitution of motivation. It's an attempt to get results without honest effort. Motivation is not a quick fix; manipulation can be.

Motivation can be bad

This brings us to a significant point in the world of motivation because there are many things that activate the brain to produce the chemicals I'm discussing. Loud rock music, inspiring patriotic songs, or songs of faith have that same impact; so does the excitement of a highly contested athletic event. For some people pornography serves as the trigger. For others, the excitement of gambling activates the brain, which produces those chemicals. However, according to Dr. Tennant, the difference in being motivated with the type of information I'm sharing with you in this book is this: You are charged up on ethical, moral values that give direction and hope on how to be more, do more, and have more. That's good.

Listening to loud rock music makes many people feel good because the music stimulates the brain, which is flooded with dopamine, norepinephrine, endorphins, and other neurotransmitters. The problem is that those recordings frequently encourage us, directly or indirectly, to do things that are of an unhealthy or illegal nature, like getting high on booze or drugs; some, such as gangsta rap, even advocate the killing of policemen. Think about the picture those lyrics paint in your mind of killing a cop, burning a building, abusing women, or committing suicide. Ask yourself, Is there a chance that this could be one of the factors in much of the senseless violence and suicide we're encountering in our society today?

William H. Philpott, M.D., says that rock music, especially hard rock, is disorganizing to the central nervous system because it comes to such an abrupt end, then starts over and has extremely disorganized patterns.

This thinking is reinforced by concert pianist Stephen Nielson, who says that the "beat of rock music is agitative and antithetical, which literally works not to build harmony in the body but rather disharmony and possibly creates antisocial thoughts and actions within us. At the same time, the pure excitement of the beat floods our very productive brain with neurotransmitters, and as a result we're energized and charged up to do some foolish things."

The evidence is growing that repetitive listening to immoral, antisocial, or self-destructive music can be disastrous. Psychiatrist Louis B. Cady, M.D., who is a former concert pianist and an authority on the subject, states:

> *Heavy metal rock music, the even more potent acid rock, and "gangsta rap" have an insidious and devastating effect on the minds of young people. Most people don't realize that youngsters' brains are growing and developing until they are at least twenty-one years old. During this steady evolution of brain development, when kids and teens subject themselves to a constant "mental diet" of suggestions that sex, drugs, and criminal activities are not only acceptable but even desirable, they are actually accomplishing a sort of "self-brainwashing" where they begin to feel that even thoughts and feelings expressed in the lyrics of the music which they might* initially not consciously believe *begin to become the accepted way of thinking—where unlimited premarital sex, experimentation with drugs and alcohol and even dabbling in criminal activities seem to be a "normal" idea rather than a deviant from societal norms. Tragically, these lyrics of anarchy are driven even further into young people's minds and their unconscious thoughts and fantasies by the heavy and rhythmic beat of the music. Another factor causing increased potency of these lyrics and music to do harm is the advent of the "Walkman" type stereo where kids can literally program themselves during every waking moment—or at least while the batteries still hold a charge.*

P.S. The rock music of the sixties and seventies bears no resemblance to the rock and rap music of today.

Now for the good news

The right music can be a real picker-upper and keeper-upper. An article in the July/August 1993 issue of *Psychology Today* says,

> *Play some toe-tapping tunes to toddlers and it may go straight to their brains. If University of California researchers are right, teaching music basics to babes opens their minds to science and math.*

When neurobiologist Frances Rauscher, Ph.D., tested the reasoning ability of three-year-olds, she found them sorely lacking. But after three months of music lessons, they were snapping together puzzles and blocks quite adeptly. Dr. Rauscher believes music "exercises" basic inborn neural connections related to abstract reasoning.

In her studies, kids from three different schools all tested better after music regardless of socioeconomic status. They'd upscaled their brains with rhythmic beats learned on a keyboard—musical push-ups for the mind. "Consider music as a sort of prelanguage which, at an early age, excites the inherent brain patterns and enhances their use in other higher cognitive functions."

Rauscher recently played some Mozart concertos to Irvine collegians, and just as predicted, they whizzed through math homework afterward. It's the linear and patterned format of his pieces like *Eine Kleine Nachtmusik* that put people in that mathy frame of mind. Mozart's musical passages repeat themselves in a very logical and rhythmic way.

According to noted Hungarian music expert Dr. Klara Kokas, formal music training enhances performance in all other school subjects. She found that children who have received formal music training perform up to 30 percent better in all their other school subjects. The doctor's findings revealed that the effort required to study music in the abstract enables children to master more easily such subjects as mathematics and languages. It is safe to say that some music inspires us to do better and moves us into a higher level of thinking and performance. However, across the board, the music that effectively functions that way is of the same rhythm as that of our bodies, the melodies, the marches, the patriotic and religious music, as well as the classics of Chopin, Schubert, Beethoven, and a host of the masters.

There's more

An article in *Sky Magazine,* February 1993, points out that therapists say music is nature's tranquilizer and that's why many people turn to a favorite piece of music to help them unwind at the end of the day.

Perhaps one of the oldest examples of the impact of music is that of King David, who resorted to his harp to soothe King Saul of evil spirits. Pythagoras, the sixth-century B.C. philosopher and mathematician, is often credited with founding the practice of music therapy, though he was most likely building on a still more ancient tradition.

Howard Martin, vice president of the Institute of Heart Math, a stress-management think tank based in Boulder Creek, California, says that for drivers with long commutes, music with a calming message is just what the doctor ordered. "If somebody has to deal with traffic jams, they can be losing energy if they constantly grumble and gripe through it. That energy drain accumulates over time, and people really do pay some dues of a mental and emotional nature which affects them physiologically as well."

The message seems to be clear. One of the ways to stay up—to have more control over our feelings and emotions, to be more enthusiastic and physically, mentally, and emotionally prepared—is to be careful about the music we hear. Soft, soothing melodies when we need to relax and wind down and a peppy, cheerful, upbeat, positive message in song when we need to get up in the morning and get started for the day can make a difference.

Motivation—the weight reducer

When we listen to a motivational tape that activates the brain, the serotonin (a chemical that enhances self-esteem) increases—as do the endorphins, dopamine, norepinephrine, and other neurotransmitters. This not only makes us feel better about ourselves but, as stated earlier, increases our energy and endurance. This is significant because the obese person uses enormous amounts of energy. By five o'clock in the afternoon, these energy-producing chemicals are in short supply. At this point, Dr. Tennant says, another brain-produced substance called galanin literally devours the remaining dopamine and norepinephrine. In a nutshell, dopamine and norepinephrine are fat burners, and galanin is a fat producer.

The net result is that by the end of the day, obese people are literally starved for rich desserts and other foods loaded with fats. They are not lazy, but their energy bucket is within a whisper of being empty, so they fill the bucket with a heavy meal loaded with fat. Then they have the energy to do the absolute necessities before collapsing in bed. Unfortunately, they regularly eat several hundred more calories than they burn, and the vicious cycle gets more vicious.

Taking control

Many times people at my motivational seminars have said to me that since listening to my motivational tapes, they have lost x number of pounds. Many of them used figures over fifty or one hundred pounds. Until now I had always assumed they had been inspired to change their eating and exercise habits when actually the body's chemical response to motivation itself was an important factor.

By listening to motivational tapes during the course of the day and especially on the ride home from work when the energy level is so low, you will receive the psychological lift that motivation provides *and* a physiological lift as well. That means you will arrive home with slightly more of that energy I mentioned earlier than you otherwise would have because you would have replenished the energy-producing brain chemicals. When you take a walk and do exercises in the evening, you are burning excess calories. You are also suppressing your appetite because the brain releases still more replacement endorphins, dopamine, and norepinephrine, as well as the other neurotransmitters, to keep your body in balance.

Evidence is solid that when you combine good eating habits with a sensible exercise program, your chances of better health and permanent weight loss are excellent. However, when you add the encouragement, direction, and excitement of listening daily to exciting motivational tapes, your odds go up dramatically.

If you have a weight problem, let me encourage you to make a conscious decision to change your eating and exercise habits. The major culprit in almost all cases is the habit of eating too much food and too many foods loaded with fat. Combine that with not getting enough exercise on a regular basis. That's where a skilled physician is needed to recommend the proper diet and exercise and to make sure you are not the exception with medical reasons for being overweight.

CHAPTER EIGHT

Attitude makes the difference

The longer I live, the more I realize the impact of attitude on life. Attitude, to me, is more important than facts. It is more important than the past, than education, than money, than circumstances, than failures, than successes, than what other people think or say or do. It is more important than appearance, gifted ability, or skill. It will make or break a company, a church, a home. The remarkable thing is we have a choice every day regarding the attitude we will embrace from that day. We cannot change our past, we cannot change the fact that people will act in a certain way. We cannot change the inevitable. The only thing that we can do is play on the one string that we have and this string is, attitude. I am convinced that life is ten percent what happens to me and ninety percent how I react to it. And so it is with you . . . WE ARE IN CHARGE OF OUR ATTITUDES.

Charles Swindoll

Your attitude, as I've indicated, is important, but positive thinking is misunderstood by far too many people, including the media, the uninformed, and the misinformed. Some people honestly believe that with positive thinking you can do anything, while others honestly believe that positive thinking is no help at all. Let's explore the subject and find out just what positive thinking will—and won't—do.

WHAT POSITIVE THINKING WILL AND WON'T LET YOU DO

This is an all-too-common scenario for the high-handicap golfer: The golfer stands on the first tee box with a driver in his hands, a fairway sixty yards wide in front of him, and the hole 397 yards away. He tees the ball up, chooses a spot 230 yards straight ahead, carefully lines up the ball with his target, makes a slow backswing, keeps his head down, follows through, and hits the ball more than two hundred yards out—and to the right. The ball comes to rest behind several large trees, but there is an opening to the fairway about four feet wide.

Our hero surveys the situation and decides that, even though he just missed a sixty-yard-wide fairway with his ball teed up and in perfect position, he can now reach the green that's 197 yards away with that same little ball by hitting it through those trees, over the pond, and to the right of the sand trap. By the time the shot ricochets off the trees, takes a dip in the pond, and spends some time on the beach, he ends up with a quadruple-bogey eight.

This golfer who makes million-dollar decisions all week long has just made a decision that converted a routine bogey (if he had simply chipped the ball thirty or forty yards back into the fairway) into a disastrous eight. Obviously, this golfer mistook positive thinking for positive skill. Positive thinking enables you to maximize your skill, but all the positive thinking in the world won't carry a golf ball through the trees, over the pond, and around the sand trap if the skill necessary to execute the shot is not present.

Most people who know him would agree that Shaquille "Shaq" O'Neal, the seven-foot one-inch, 312-pound all-star center who signed a $120 million contract to play basketball for the Los Angeles Lakers, is an optimistic, positive thinker. However, I can tell you with confidence that with all his positive thinking he would be a complete failure as a jockey. As a matter of fact, he would have to carry the horse across the finish line! Over the years I have established a reputation as an optimistic, positive thinker, but if you needed major surgery, I would not recommend me to perform it.

QUESTION: What will positive thinking let you do?

ANSWER: Positive thinking will let you use your ability and experience to the maximum. That is realistic. To believe that positive thinking will let you do anything is tantamount to disaster. It's untrue and very damaging because it creates false hope and unrealistic expectations. And unrealistic expectations are the seedbed of depression.

THIS MAKES SENSE

However, despite the obvious fact that as human beings we have certain limitations, there is a persistent belief that if you can conceive an idea and believe you can accomplish it, you will be able to do so. I will be the first to concede that if the idea is yours and if you really believe that you can do it, your chances for accomplishing it go up dramatically.

Unfortunately, there are many bankruptcies filed every year by people who conceived "marvelous" ideas and believed with all their hearts they could achieve them. They poured their hearts and souls into their endeavors and still ended in bankruptcy. Perhaps the idea was not sound, or they did not have the skills, ability, or training necessary to make the idea work. It could be that circumstances beyond their control prevented them from bringing their idea to a successful conclusion.

Our jails and prisons are filled with people who conceived what they believed to be marvelous ideas, visions, or dreams. They believed with all their hearts they could reach them, worked extremely hard and ended up behind the eight ball, compromised their integrity, and landed in prison.

> **"** *Since your thinking has a direct bearing on your performance, your thinking must be based on sound input.* **"**

We were given minds so that we can gather information, mix it with common sense, and ultimately make sound judgments about what we can and want to do. Then we can plan accordingly.

NEGATIVE THINKING

There is also considerable confusion about negative thinking. Some positive thinkers sincerely believe that if you even speak of a problem or challenge, you're being negative. That is being naive. Actually, you're being realistic when you recognize that you are faced with a problem or challenge. Would you want your doctor to tell you the lump in your thigh is a cyst because she doesn't want to be negative and tell you it is cancer? Or your positive-thinking accountant to tell you things are fine because he doesn't want to be negative and tell you the company owes $68,000 in back taxes?

The first step in solving any problem or meeting any challenge is to be sure it is properly identified. Negative thinking is when you throw up your hands in despair and say, "I've never been able to do this before," "This is a hopeless situation," or "There's nothing I can do." The picture these words paint in your mind will stifle your creative imagination and create an even bigger problem than the one that already exists.

YOUR CHOICE: BOOM ATTITUDE OR DEPRESSION ATTITUDE

As most of you know, in late 1992 and early 1993, we were just coming out of a prolonged recession. Many people suffered severely because of high unemployment caused by downsizing and the bankruptcies of some major companies and thousands of small ones. My heart goes out to those of you who suffered, and much of *Over the Top* is written to help you prepare yourself for any future difficulties. I do firmly believe that regardless of what is going on "out there," your attitude can give you a competitive advantage.

Even as a child of the depression of the 1930s, I noticed that some people wore nice clothes, drove nice cars, lived in nice houses, took great vacations, and even played golf at the country club.

Throughout my lifetime I have noticed that some people pay no attention to the economy. I've seen occasions when the economy was really bad. The rate of inflation and the rate of interest were both over 20 percent. Yet in those difficult times some people were doing extremely well financially—actually, they got rich! I've also noticed that during the most incredible boom times, when money almost grew on trees, that some people couldn't find jobs and others went bankrupt. I believe the difference was in their attitude. Some looked "out there," grew despondent, and had financial as well as other difficulties. Others looked "out there," saw opportunity, and recognized that it was up to them to take advantage of it. Attitude did make the difference.

MOMENTUM—KEEP IT GOING—OR STOP IT

I touched on this subject in chapter 7, but it's so important that I wanted to hit it again. Positive momentum is so beneficial we want to sustain it, and negative momentum is so destructive we want to quickly stop it.

FOR EXAMPLE: In the world of athletics an enormous amount of emphasis has been placed on the importance of momentum and how it can change in a split second. I would like to point out that momentum is involved in every facet of life, on both a positive and a negative plane. When the momentum is downhill, it is fueled by downhill thinking. One negative thought breeds another, which breeds another, until you have an entire family of negative thoughts. When you get enough of them, PLOM disease moves in and takes control.

In baseball, when a team has lost several games in a row, the manager looks his staff over to find a stopper. Some pitchers are famous for their ability, almost regardless of their won-lost record, to win the big ones and to provide that stopper.

In life, action with the right attitude is the best possible stopper for a downhill slide and the best insurance for keeping momentum going when it's of a positive nature. This chapter on attitude is filled with momentum builders and negative stoppers. Latch on to the ones that appeal to you the most, and if things ever start to slide (in a lifetime all of us have our peaks and valleys), go to the stopper and grab hold of that procedure. When things are going well, keep doing the things that started you in that direction.

Maintaining the right attitude is easier than regaining the right mental attitude.

One of the things that has mystified me most over the years is the incredible number of people who have said to me, "Zig, when I get a little down, I pop in one of your tapes or pick up one of your books, and invariably, it gives me the lift I need." What puzzles me about that statement is that if they were to keep doing the things that got them going, they would keep on going, and their chances of getting a little down would be dramatically reduced. Maintaining the right attitude is easier than regaining the right mental attitude.

PMA + POSITIVE TEACHING WORKS IN SCHOOL

No, positive thinking won't let you do anything, but it will let you do everything . . . better than negative thinking will. That makes sense. What will positive thinking do? Positive thinking will let you use the ability you have. For example, 46 percent of the students in a study of fifteen hundred who had taken our I CAN school course, increased their positive thinking and made better grades in their other subjects.

Does positive thinking make you smarter? I didn't say that. I said the students made better grades in their other subjects, because of a four-letter word called *hope*. A youngster who does not think he can learn enough to pass will not study. Change his attitude, convince him he can learn, and he will open his books and study. It is the attitude change that got him into the books; it is the working (studying) with the right attitude that produces the results.

A more recent and comprehensive survey involving 492 male students and 510 female students in the eighth grade I CAN class at Bridgeview Middle School in Sidney, Ohio, revealed some tremendously exciting results. David Gates is the teacher, and the report is as of June 7, 1992. I include this information in *Over the Top* because I have contended from the beginning of the book that these are things that can be taught. Mr. Gates submitted 31 measurable results, but I include only the following ones because I believe the point is made.

Of those 1,002 students,

- 64.1 percent reported using what they learned from one to several times a day.
- 76.1 percent reported improved performance at school, home, or work.

- 79.1 percent reported having a better self-image since taking I CAN.
- 82.8 percent reported a more positive attitude after taking I CAN.
- 52.2 percent reported having a better attitude toward school.
- 63.5 percent said they're more optimistic about their future.
- 65.7 percent indicated they are setting and reaching goals.
- 65.4 percent reported they are happier since they've learned these concepts.
- 72.4 percent reported understanding that among drug users, smoking cigarettes is almost always the first step leading to drug use.
- 58.3 percent reported a reduction in the use of drugs and alcohol.
- 54.5 percent said they are more honest and loyal.
- 59.7 percent reported making better choices.
- 66.4 percent felt they're more kind and helpful to others.
- over 50 percent reported getting along better with friends, family, and others their age.

FLIP THE SWITCH

This is the way positive thinking works. Last night I walked into a dark hotel room and flipped the light switch, and the room was flooded with light. Flipping the switch did not generate electricity; the electricity had already been generated and stored. The flip of the switch released the electricity. But had there been no electricity stored, I could have flipped that switch forever and still had no light.

When you flip the switch of positive thinking, you release—or make available—the knowledge and experience that you have previously stored. That's the reason the students in the hundreds of schools that teach our concepts and principles make better grades in their other subjects.

NOTE: If the student hasn't studied and learned the material, all the positive thinking in the world won't help.

The exciting thing is the fact that this I CAN way of thinking and working will improve your performance, too, whether you are seeking a job or a promotion or making a sale.

EXAMPLE: Many unemployed people, who would be delighted to go to work if a job were offered them, often remain unemployed for a simple reason: They have PLOM disease. They don't think a job is available (everybody has told them so), or they don't think they would be lucky enough to get one. With this kind of thinking the inevitable happens. Their job-seeking efforts, if any, will confirm what they already know ("I told you no jobs were available!"). Change that thinking and the job applicants will work much harder to get a job, and they will work with the expectancy of getting a job. Now let's look at a specific example to validate this point.

> Many unemployed people remain unemployed because they don't think a job is available (everybody has told them so), or they don't think they would be lucky enough to get one. With this kind of thinking the inevitable happens.

SHE IMPROVED HERS AND HELPED CHANGE THEIRS

Our company donated our Strategies for Success video training series to the Interfaith Job Search Council whose purpose is to help unemployed people qualify for and obtain jobs.

Aletha Beane, from the Fort Worth office of the Texas Employment Commission, had just been promoted and was once removed from dealing directly with unemployed people. She realized she needed more direct contact with the people she ultimately helps as well as more motivation, new thoughts, and ideas, so she went to the Interfaith Job Search Council and took the training to qualify as a "Strategies for Success" facilitator. Once a week she volunteers to teach the class to the unemployed and work with the various breakout groups.

In 1989 when she adopted our philosophy, as well as the procedures and techniques you are learning in this book, the Employment Commission's Fort Worth office was running 81 percent of the standard for placement. By the end of the year, it was 102 percent. In 1990, her office was 136 percent of standard, and in 1991, the most significant year, it was 114 percent. I say most significant because in 1991, General Dynamics laid off over 10,000 employees. Four major companies laid off over 500 employees, and scores of companies laid off anywhere from 2 to 50 employees each. I don't need to remind you that '91 and '92 were pretty tough years for the economy. In 1992, the Fort Worth office hit 109 percent of the standard for placement despite the fact that General Dynamics laid off 4,000 more employees, and many other industries were downsizing or closing. In 1993, Aletha's office hit 122 percent of the goal.

LESSONS FROM ALETHA

FIRST: The philosophy that you can have everything in life you want if you will just help enough other people get what they want comes alive in this story. As a result of helping others in 1991, Aletha received the highest award given to an individual by the state chapter of the International Association of Personnel in Employment Security, and she was later recognized by the international chapter at the annual meeting in Charleston, South Carolina. In 1993, she was recognized by Governor Ann Richards as one of the 100 Outstanding Women in Texas Government (180,000 women were involved).

SECOND: What she did off the job (teaching unemployed

people at the Interfaith Job Search Council how to get a job) made her more effective in teaching those principles and procedures at her job with the Texas Employment Commission.

THIRD: The goal-setting procedures she learned and taught the unemployed were beneficial to her personal life.

FOURTH: According to a study done at the University of Michigan Survey Research Center, regular volunteer work more than any other activity dramatically increases life expectancy. Volunteer activities reduce stress, improve the cardiovascular system, and boost immune functions.

Don't miss this: Unemployed people got jobs because they changed a negative expectancy to a positive one, and when their attitudes improved, they became employable. Their attitudes, pictures, direction, and enthusiasm for life combined with the emphasis on character qualities made them valuable commodities in the job market. That's employment security.

When people are unemployed, it is difficult for them to keep a positive attitude. That's why classes that teach attitude and self-image improvement are vital to their placement. The percentages speak for themselves. By helping her clients learn how to be more employable, Aletha helped the Fort Worth Employment Commission's success rate.

Aletha is one more happy woman who bubbles with excitement as she talks about the benefits of helping others and staying involved in a growth program. She clearly understands that the teacher really does learn and benefit more than the student, and her attitude reflects Dr. Albert Schweitzer's statement that "the only ones among you who will be really happy are those who will have sought and found how to serve."

ACTION CHANGES ATTITUDES—AND PERFORMANCE

One of the most intriguing examples I've encountered is the story of the two women who, several years ago, worked for Western Union, and to say they were not overly excited about their jobs would be a gross understatement. One evening over coffee they started discussing the issue and decided that, even though they did not have other job offers, they simply could not tolerate that place any longer and were going to leave. Then since the evening was young, they started planning how they were going to make their grand exit. One thought led to another and another and another until they had devised a rather elaborate plan: They were going to leave without notice after work on Friday of the next week. During the intervening days, they talked about it, laughed about it, and in general had a good time.

YOU CHANGE AND THEY CHANGE

On the appointed day, by plan, they dressed in their best clothes and met at the office an hour early. They had the coffee brewed and the kitchen tidied up by the time their first coworker arrived. They greeted her with considerable excitement and invited her to sit down and let them get her a cup of coffee. The new arrival expressed surprise and delight and wanted to know what was going on. The two culprits just laughed and said everybody had been so nice to them they had decided that they were going to turn the tables.

A moment or two later another employee came in, and the process was repeated, perhaps with even more enthusiasm, then a third and a fourth, with the same result. The two plotters were at the front counter when the doors opened for business. They greeted the first customer with broad smiles and a cheerful "Good morning!" They told him how delighted they were that he was their first customer of the day, that they felt it was a good omen. The man exchanged some pleasantries, took care of his business, bid them a cheerful "Good day," and made his departure.

A few moments later another customer came in. They greeted him with equal enthusiasm and courtesy and rendered superb service, thanked him profusely for coming in, invited him to come back, and so it went all day long. They were highly motivated, enthusiastic, and very gracious to everyone. The rest of the employees were in absolute shock. All the customers were pleased and delighted; things went unbelievably well with no glitches of any kind.

At about 4:30 one of the women said to the other, "Well, are we going to walk out and not say anything and never come back, or do we make our grand exit and tell them this is the last time they will ever see us?"

Her partner in crime, somewhat astonished, said, "What are you talking about?"

The first one said, "Well, you know, we're quitting today."

Her partner said, "Quitting! Are you kidding? Quitting the best job where I have the most fun I've ever had in my life? No way!" (They both stayed.)

NOTE: Nothing had changed about the job, the management, or the economy. However, everything had changed for the better because the women's attitudes had changed.

MAJOR POINT: Their attitudes changed because their actions changed.

> **“** *Feelings follow actions. So when you don't really want to or feel like doing what needs to be done—do it and then you will feel like doing it.* **”**

In the end the two women were much happier, felt better about themselves, and were considerably more valuable to their employer. That's why numerous studies have validated the fact that 85 percent of the reason people get jobs and get ahead in those jobs is attitude. Fortunately, your attitude is something you can control.

A SENSE OF HUMOR INCREASES YOUR EMPLOYMENT SECURITY

If you want to increase your employment security, take action and employ humor. Roger Ailes wrote in a *Success* magazine article titled "Lighten Up: Stuffed Shirts Have Short Careers": "The only advice some of my clients need when they come to see me can be summed up in two words: Lighten up. It's ironic, but your career can depend on whether you get serious about taking yourself less seriously."

According to Executive Recruiters, for seven out of ten people who lose their jobs, the cause isn't lack of skill: It's personality conflicts. As an executive reaches middle management and beyond, the primary criteria for advancement are communication and motivation skills rather than job performance. Relations with superiors and peers are also critical; historically, top management promotes people it likes. The number one reason someone isn't liked in business? He takes himself too seriously. He has no sense of humor.

Emerson said, "If you would rule the world quietly, you must keep it amused." Humor shows that you are human, and the records clearly show that all of us prefer to work for people who are human. The benefits that go with humor and laughter are well known.

In the March 1992 issue of *Florida Trend* magazine, an article about corporate humor by consultant Leslie Gibson contains some interesting data. She reports that the average four-year-old laughs 400 times a day, while adults laugh only 15 to 16 times.

That's a shame because, Gibson says, "Laughter is also good for business. It can reduce stress, enliven presentations, and spur creativity. In a corporate setting, when people are allowed to laugh, even if it's only for fifteen seconds, they're getting more oxygen to the brain and that lets them think more clearly." Gibson warns against any jokes that involve ridicule, slander, or sarcasm. (Don't start a joke you can't finish, regardless of who walks in the room.) She also says the most positive use of humor in the workplace may be to create a spirit of social equality by stripping away pretension.

LOTS OF ADVANTAGES

A sense of humor gives us many advantages. A study at the University of Michigan concluded that people with a good sense of humor tend to be more creative, emotionally stable, realistic, and self-confident. You can also have fun and make friends by sharing humorous incidents from daily experiences. I'm not just talking about telling jokes but appreciating them as well.

For several years Graydene Patterson worked with us, and when we produced customized recordings, she was always invited to be in the audience because her laughter was so natural and spontaneous that she immediately had the rest of the audience laughing with her. She always made a good audience great.

I love the story of the little fellow who did not realize the preacher was visiting and he came charging into the house and said, "Mama, Mama, I just found a rat in our backyard and I took a board and I hit him and I hit him and I hit him and then I stomped him and stomped him and stomped him." At that point he looked over, saw the preacher, and piously said, "And then the Lord called him home."

I hope you got a little chuckle out of that or at least smiled broadly. Medically speaking, we know that laughter releases endorphins that energize us, increase our endurance, and act as nature's painkiller. When you hear something really funny, I sincerely hope you will laugh out loud because if you don't, you won't like the consequences. I feel I must warn you that when you really want to laugh but stifle it, the full force of that laughter reverses itself, comes back inside, and spreads the hips! And as you well know, obesity is widespread, so failure to laugh could force you to buy a new wardrobe.

Dr. John Maxwell remarked, "A person who can laugh at

life and laugh at himself, will have less stress in life. If you have a good sense of humor, you'll climb the ladder faster and enjoy the climb more. It increases your effectiveness with others because people who have a sense of humor have good relationships; team spirit is enhanced, and productivity goes up."

The effective use of humor has yet another advantage: It increases our persuasion effectiveness. Here is a letter sent out by Methodist minister Charles Allen under the pretense that he had received it himself:

In reply to your request to send a check I wish to inform you that the present condition of my bank account makes it almost impossible. My shattered financial condition is due to Federal laws, state laws, county laws, corporation laws, in-laws, and outlaws. Through these laws I'm compelled to pay a business tax, amusement tax, head tax, school tax, gas tax, light tax, water tax, sales tax, even my brains are taxed.

I'm required to get a business license, dog license, and marriage license while contributing to every organization or society that the genius of man is capable of bringing to light: comic relief, unemployment relief, every hospital and charitable institution in the city, including the Red Cross, the Black Cross, the Purple Cross, and the Double Cross.

For my own safety I'm required to carry life insurance, property insurance, liability insurance, burglar insurance, accident insurance, business insurance, earthquake insurance, tornado insurance, unemployment insurance, and fire insurance.

I'm inspected, expected, disrespected, rejected, dejected, examined, re-examined, informed, reformed, summoned, fined, commanded, compelled until I've provided an exhaustible supply of money for every known need, desire, and hope of the human race.

And if I refuse to donate something or other I'm boycotted, talked about, lied about, held up, held down, robbed until I am ruined.

I can tell you honestly that until the unexpected happened I could not enclose this check. The wolf that comes to so many doors nowadays, fortunately, came to ours and just had pups in the kitchen. I sold them and here's the money.

Result—an enormously effective fund-raising campaign. There's evidence that the fastest and surest way to the heart, head, and hip pocket as well as a step up the ladder is often through the funny bone.

QUESTION: Seriously now, don't you already feel better than you did when you started the chapter?

When we speak of attitude and gaining the most benefit from the procedures covered in *Over the Top,* we need to insert a big plug for the use of genuinely humorous cassette recordings. Humor, as you've been reading, relaxes us, relieves stress, is good for our health, and does wonders for our attitudes. I especially encourage you to listen to good, clean humor the last few minutes of your drive home from work. People like Ken Davis, Andy Andrews, Dr. Charles Jarvis, Jeanne Robertson, Joe Griffith, Dr. Herb True, Bob Murphy, Doc Blakely, Charlie "Tremendous" Jones, and Rick Nielsen can get you in a marvelous frame of mind and make you easier to get along with when you return to your family.

NOTE: Ken Davis can be reached at Ken Davis Productions, 6080 West 82d Drive, Arvada, Colorado 80003; Andy Andrews can be reached at P.O. Box 2761, Gulf Shores, Alabama 36547. All other humorists can be reached through the National Speakers Association, 1500 South Priest Drive, Tempe, Arizona 85281.

My other favorite sources of humor are the *Reader's Digest* and the daily comics. "Humor in Uniform" and "Life in These United States," as well as the numerous little inserts throughout *Reader's Digest,* make it a real upper every time I pick it up. In the daily comics I love "Dennis the Menace," "Peanuts," "B.C.," "Garfield," "Family Circus," "Marmaduke," "The Lockhorns," "Pavlov," and "Cathy." They only take a moment to read, and they always bring a smile and frequently a real chuckle.

START—OR FINISH—THE DAY THIS WAY

Read something funny. The one-frame comics will bring a smile, but if you want to have real fun, draw the family closer together and teach the kids how to appreciate humor and develop a "sense" for it. Pick up a copy of *Anguished English, More Anguished English,* and *Even More Anguished English,* all by Richard Lederer. They will need a little screening for the family, but each day if you take turns reading three or four of the "mis-speaks," you will have everyone laughing, and that helps create a relaxed, loving appetite for humor. Here are three examples:

"Benign—what you do after you be eight."
"Nitrate—lower than the day rate."
"Vertigo—what a tour guidebook tells you."

As Diane Johnson says, "Laughter is the jam on the toast of life. It adds flavor, keeps it from being too dry, and makes it easier to swallow."

BE A GOOD-FINDER

For years I have been encouraging individuals who are unhappy to change from being faultfinders to being good-finders. I suggest they make a list of all the things they like, admire, or appreciate about their job, mate, or city. Then I encourage them to enthusiastically verbalize those things in front of a mirror each morning and evening. Results in the lives of those who participate are often immediate and dramatic.

You should know that the more you complain about your problems, the more problems you will have to complain about. The constant complainer at home is likely to destroy any hopes for good relationships with his mate and children. The person who is always griping and complaining on the job is the least productive person on the payroll, and when staff reductions take place, he is the first one to be discharged. The person who gains a reputation in the community for griping and complaining is less likely to establish friendships and, as a result, has no support system to build on.

So don't complain. Become a good-finder instead by following this approach with your mate or parents or children. List what you like about them, and review the list on a regular basis. The more you emphasize their good qualities, the more good qualities you will find to like—or love. As a result, you will treat those family members with more respect, courtesy, and appreciation. This procedure improves your chances of having more meaningful relationships and more happiness on the home front—and happiness is an attitude all of us want to have.

Part of the solution to maintaining an up attitude and eliminating problems is putting your list on paper. For instance, write down the things you really like about your community. Then, when people ask you where you're from, tell them with pride and enthusiasm where you live and, if time permits, some of the reasons you're so pleased to live there.

Follow the same procedure regarding your job, your company, and the people who work there. When somebody asks you where you work, respond enthusiastically that you work for the XYZ Company and you really appreciate your job. Then verbalize what you like about your job. It will increase your appreciation for the employment opportunity you already have.

Recently, in a presentation in Dallas, I suggested that audience members list things they liked about their jobs. Two weeks later a woman who worked with JCPenney told me she followed through on my suggestion, and in less than a week her supervisor was complimenting her on her new attitude and the improvement in her performance. This procedure does wonders for the attitude because one of the great truths of life is that the more you recognize and express gratitude for the things you have, the more things you will have to express gratitude for.

ATTITUDE STARTS WITH YOU

The next step for maintaining the right attitude and giving ourselves a better chance at total success is exercising careful control over our language. The words we use on others and on ourselves make a dramatic difference in that attitude. People frequently ask me how I manage to stay up so much of the time. My response is always that I listen to myself. Sounds funny—even egotistical—but you do exactly the same thing, and what you say to yourself has a major influence on whether you are up or down.

I do have one advantage over most of you. My career is built on words—saying them, writing them, and reading them. Most of the input into my mind is of an informational or inspirational nature. What I dictate in letters and verbalize in one-on-one conversations, what I voice when I'm making my talks, has a significant bearing on my own attitude. My speech to you is my self-talk to me.

If you've ever heard me speak, you know I deliver those talks with considerable excitement and enthusiasm. That's the way our self-talk should be delivered—with passion, with excitement, with conviction. When you do that, the impact it has on your own thinking is substantial.

On the other hand, that same passion, excitement, and conviction, when applied to negative words, thoughts, and expressions, can have a significantly negative impact on your attitude.

Let's explore some comments Rabbi Daniel Lapin makes in his publication, *Thought Tool,* about putting the positive things in and avoiding the negative ones:

If we listen as others are maligned, in spite of our disinclination to believe what we hear, our relationship with the vilified individual is forever altered. In other words, we are involuntarily influenced by everything we hear. Harmless gossip does not exist. Listening to gossip will usually leave us feeling dissatisfied with our spouse, children, employees, friends, or life in general. Speaking gossip usually leaves us feeling less worthy. Words penetrate to our souls and cannot be erased or ignored.

Leviticus 19:14 says, "Thou shalt not curse a deaf man." Since he cannot hear what harm has been done, the prohibition is due to the effect on the curser himself. He hears his own words and they reduce his worth as a human being.

Overcome your inhibitions about talking to yourself. Speak passionately to yourself. Prepare speeches by actually saying them out loud. A winning mind-set is the consequence of hearing words that penetrate right to the core of personality.

If we truly wish to believe something, we should tell it to ourselves audibly, rather than think it silently.

Since we remember far better that which we hear, reading aloud increases our vocabulary, fluency, and range of ideas. Above all, it inspires.

Each time you say something good about someone in your life, you increasingly believe it yourself.

Self-censorship benefits one's soul. Since everything that enters the mind through the ears has an effect, it is better not to hear certain things.

Through speech one can substantially increase inner feelings of harmony and satisfaction with certain unchangeable facts of one's life. Praising God makes for a close relationship with Him. This is part of the basis for praying out loud.

P.S. Our own language should be so clean we could give our talkative parrot to our preacher, priest, or rabbi.

IT'S IMPORTANT

I include the importance of self-talk in this chapter on attitude because you are the only one who can control what you say to yourself. A positive attitude starts with you. Once you develop, maintain, and apply that attitude, life's inconsistencies won't have the power to disrupt your positive outlook. The next chapter is designed to get you focused on claiming positive qualities, and your attitude dictates how effectively you can use those qualities in your day-to-day affairs. Claiming the qualities takes effort, and the next story will reveal why effort is a necessary ingredient for over-the-top living.

FRONT-ROW SEATS AVAILABLE

In January of 1992, I had the privilege of speaking at Hinds Community College in Raymond, Mississippi. As a sixteen-year-old back in 1943, I was also privileged to attend Hinds Community College, which was then known as Hinds Junior College. While I was there, Coach Joby Harris had a profound impact on my life.

The purpose of my engagement in Raymond and later that evening in Jackson was to establish the Joby and Jim El Harris Scholarship Fund. Students and others were lined up around the back of the room and part of the way around the auditorium. As I began to speak, I noticed seven vacant seats on the front row and five seats on the other side on the second row that were also vacant. Early in my talk I pointed out the empty seats and encouraged the students who were standing to come on down. No one moved.

Then I said, "You know, I wish I had the strength and the time to step off the stage, lift those seats, and take them back to you so that you would be more comfortable for this presentation. But I'm not strong enough, time will not permit it, and I have a sneaking suspicion that the administration would be visibly upset if I actually did that. However, I just want to say to you that all you have to do is put one foot in front of the other about twenty times and you will have a front-row seat.

"On the other side of the auditorium, unfortunately, you will have a little more trouble because those five empty seats are in the middle, and you will have to climb over three or four people. However, that's the way life is. Opportunity seldom comes to you. You have to go to it. In most cases there are obstacles standing between you and those opportunities in life, but I want you to know that front-row seats are available everywhere. There is plenty of room at the top. There's just not enough room to sit down. And those 'spots' or seats are not going to come to you. You have to go to them."

Remember, it's not where you start; it's where you go that counts. Colin Powell's first job was mopping floors in a soft drink plant. He decided to be the best floor mopper anywhere. He took that same attitude into the military and, as I mentioned earlier, retired in 1993 as the much decorated, highly regarded chairman of the Joint Chiefs of Staff.

CLIMBING THOSE OBSTACLES

Although I probably embarrassed some of the students, my intention was to make a point and offer some encouragement for them to move toward the front. Many good things in life are available (even when the economy is reportedly bad), but we are going to have to go after them to make them ours. It's also significant that the seven front-row seats involved climbing over no one. The smaller number of seats (five) involved a little climbing, but there would have been no resistance. The trip would have been easy.

I know you are wondering how many of the standing students had the courage to walk fifteen or twenty steps under the eyes of everyone there and claim those choice seats. The answer is one. It would be neat if I'd had the foresight to get that person's name and followed him through life. I have an idea that with his attitude he's probably doing all right.

What about the other students? They could learn something from these two old boys down home who had an interesting encounter one day. One was lying down and relaxing under a tree; the other was standing there, just looking at him. After several moments, the one lying down said, "Now, look here. I know you want to be lying down on the ground like I am, but, man, you gotta make some effort in order to do it!"

An important part of attitude is the concept "you gotta make some effort" to develop and maintain a positive attitude. Remember, if you make positive deposits every day, you will be motivated to flip the switch to release the electricity (positive thinking) to turn on the lights so you'll be able to see your way to that front-row seat.

IMPORTANT: The next chapter is so significant and potentially life-changing that I encourage you to make certain you are alert and at least reasonably well rested before you get started. It's dynamite.

CHAPTER NINE

You—yes, you— have got what it takes

You are the way you are because that's the way you want to be. If you really wanted to be any different, you would be in the process of changing right now.

Fred Smith

O ver the years I have researched a number of individuals from many walks of life who have by every standard been successful. The list includes U.S. presidents, three hundred world-class leaders, Rhodes scholars, CEOs of the Fortune 500 companies, astronauts, athletes, businesspeople, mothers, fathers, coaches, teachers, physicians, entrepreneurs, and ministers. My prime objective has been to identify the foundational qualities that made them successful in their lives. I wanted to know what qualities they developed that enabled them to get at least a portion of the things money will buy without losing the things that money can't buy. The next example helps us identify some additional success qualities and see what happens when they are combined with love and encouragement from a caring and concerned teacher who is truly making a difference.

YOU, TOO, CAN STAND AND DELIVER

You probably saw the movie in the theater or on television. You may have read his book or heard about Jaime Escalante from some other source. He's an immigrant from Bolivia who taught school at Garfield High in the barrio (which is a Hispanic neighborhood) in Los Angeles. Drug usage was rampant; violence was a daily occurrence; the rate of teenage pregnancy was extremely high; the number of high-school dropouts was a major problem. Many of the kids who got diplomas did not necessarily have an education.

Escalante came up with a preposterous idea. He wanted to teach the kids advanced calculus. The school administrators scoffed at the idea. Some of the kids were having trouble with their multiplication tables, and Escalante wanted to teach them advanced calculus! Escalante was persistent (remember, that's one of those qualities) and finally prevailed.

The third year he taught advanced calculus, eighteen of his students took an exam in advanced calculus in an effort to win college scholarships. The exam is so difficult that less than 2 percent of the high-school seniors in America will even attempt it. Eighteen of his students took it and eighteen of them passed it, seven of them with the highest possible score. The administrators of the test screamed foul! That had never happened before so they knew the students must have cheated to accomplish their scores. They demanded that fourteen of them retake the exam.

Everyone at Garfield High was furious! The school officials and parents were incensed! For many weeks they debated back and forth as to whether or not the students would or should retake the exam. There were ugly cries of racism and prejudice. One of the students accepted a college scholarship, and one chose to pursue a military career before a decision could be made.

After much persuasion from Escalante, the remaining

twelve students reluctantly decided to take the exam again. They all passed it with the same grades and won their college scholarships. Seven years later, 85 percent of these young people are professionals. MESSAGE: Successful people come in all shapes, sizes, and colors, and they can come from any neighborhood or country. They can be male or female, and success can come to them at any age.

Let's look at the qualities the students acquired while pursuing the goal of mastering calculus. They learned to be committed, competent, convicted, courageous, disciplined, bold, ambitious, and energetic. They discovered they were intelligent, loyal, patient, and resourceful team players. They became educated, goal-directed, hardworking, knowledgeable, and responsible self-starters who understood the importance of living a sober life.

By watching Mr. Escalante give freely of his time (he invested many extra hours teaching his students before and after school), they learned how to be generous and unselfish. They became organized, punctual, persistent, and obedient. Over time the students developed hope for the future and healthy pride in their accomplishments. Ultimately, they discovered the honor and the rewards that come with successfully completing a difficult task and doing it with integrity.

Yes, these young people from the barrio truly understand failure is an event, not a person. They know that yesterday ended last night, and it's not where you start, but where you finish that counts.

NOTE: Mr. Escalante already has the qualities we are talking about. That's why he was able to be a catalyst in the lives of his students.

If you missed the movie *Stand and Deliver*, I encourage you to go to the video store and rent a copy. You will clearly recognize every quality mentioned above as you watch. When you get past the foul, violent language and concentrate on the message, it is powerful and inspiring.

THE REAL YOU

A s we get into the heart of this chapter, let me remind you that I have noted the qualities that contributed to the success of individuals as well as members of certain groups such as the youngsters from the barrio. Now let's look at the qualities we've identified throughout the book, including the qualities that you already have and that you used on the day before your vacation.

From the beginning of *Over the Top* I have repeated several phrases, such as, "You've got to be before you can do and do before you can have." It's also my conviction that the statement, "You can have everything in life you want if you will just help enough other people get what they want," applies to all areas of life. In my mind, everything I have written comes to a head in this chapter.

The emphasis has been on attitude combined with skill, built on character. What I would like to do as we identify these qualities is start with you and what you were able to accomplish with the qualities you used on the day before you went on vacation: honesty, intelligence, goal-directed, organized, responsible, committed, punctual, self-starter, motivated, optimistic, enthusiastic, decisive, make good choices, disciplined, persistent, positive, good self-image, manage self well, confident, competent, energized, resourceful, creative, knowledgeable, focused, believer, emotionally intelligent, self-controled, extra-miler, and team player with momentum.

THE "SEED" IS THE KEY

I would like to emphasize that you and each one of the people named in the earlier chapters have at least the seed of all of these qualities. I have identified the ones in each individual example that I felt were the greatest—but by no means all—strengths.

Next, we look at the list of qualities not already mentioned but ones manifested by Richard Oates, John Foppe, Gerry Arrowood, Pam Lontos, Pious Obioha, military leaders, business leaders, and others: promptness, courage, humor, adaptability, vision, faith, gentle, thoughtful, determination, responsiveness, open mind, unselfish, trustworthy, passionate, kind, caring, generous, teachable, assertive, giving, forgiving, conscientious, personable, desire, educated, conviction, maturity, patient, "Gosh!" attitude, student, sound judgment, flexibility, mannerly, versatile, trust, curiosity, empathy, sympathy, action oriented, communicator, friendly, consistent, sober, good-finder, ambitious, authoritative, courteous, obedient, loving, affectionate, neat, wisdom, cheerful, respectful, compassionate, diligent, and integrity.

The list also includes qualities identified by audiences all over the world that the *ideal* husband, wife, child, teacher, student, leader, employer, or employee would have.

The ideal mate would demonstrate the qualities of affection, caring, loving, kindness, and generosity, and the military commander would demonstrate the qualities of more authority, organization, assertiveness, focus, and decisiveness. However, regardless of what you do, every quality we've identified would be valuable to you.

SPECIFIC SKILLS ARE A MUST

NOTE: In addition to the skills (qualities) we've identified you will need specific skills to be a physician, teacher, lawyer, truck driver, computer whiz, or whatever you choose. However, I know you will agree that any job or profession (doctor, mechanic, etc.) would be more effective *and* rewarding when built on these character qualities.

Take a careful look at these qualities with a pen in your hand, and check each of the qualities you feel you have—even if you have only the seed of that quality.

If you're completely objective, you put a check mark by all of the qualities because you really do have the seed of each one, and that is the critical point. Now we need to water and fertilize that seed, encourage, nurture, and use it so it will grow stronger and stronger.

I want to emphasize that I am not implying this is easy and instantaneous because complete success comes over time—not overnight—but the growth process is exhilarating and *some* changes and rewards will come almost immediately. Psychiatrist Louis Cady, referenced in another part of the book, said, "The results of the process [which I'll finish describing in this chapter] after three days were frightening—because they were so good—so fast." Just remember, success requires commitment, discipline, persistence, and patience. The key is getting started.

NOW—RIGHT NOW—IT'S TIME FOR YOU TO TAKE ACTION

I hope you are ready because now is action time. So turn back to the list of qualities you checked on page 160; go down that list slowly, and place the letter *A* by the words that you consider to be attitudes. Write an *S* by the words that you consider to be skills. If you're not certain whether the word denotes an attitude or a skill, write *A/S* by it. If you think it is a gift, place a *G* beside the word. Go down the list and mark your first instinctive choice. In all probability it is going to be the right one. Please do it now.

Here is some good news. *All* of the qualities we have identified are skills. The Scouts were taught those qualities/skills we identified in the Scout Motto, Oath, and Law. You were taught the qualities/skills you used the day before vacation. Gerry Arrowood was taught the qualities/skills she used to move from cake baker/seamstress to vice president of sales. The kids from the barrio were taught the qualities/skills they used to move from potential high-school dropouts to successful professionals.

That information might be surprising to you because in public seminars most people identify virtually all of the qualities as attitudes. The news is good—incredibly good—for you. It's good because it means that you—almost regardless of what your past has been—have a legitimate chance to succeed big time.

THIS IS PROFOUND

The most significant and exciting news I could possibly give you is this: *Since they are skills* that can be taught, not only you but your children and your grandchildren can develop them. That also means that children in the inner city who encounter a Jaime Escalante somewhere along the way can develop them, which means they, too, have a chance.

You have the seeds of *all* these skills, but you need to do something with those seeds.

The acorn has an oak tree in it, but if we just let that acorn lie around, the oak tree will never come to life. That's also true of the success seeds in you. Now you have a choice—develop and use the seeds and bring your "oak tree" to full maturity, or let them lie around and watch your oak tree die. Keep reading. The fertilizer, fuel, and hope your seeds need to reach full maturity are in your hands.

At this point let me remind you of something you already know: My objective is to get you involved and into action because until you do something, the benefits of *Over the Top* will be primarily limited to just helping you feel good. These feelings are important and provide the starting point. However, feelings are short-term and frequently change. Action that produces growth is necessary to achieve long-term beneficial changes—and that's what you want.

QUESTIONS, QUESTIONS, AND MORE QUESTIONS

QUESTION: As you review the list, do you believe that anyone who develops these qualities would make a good spouse?

SECOND QUESTION: If you're married, do you believe that anyone who develops these qualities could get along with you and you with that person?

THIRD QUESTION: Would you love to have children with all of these qualities? Do you believe that a family consisting of people who have all of these qualities would be a warm, loving, happy, successful family? Yes or no? Specifically, do you believe anyone who has recognized, confessed, developed, and used these qualities would have an excellent chance of being happy, healthy, reasonably prosperous, and secure? Would someone have more friends, more peace of mind, better family relationships, and a realistic hope that the future was going to be even better?

Let me pause and say that if you've answered yes to the preceding questions (and unless you're the most unusual person on earth, you did answer yes), you have done something that none of our three presidential candidates in 1992 were able to do. You have identified family values.

If you said yes, and surely you did, you have also just identified educational values. Do you believe anybody with all of these qualities could take your job or enter your profession and literally go to the top in that job or profession? If you do, you've just identified business, leadership, and professional values. Do you believe an individual with all of these qualities would be successful in a governmental or political position? If you do, you've just identified governmental and political values.

By now you have undoubtedly realized that there are no such things as family values, educational values, business values, governmental values, or political values. They are life values. You cannot separate successful family or life values from successful educational, business, or governmental values. Nor can you separate your personal, family, and business lives any more than you can separate your physical, mental, and spiritual lives. You are a package deal and a marvelous package at that! And the package is getting more valuable by the minute.

You—yes, you—have got what it takes 163

WHOSE VALUES?

By now you might well be thinking, *But, Zig, you're talking about values.* So my question is, Whose values do you want taught in the schools and practiced at home and in the business community? Here's my challenge to you: Go back to the list of words. Specifically evaluate each word and ask yourself, Is there any quality here [now remember, the courts have taken faith out, and after two hundred years, we can no longer teach it in our schools] that I would not want my child taught in school? Is there any quality here that I would not want practiced at home? Is there any quality here that I would not want implemented in the business or job where I am working? I'm convinced you'd be hard-pressed to list even one quality you would want removed.

THIS WAY TO SOLVING OUR PROBLEMS

Our country was built on positive ethical values and qualities. These are the values that, according to the *Wall Street Journal,* 84 percent of the people in America want their children taught. A September 29, 1993, report in *USA Today* reveals that 97 percent of the public want honesty taught, 93 percent want democracy taught, 91 percent want caring for friends and family, patriotism, moral courage, and the golden rule taught. If these values were taught at home and reinforced in school, then implemented in the business community, think about what a dramatic difference it would make in our society.

HIRE THAT ONE

In all of the years I've been beating the bushes, I've never met a businessperson who said to me, "Well, Zig, I disagree with what you're saying. As a matter of fact, just the other day, I interviewed a person who had all of the qualities you mentioned, and we obviously could not give the interviewee a job. We have no place in our organization for someone who is honest, has a positive mental attitude, is a team player, is disciplined and committed, has character, is hardworking, is a good communicator, and is goal directed. No, Zig, we just couldn't use anybody like that."

In my lifetime I've never had anybody say that to me. Actually, people have always said, "Send me somebody with these qualities, and I'll teach the specific skills the person needs to fill the vacancy we have."

As you have undoubtedly noticed, I've been using the word *teach*. Teach these qualities at home; teach them in school. Reinforce them and implement them in the business community. The question is, Can you teach these things? The answer is a definite, emphatic, positive, no-question-about-it yes, you definitely can teach all of them because as we have already indicated, they are all skills. In the process you will also raise your level of intelligence. My own IQ, for example, is well over twenty points higher than it was when I graduated from high school.

Am I saying that everybody is equal? Obviously not. We have different natural abilities, and the mix and amount of each quality we have will vary considerably. The tragedy is, most people never recognize, confess, develop, and use the abilities (qualities) they have. That's a major objective of this book—to encourage you to develop what you have. And to do that, you must recognize and confess what you have.

VINCE ROBERT FOUND OUT WHAT HE HAD

I briefly told the Vince Robert story in *Ziglar on Selling,* but this point is so significant, I want to expand it. Like all of us, Vince wanted more of the things money would buy and all of the things money won't buy, but he simply was not qualified in many ways to get those things because he had not recognized, developed, and used what he had.

He was thirty-seven years old, had a fifth-grade education, and was driving a taxi. On a daily basis he spent hours at the airport and in front of hotels, waiting for fares. Something happened, however, when Vince Robert went into a bookstore and purchased a twenty-pound *Webster's Dictionary* (incidentally, Webster wrote the dictionary because his wife kept asking him, "Now, what does that mean?").

Vince set the dictionary on the front seat of his taxi, and starting on page one, word one, he began memorizing the words one by one. Before Vince Robert had gotten more than an eighth of an inch deep into the dictionary, he started understanding things he'd only been hearing and reading. As a result, he got interested in the stock market and started investing every dime he could. His personal fortune grew, and he ended up buying the nineteen-car cab company. Today he is a wealthy man and tells others how it happened.

TWO OBSERVATIONS: First, he did not start investing in the stock market one day and buy the cab company the next; it took several years for that to happen. Second, in that process he displayed patience by denying himself certain luxuries of life in order to realize that major objective. This is a sign of maturity.

> *The chief cause of failure and unhappiness is trading what you want most for what you want now.*

Hope is born when we see or hear about someone who overcame difficult odds to become successful, and we say, "Maybe I can do that, too."

FIRST THE QUESTIONS—THEN THE PLAN

Before I give you the plan of action, I'm going to give you the most important sales talk I've ever given. I'm going to sell you on why you should and how you can develop these qualities of success. I start with two questions that on the surface might appear to be foolishness personified. First, if I could give you one procedure that would require roughly fifteen minutes every day, could you find the fifteen minutes? Think about it. Second, suppose the fifteen minutes and the procedure would have a dramatic impact on your life, giving you an infinitely better chance at being happy, healthy, reasonably prosperous, and secure, and having friends and peace of mind, and you would see results within ten days after you started the procedure. Are you willing to commit yourself to invest fifteen minutes every day for immediate results and long-term benefits?

You may have hesitated as you answered, "Of course." Human nature being what it is, you probably had a little thought in the back of your mind: *What's the catch?* Well, there are no catches, and best of all, the results have been well established. I'm going to tell you in advance it definitely, absolutely, positively has worked, is working, and will work for you. I leave myself absolutely no room for retreat—it will work. Here are some reasons I know the procedure works.

> **Are you willing to commit yourself to invest fifteen minutes every day for immediate results and long-term benefits?**

The first reason involves my personal experience: It has worked, is working, and will continue to work in my life. Second, each year we receive many pounds of unsolicited testimonial letters plus hundreds of telephone and personal contact testimonials from people all over the world. In a thousand different ways, they say this philosophy and procedure work. Here are some specific examples.

THIS HAS BEEN TESTED AND PROVEN

One of the most revealing incidents occurred in 1993 after I had spoken on Tuesday morning in Los Angeles. Two days later my administrative assistant, Laurie Magers, received a phone call from a gentleman who had attended the seminar. He told Laurie that he did well in claiming the qualities on the night of the seminar until he got to the word *integrity,* which disturbed him and caused him to turn over a few times that night.

He claimed the qualities on Wednesday morning, and again when he got to the word *integrity,* it bothered him. Wednesday evening, when he claimed to be a man of "integrity," he confessed that he had a sleepless night. After repeating the process on Thursday morning, he knew he had to call us.

He confessed to Laurie that he had bought and paid for our motivational series, which included the self-affirmation card, but that when he got home, he found our video training program—which also teaches the development of these qualities—in his bag; he had not paid for that series. He confessed his embarrassment, and Laurie assured him that "accidents happen to all of us."

After a brief moment of silence, he said, "Laurie, it was no accident. When no one was looking, I slipped that video series into my bag—and I must pay for it."

What had happened is simple but significant. Because the eyes are literally the windows of the soul, when the young man looked himself in the eye and claimed to have integrity, he knew it was not true because he had stolen the training program. He then paid for the video series and from that point on has been free to claim the qualities and enjoy the benefits thereof.

DEFINITELY NOT "NEW AGE"

Factually, you cannot look yourself in the eye and claim to be kind, generous, compassionate, caring, loving, understanding, and so on, and then abuse your mate, the waitperson at the restaurant, or someone you work with. Claiming these qualities is a life-changing, enriching procedure. For those of you who might believe this is some "New Age" approach to life, let me remind you of a couple of things.

First, remember the Scout Oath is pure self-talk, and it has been around a long time. Its effectiveness has already been validated. The Twenty-third Psalm and much of the Bible are pure self-talk and are several thousand years old. Go to the church or synagogue and get one of the hymnals; read the incredible number of songs that are self-talk set to music. Listen to the songs of the day for that matter—those that are sung in the first-person present tense and depict us at our best inspire us to perform better; those that degrade us influence us to perform at our worst. Self-talk works whether it is a positive, "I can" approach or a negative, "I can't" approach.

Think about it this way. You repeatedly say, "I feel really bad—I'm getting sick—I'm afraid something is really wrong," or you repeatedly say, "I feel good—really good—my energy level is high and getting higher all the time." QUESTION: Which one do you think will produce more positive results?

In addition, *Psychology Today* reports that self-talk is more effective than visualization, and many of us still remember from our childhood *The Little Engine That Could,* which is self-talk in its most basic form.

On January 14, 1992, I spoke in Las Vegas, Nevada. After I made the presentation, a very enthusiastic woman came up to me and said, "Mr. Ziglar, let me tell you how excited I am about what you're talking about. I have three daughters; two of them are straight-A students. They have always excelled academically. Our third daughter has been an average student, mostly making C's and occasionally B's. She had never been competitive with her sisters and had never felt she was as smart as they were. However, we bought your philosophy and started claiming these qualities. Results have been outstanding. This past semester her grades were even better than her sisters'. More important, it changed several areas of her life for the better. She now has an entirely different picture of herself and is performing accordingly."

500 PERCENT INCREASE DURING A RECESSION

Another example took place in Birmingham, Alabama. I spoke there on October 6, 1992, and when the seminar was over a gentleman came up to me and said, "Mr. Ziglar, three years ago when you were in Montgomery doing this seminar, I took you seriously. Every morning and every evening for the last three years I've taken a 5" × 7" card I prepared by listing the qualities I wanted, looked myself in the eye, and claimed all of them aloud.

"I will confess, Mr. Ziglar, that when I got to the word *punctual,* I laughed out loud. All of my life I've been late for everything—school, breakfast, lunch, dinner, church, appointments, even golf games. My friends and family knew that if they wanted to see me at twelve o'clock, they should make the appointment for 11:30.

"As I said the word *punctual* and started laughing, a somber thought hit me: I was late by choice, and I was now in position to make another choice. Even more sobering was the fact that it dawned on me that I was late because I was selfish, self-centered, and arrogant. I never verbalized it, but I realized I felt that my time was more valuable than theirs, and so it was no big deal if they waited for me, but it would be very bad if I had to wait for them. What an arrogant attitude!"

He said, "At that moment I decided to never be late again." He went on to say that in the last three years he had not been late for anything. "This procedure completely changed my life, not only financially but in more important aspects as well. In the last three years my income is up over 500 percent, and in the last year alone it's up over 300 percent."

This gentleman is in the real estate business, and I don't need to tell you where the real estate market was in 1990, 1991, and 1992. "Now," he said, "obviously, that extra income is tremendously exciting to me. But the other benefits are infinitely greater. It's amazing what that's done to my attitude about everything else, especially my relationships with my family, friends, clients, and associates."

THIS IS TRULY LIFE-CHANGING

The next example I'd like to share with you is the most moving one (and explains why my passion for spreading these concepts is so strong). On January 6, 1990, I conducted a very large seminar in New Orleans and covered these qualities and procedures. A few weeks later I received a very touching letter from a mother who enclosed a laminated card her daughter made. It listed the qualities we're covering in this book. The mother wrote that her daughter had been at the New Orleans seminar, had accepted the idea about claiming and developing the qualities, had done exactly what I suggested and experienced a dramatic turnaround in her life. She explained that as a direct result of the changes, her daughter found faith in God, accepted His offer of salvation, and was secure in her eternity. Her daughter had recently died in a tragic automobile accident.

When you receive that kind of correspondence, it convinces you beyond any doubt that the process works and that you're on the right track as far as helping other people is concerned. This is especially true when you add the scores of examples where alcoholism, drug addiction, broken relationships, obesity, criminal activities, immoral conduct, racism, sexism, and a host of other problems have been helped—or solved.

You are probably saying, "Okay, okay, Zig, you've got me sold. Now tell me exactly what to do."

STEP #1: Either remove or photocopy the "Claiming the Qualities" pages, which appear in the last chapter of the book (later if you prefer to have a folding laminated card with these qualities and instructions, send us a stamped, self-addressed envelope, and we will send you a card with our compliments). At this moment carefully review the qualities.

STEP #2: This next procedure is something you need to start tonight. Our experience shows that those who read these words and start immediately are far more likely to not only start but to keep it up than are the procrastinators waiting for circumstances to get right before they take action.

THIS REALLY WORKS

What is this marvelous step that's going to make such a change in your life? Well, here it is. Tonight, just before you go to bed, take this list of qualities in complete self-talk form on pages 316–19, get in a room with a large mirror by yourself, and close the door. Depending on whether you are assertive and extroverted or quiet, shy, and inhibited, stand up and look yourself in the eye, or casually take a seat in front of the mirror. Speaking in first-person present tense—it's *critical* that you enthusiastically claim these qualities aloud—you say, "I, [your name], am a completely honest person." Then you proceed to go all the way down the list, exactly as the instructions encourage you to do, firmly claiming every one of these qualities. When you get to the last one, you say, "These are the qualities of the winner I was born to be." And finish the statements on the form.

I can assure you that you will sleep better, you will dream more powerful, positive dreams, and you will awaken refreshed. Just before you go to work the next day, again go to a room alone, close the door, look yourself in the eye, and in first-person present tense say, "I, [your name]," and go right down the list, claiming every single one of these qualities. I can absolutely guarantee you that within ten days you will feel better about yourself.

TALK TO YOURSELF BUT SAY THE RIGHT THINGS

In a matter of days, by following this procedure, you will find yourself automatically thinking more positive thoughts about yourself. You will, in essence, be in your own corner. Within two to three weeks, people you see every day will start to notice changes in you. They will comment that you seem to be happier, more excited, and more enthused about life, and that you appear to feel better and have more energy.

Now, I am not a mind reader, nor is anyone else, but I do feel I know a considerable amount about human nature, and I know exactly what many of you are thinking as you read this: "Well, Zig, that's a little much! Oh, I'll admit that I'm an honest person and that I'm a hard worker. I'll even admit that I'm a forgiving, flexible individual who looks for the good in others. But, Zig, I would feel silly standing in front of a mirror claiming all of these qualities."

QUESTION: In front of whom? You are by yourself! Can't you at this point stand yourself for five minutes at a time?

Listen to the experts who really know something about you instead of those negative people who might even have ulterior motives in emphasizing your weaknesses. If your self-talk has been negative in the past, maybe you have literally been your own worst enemy, so now you need to get on your own side and become your own best friend. One way to do this is to follow speaker Mamie McCullough's advice. She says that when you bid someone good-bye, you should give that person a "thumbs-up." As you do, look at your thumb and remember that you are "thumb-body."

The psalmist David used these words: You are "fearfully and wonderfully made." That means that you were born to win, but you must plan to win, prepare to win, and expect to win. What you're now doing is following the plan.

NOW YOU'RE READY FOR THE NEXT STEP

This brings us to phase two of claiming the qualities. The first thirty days, every morning and every night, you continue to claim all these qualities. Beginning with the second thirty days, you keep the pages handy and reference it every day, but you concentrate on the specific areas where you need the most help.

Let's say, for example, that you are a very enthusiastic person, but your organizational skills are suspect. To be completely honest, you were (that's past tense) the kind of person who could lose your glasses on your face, so your greatest strength is your enthusiasm; your greatest need is to become better organized. You write out your own 3" × 5" card and say: "I, [your name], am a tremendously enthusiastic person, and every day I am getting better and better organized." You look at that card a number of times throughout the day, and an exciting—even amazing—thing will happen to you.

I'm sure you've already noticed that whatever you focus on and become sensitive to suddenly becomes the hot item or issue of the day. Newspapers, magazines, books, seminars, meetings, and even radio and television will seem to have your needs in mind when they do their programming. They will give you suggestions and ideas that will be helpful in developing your organizational skills.

Actually, you will get the feeling that there is a conspiracy to help you develop the very qualities you've written on your card and to help you get the things you want. And you will be right. It has always been true that the right kind of person heading in the right direction with the right motives will receive a push forward from unseen hands or others will step aside to keep from slowing him down. That's an exciting and amazing turnaround because until now you might have thought everyone was conspiring to keep you from getting the things you want. And you were right on that one, too. The good guys and gals, over the long haul, really do win.

The second week of your second thirty days you concentrate on your second most outstanding quality and your second greatest need. For example, you might be a very motivated individual, but you need some help in your listening skills. The second week your card would read, "I, [your name], am a highly motivated person, and I am daily improving my skills as a good listener."

You may have a question for me now: "Ziglar, how long do I

> **"** *It's amazing what happens when you recognize your good qualities, accept responsibility for your future, and take positive action to make that future even brighter.* **"**

keep this up (claiming the qualities)?" THE ANSWER: As long as you want more of the things money will buy and all of the things money won't buy.

ONE MORE THOUGHT: Record this procedure, claiming your qualities on a cassette recorder, and listen to them as you drive back and forth to work.

I KNOW IT WORKS

Another reason I know claiming the qualities works is that every one of them is a biblical quality. The Bible itself, in Philippians 4:8, says, "Finally, brethren, whatever things are true, whatever things are noble, whatever things are just, whatever things are pure, whatever things are lovely, whatever things are of good report, if there is any virtue and if there is anything praiseworthy—meditate on these things."

We need to listen to what a prophet named Joel said several thousand years ago: "Let the weak say, 'I am strong'"(Joel 3:10). Pretty clear, direct, and very simple. What do you have to lose by giving it a shot compared to what you have to gain?

Now just in case you're not quite as enthusiastic as I am about the value of biblical advice, I encourage you to remember this. According to the April 28, 1986, issue of *Fortune* magazine, 91 percent of the CEOs of Fortune 500 companies apparently learned their values, ethics, and morals from the same source—the Bible and the church. At least they claimed affiliation with a Catholic or Protestant church or Jewish synagogue. (Less than 7 percent said they had no religion.)

THOUGHT: If W. Edwards Deming, Tom Peters, Warren Bennis, or Fred Smith had written a book that had positively affected the lives of 91 percent of the CEOs of the Fortune 500 companies, you would undoubtedly head for the bookstore and pick up a copy. For that matter if you thought *Moby Dick* or *Black Beauty* had been their source of inspiration, you probably would quickly read or reread those books.

THIS CHANGES EVERY AREA OF LIFE

One of the beautiful things about claiming these qualities of success is that as you claim specific qualities and they become a part of you, you will transfer this feeling to every area of your life. For example, if you have just claimed that you are a patient person and then you lose your patience and blow your cool, you will immediately remember your claim and make a new resolution to do better in the future. When you take any action that is inconsistent with the qualities you claimed that morning or evening, you will immediately be reminded of the inconsistency. It won't take many incidents for you to start making significant changes in your life. As you read

Gloria Hogg's story, and think about the examples I've already shared in this chapter, you'll understand that what I say is true.

FROM RACIST TO LOVER OF ALL HUMANKIND

In October of 1992, Gloria Hogg from Tri-Cities Hospital in Dallas was a guest speaker at our People Builders Meeting that we have every three months to recognize top achievers in our company. We knew from information Gloria's supervisors had given us that she was a top achiever and a loving, personable, enthusiastic African-American with a great sense of humor. All of that was confirmed as she entered the meeting room smiling broadly and taking time to hug several of our staff members. After her introduction, she told several jokes, mostly poking fun at herself. Then we were all stunned as Gloria started talking about a side of her life we had heard nothing about!

Gloria confessed that she had been a racist, and she did not like or really trust anyone who was not African-American. In her own words, she looked for a chance to verbally get after people of other races when they did or said anything that was not pleasing to her.

Gloria explained that Tri-Cities Hospital had implemented our Strategies for Success personal growth, team-building programs teaching these *Over the Top* principles. She began to notice positive changes in her coworkers. She realized she had a serious problem when her coworkers' new behavior made her own attitude and behavior seem out of line by comparison. Because she had always professed a belief in the Bible and its teachings, of "Love thy neighbor," and the golden rule, Gloria became acutely aware of the inconsistencies in her life and resolved to make some changes and develop the qualities that were effectively making improvements in her coworkers.

What happened? Well, let me put it this way. Her progress, growth, and results were so spectacular that not only did she receive a significant promotion, but Governor Ann Richards recognized her as one of the 100 Women of Distinction in Texas.

Perhaps even more significant than her promotion or her recognition is the fact that every morning at 5:30, Gloria Hogg gets up to start her day. Her first step is to make three house calls to give insulin shots: one to an African-American woman, one to a white woman, and one to a Mexican-American woman. Gloria can look you in the eye today and with complete conviction tell you that she loves all people of all races. Every month she draws the name of a senior citizen and pays his or her electricity bill for that month. As Gloria told our group that day, she is grateful for her good job, and she wants to do something for someone else.

Racism was Gloria's attitude before she was influenced to make some changes and develop the qualities we're emphasizing throughout *Over the Top*. It's true that if you don't like who you are and where you are, you can change. I am convinced that if adopting this philosophy and developing these qualities can cure racism, which is one of the ugliest realities in our society, they can be helpful to you in your life.

GUARANTEE: The day will come as a direct result of this procedure that your patience, attitude, positive "picture," and the other qualities you have claimed will get stronger and stronger.

OTHER BENEFITS: It could be that over a period of time, you have fallen out of love with your mate, or you don't really like to be with or around a certain person. As time passes and you claim these various qualities and begin to see them in yourself, you will start using a different yardstick in your measurement of others. Instead of being critical of the faults of other people (as Gloria Hogg used to be), you will start looking for and finding the good qualities in the other person. As you come to admire the qualities and treat your mate, friend, boss, or employee as having these qualities, you'll be amazed at how much better you get along with that person.

ONE MORE WORD ABOUT QUALITIES

I am frequently asked in private conversations, "What is the most important thing I can do to be completely successful?" Or, "What one thing do you believe has contributed most to your success?" A moment's thought will reveal that more than one thing is involved in the success of anyone; however, some things are more important than others. The same thing could be said about *Over the Top.* I believe all I have written in this book is important for a person to have a balanced success. Nevertheless, I believe this chapter will have a more dramatic impact on your life than any other single chapter.

If this were the only chapter, though, the benefits would be dramatically less than they will be if you follow the total philosophy. What has been written preceding this chapter, and what will be written after this chapter, tie it all together. The action I so strongly encourage in this chapter is the one single action that will make the biggest difference in your life. For that reason, I encourage you to take it very seriously and to follow through on the action steps, because these steps will help you "be" to a greater degree than any other steps in the book.

NOTE: Because of some negative or even traumatic experience, one or more of the qualities we've identified could bring back painful memories. EXAMPLE: *Discipline* might be confused with *punishment,* and if you were brutally "disciplined" (beaten), the word *discipline* might be a downer. PROCEDURE: Temporarily eliminate that word from the list; then do a comprehensive word study to learn the real meaning of the word. *Discipline* (in this context I'm speaking of self-discipline) is a very positive word, as are all the words on the list.

The exciting thing about this specific step is that it will help you eliminate one or more "ghosts" of the past. This will help you to focus on the present, which you must do in order for your future to be as bright as you are capable of making it.

The procedures described in this chapter will get you

excited, but since life is an endurance race and not a sprint, you need to have a goals program to become the person you are capable of becoming, do the things you are capable of doing, and have the things that are truly important to you. The next three chapters will show you that when life deals you those inevitable and unexpected blows, you can handle them as challenges and not as crises.

CHAPTER TEN

A goals program is a must

If one advances confidently in the direction of his dreams, he will meet with a success unexpected in common hours. If you build castles in the air, your work will not be lost. That is where they should be. Now put the foundations under them.   Thoreau

Everyone has individual goals that might be positive or negative, but 97 percent of the people in our society do not have an organized goals program.

INDIVIDUAL GOALS BUT NO GOALS PROGRAM

There is a difference. Individual goals focus on a specific objective and can cause us to neglect many other areas of our lives. Although we might reach the one, we might overlook or fail in other areas that could be even more important.

EXAMPLE: The drug addict has a goal for another fix, the alcoholic for another drink, and most of us for another meal. Many people have worthwhile goals like finishing school, getting a job, or losing twenty pounds. Single goals like the ones mentioned above or individual goals (like the day before vaca-tion) are relatively easy to set. However, a balanced goals pro-gram is a different matter.

That's one reason only 3 percent of all Americans have goals programs designed to reap the most benefits from life it-self. I'll deal with these reasons in more detail as we go along, but here's a quick overview.

The first reason most people do not have a goals program is fear. Fear is the great inhibitor. Fortunately, most of our fears are groundless, and as we explore why you should have your own goals program and how you can establish one, those fears will vanish.

The second reason people do not have a goals program is that they have a poor self-image (the picture they have of themselves). They cannot possibly imagine getting the eight things we have identified throughout *Over the Top* (happi-ness, health, reasonable prosperity, security, friends, peace of mind, good family relationships, and hope). They can see where other people could, but for them, no way! That's why so much of *Over the Top,* including the goals program infor-mation, is geared to help you change your picture of your-self.

The third reason most people do not have a goals program is that they have never completely understood the benefits. If that reason applies to you, get ready because by the end of these three chapters on goals, you're going to want your own goals program. As Jim Paluch says, "The instant you set a goal a light goes on in your future."

The fourth reason 97 percent of the people do not have a goals program is that they do not know exactly how to de-velop that program. The steps you will learn in these next three chapters are very specific and will remove lack of know-how as an excuse not to have a goals program.

FEAR

Fear, to a degree, makes procrastinators and cowards of us all. To be candid, fear and a poor self-image are so interwoven that it is difficult, if not impossible, to separate them. Assuming you have been following through on the suggestions I have been making, your image is improving steadily. That means your confidence is growing, and confidence drives out fear. That's important because according to speaker and author Bob Couch, Ph.D., "Fear is the dark room where we develop our negatives."

Direction also drives out fear.

EXAMPLE: If we had to drive from Dallas to Boston with no directions, maps, or signs, we would have a degree of fear. With directions, good maps, and clear road signs, that fear would largely disappear. Actually, very few of us would attempt that trip without directions and maps. Unfortunately, very few people are equipped with specific directions on how to navigate the highways of life. No wonder the overwhelming majority of people end up at the end of life's journey with just a fraction of what life has to offer.

A few bits of good news: Dr. Karl A. Menninger said, "Fears are educated into us and can, if we wish, be educated out." James Allen, author of *As a Man Thinketh,* stated, "He who has conquered doubt and fear has conquered failure."

YOUR PICTURE AND YOUR GOALS

The second reason very few people have a complete goals program, as stated earlier, is because of the picture or image they have of themselves. Dr. Joyce Brothers says that your self-image has a direct influence on the clothes you wear, the way you look, the profession you choose, the mate you select, the habits you acquire, and your moral conduct. That's strong motivation for doing something about that picture you have of yourself.

Now let's look at an example that deals indirectly, but with

A goals program is a must 183

very direct results, with reducing or eliminating fear, changing attitudes, improving the self-image, and is in many ways one of the most inspiring I've ever been associated with. It ties directly into self-image, and it should convince you that regardless of your condition and circumstances today, there is legitimate hope that you can overcome the obstacles, starting from where you are, with what you have, and make it happen.

SOUNDS LIKE A BUNCH OF BALONEY

Several years ago, I was speaking in Oklahoma City at an all-day seminar. We had roughly 1,600 very enthusiastic, responsive people in the audience. Approximately eighteen months later, I received a letter from a man named Tom Hartman. The letter was the beginning of a relationship and correspondence that lasted for ten years. Unfortunately, I lost touch with him several years ago.

I well remember the first letter, phone conversation, and personal visits we had. In essence, here is the way it went, and I'm going to periodically shift between dialogue and an explanation of the sequence of events. The first letter from Tom started,

Dear Zig,

On January 28, 1978, I was in your audience for the all-day seminar in Oklahoma City. It was my day off and my brother had given me a ticket to attend in the hopes that I might find some hope and encouragement. There I sat, skeptical but still hopeful that something would happen that would give me that "shot in the arm" my brother felt I needed (deep down I knew I needed it, too).

You opened the presentation with an enormous amount of enthusiasm as you said, "You can go where you want to go, do what you want to do, and be like you want to be." I confess, Zig, I was surprised that you came on so strong and immediately decided that I was not going to sit there all day and lis-

ten to a bunch of hype from some super-excited, turned-on, enthusiastic guy who didn't know the first thing about me. I knew that what you were saying didn't apply to me so I looked around for a way to get out. However, I was in the midst of about 1,600 people and I knew that it would create a disturbance if I left so I decided to keep my seat until the first break. Then I planned to quietly make my exit, never to be seen or heard from again as far as you were concerned.

A few minutes later you had the gall to say that God loved me and I knew that couldn't be the truth so I started to squirm even more. Then you made the observation that man was "designed for accomplishment, engineered for success, and endowed with the seeds of greatness." As you said those words I literally thought to myself, Well, the old boy is finally getting reasonably close to the truth, because as I looked down I could truly see greatness. A 63½" waist-line and 406 pounds of bulk spoke volumes about my "greatness."

At that point, Zig, I was just coming off a devastating divorce. I had a job only because my boss was my friend and not because I was productive and earning my paycheck. I was literally so broke [and you could do this in 1978] that I was writing "hot" checks on Friday evening to buy my groceries for the weekend. I would rush to the bank on Monday morning to cover the check. I had not been to church in years. I was financially bankrupt, spiritually bankrupt, physically bankrupt—no family, only one friend, a dismal future staring me in the face, and you were telling me there was hope for me.

YES—THERE IS HOPE FOR YOU

I wasn't buying it but you are a persistent guy and you kept emphasizing the "you can do it" theme. And then you said something that I do not remember but it was reinforced by a woman behind me who said, "That's right," or "Amen," or whatever it is you Christians say when you're in agreement with someone. When she made her comment my mind sprung wide open, I reached for my yellow pad, and started taking notes.

As an aside, it's a fact that some people are so narrow-minded they can look through a keyhole with both eyes at the same time. And I'll bet you've noticed that a narrow mind and a fat head are generally found on the same person.

For the rest of the day I wrote fast and furiously with a sense of excitement growing within me. For the first time in my adult life I had just the slightest glimmer of hope that maybe, just maybe, I could do something with my life.

By the end of the day I was truly excited and wanted badly to buy your set of tapes on motivation, but I was struggling for financial survival. Again, my brother proved to be a life-saver. He loaned me the money and I made the purchase. That day I had already listened to you for over six hours but that evening I went home and listened an additional seven hours. Before I turned the lights out that night I had a feeling I was going to make it. Hope, for the first time in my adult life, had reared its head—and it looked good.

The next morning the first thing I did was tell my boss that he had a brand-new employee. I even told him that I was going to "carry my own weight." In retrospect I realize that was quite a statement for a 406-pounder to make!

That afternoon I went to Oklahoma City University and switched from the two courses in history I was already taking to two psychology courses so I could learn more about myself and my fellow man. The next day I went to the Nautilus Health Center to do something about bringing this body of mine into shape.

On Thursday I went to the store where I had in the past bought clothing and laid aside $700 worth with a minute down payment. When I chose size 47 coats and 39 slacks, the owner of the store asked me who I was buying the clothes for. When I told him I was buying them for myself and that one day I would walk out wearing them, he looked skeptical but said nothing.

Now let's pause for a minute and look at what Tom has already done.

Mentally. Course changes at the university, and listening to the tapes.

Physically. Exercise and diet program at a health studio.

Career. Carry his own weight; be productive.

Commitment. New clothes for a much slimmer man.

MAJOR POINT: He immediately took action. Now let's let Tom take up the story.

At that point, Zig, I really got involved in listening to your tapes. You had said that I should listen sixteen times in order to get the full message, but I listened to "The 25 Steps to Building a Healthy Self-Image" over 500 times and all the others over 300 times. I can literally quote you verbatim, so if you ever develop a sore throat, don't cancel an engagement—just call me and I will deliver the message!

In our personal encounters, ol' Tom would smile and say, "I can even use your accent, Zig." (Can you imagine him accusing me of having an accent?)

Tom continued,

Zig, I'm so glad that the police were not watching me as I drove down the street listening to those recordings because you and I had some conversations that were unbelievable! You would say, "You were born to win," and I would respond, "Then why am I always losing?" You would say, "You can do it!" and I would respond, "But, Zig, I never have!" You would say, "Hang in there, Tom," and I would say, "Hanging is no fun!" You would say, "You were designed for accomplishment," and I would say, "Well, how come I haven't accomplished anything?"

Well, Zig, it went back and forth but I noticed something—on those recordings you never grew weary. You were always enthusiastic, always excited, always turned on. My resistance grew weaker and weaker.

NOTE: At this point Tom's self-talk started changing from "I can't" to "I can"—fear of failure was retreating, and hope and belief were moving in to fill the void.

Then Tom said something that I believe is absolutely true because I work very hard at speaking truths that have stood the test of time.

Zig, you know, I believe anybody could argue with you as I initially did. They could disagree with you the first time, even the tenth time. However, I honestly believe that anybody who listens repeatedly to the concepts you're presenting will eventually know that what you are saying is true and take action with positive results.

NOTE: Here's why: When you hear a positive message so many times you start finishing the sentences, you are "self-talking" your way to the top.

"MAMA, LOOK AT THAT FAT MAN"

Tom had been listening about six weeks when he was in a grocery store one Friday evening, buying groceries for the weekend. Suddenly, he heard a little girl about five years old scream at the top of her voice, "Mama, look at that fat man!"

Tom said he whirled around and looked all over the place for the fat man. Then it occurred to him the little girl was talking about him, and he started laughing. He laughed until he cried—and then the realization of why he was laughing hit him and he shed a tear of a different kind. For the first time in his adult life, Tom Hartman saw hope in full bloom and knew he was going to make it.

About a month later, that conviction was reinforced in another unique way. Tom had been to a movie and was on his way back to his car. He was strolling along when a window display caught his eye. After looking at the display for a few minutes, he suddenly realized he was not alone. Some big dude was looking over his shoulder so he spun around—but there was no one there. He had seen his own reflection in the window and didn't recognize himself.

The late Dr. John Kozek, a brilliant young psychiatrist from Dunedin, Florida, told me that at that precise moment, Tom Hartman was no longer obese. Though he still weighed over 380 pounds, he no longer saw himself as an obese person. The picture had changed. (It really is true that you are what you are and where you are because of what has gone into your mind, and you can change what you are and where you are by changing what goes into your mind.)

Dr. Kozek pointed out that one of the reasons crash diets seldom work is because a person can quite easily take weight off the body. But he said even though you have lost the weight from your body, unless you've changed that picture you have of yourself, you will dream as an obese person when you go to sleep. Subconsciously, you know you are an obese person, and so you go back to eating too much to make your body conform to the picture, namely, that of an overweight person.

HE TOOK ALL THE STEPS

Tom Hartman had changed the picture in his mind. He had done it with a tremendous amount of personal effort and commitment. He followed a sound exercise program, combined with sensible eating habits. He kept feeding his mind the good, clean, pure, powerful, positive inputs that enabled him to stay focused on his objectives and provided the motivation necessary for him to get there.

What's the end of the Tom Hartman story? I have no idea because the story is still being written; I can tell you he got his degree in psychology. He graduated magna cum laude and later went into business for himself. He taught a Sunday school class every Sunday; he worked with battered women; and oh, yes, his weight came down to roughly 225 pounds.

Since he's about six feet four inches tall and has a very large frame, that's a good weight for him.

I give you all the details on the Tom Hartman story because I find it very difficult to believe that any of you who read these words have all of the difficulties and needs Tom Hartman had in his life. Remember, he was obese, broke, and going nowhere, and he was spiritually bankrupt. Here's a man who in every phase of his life—financially, physically, mentally, socially, and spiritually—became the winner he was born to be.

MESSAGE: If Tom Hartman can do what he did and overcome all those obstacles, don't you just know you can do it, too? Go ahead—make the commitment. Do it now. (Tom looked at least fifteen years younger and had infinitely more energy after he lost that weight.)

Please notice I'm not even mildly hinting that this is easy— it's difficult. But when you see the joy and excitement of a Tom Hartman who took control of his life, you will know it's worth it. He went to work and accomplished his objectives. He knows that it's worth the blood, sweat, and tears. Tom Hartman knows you don't pay the price for good health—you enjoy the benefits. In retrospect, he understands that whatever the price might be, it is temporary and eminently affordable. The benefits are long-lasting and magnificently enjoyable.

FREE YOUR RIGHT BRAIN

Perhaps the greatest advantage of having a goals program is the freedom that goes with having direction in your life. When your goals are clearly defined and intelligently set, you have, in essence, taken a major step toward programming your left brain. That frees your right brain to be its creative best.

The best analogy I can give you is the superbly conditioned and gifted athlete who is so disciplined and committed to the fundamentals of the game that he or she is free to be at the creative best. When unique situations arise where the athlete must improvise to make the big play, coaches of gifted athletes will typically say, "You can't coach that."

A Michael Jordan, for example, is confronted a number of times in every game he plays with a new situation. It might be the number of opponents around him, the number of players supporting him close by, the exact distance of the ball from the hoop, or a host of other little things that make the situations uniquely—even if minutely—different from previously encountered situations. Because Michael is so drilled in the fundamentals of dribbling, passing, shooting, faking, pumping, and looking off, he, with his superb athletic skills, can be creative in the way he handles the truly unique situations that arise.

> When your goals are clearly defined and intelligently set, you have, in essence, taken a major step toward programming your left brain. That frees your right brain to be its creative best.

The same situation happens to all of us. Only with discipline do doctors, students, and people like you and me have the freedom to give their best performance. When we are fundamentally sound with a base of moral, ethical values to work from, a goals program to focus on, and the optimistic outlook of automatically seeking the solutions to problems with the expectancy of finding them, we free the creative right brain to bring forth those solutions.

BALANCED SUCCESS

I have, on several occasions, stated that in my seminars around the world I've learned that everybody wants the same eight things. Now I would like to elaborate on them because if they really are the things we want in life, we should set them as our goals. The importance of taking this step was spelled out by Dr. Gerald Kushel in the September 30, 1991, issue of *Bottom Line Personal*.

He breaks life down into three dimensions: successful careers, satisfying work, and rich personal lives. He studied 1,200 people—lawyers, artists, blue-collar workers, teachers, and students. All had successful careers and so had achieved at least one-dimensional success. Unfortunately, 15 percent enjoyed neither their jobs nor their personal lives. Their success was superficial. Eighty percent enjoyed their work but not their personal lives, and thus had achieved two-dimensional success. The sad fact is, most of them thought that their successful, enjoyable careers resulted from a willingness to sacrifice their personal lives. Only 4 percent enjoyed their work and their personal lives. These people had achieved three-dimensional success. They were good at their jobs, enjoyed their work, and had fulfilling personal lives.

Dr. Kushel labels the 4 percent as uncommonly successful people. All of them share three important traits. Number one is an inner calm that helps them stay focused. Number two is clear goals and a sense of purpose that guide their lives. Number three is adventurousness that lets them laugh at themselves and gives them the courage to take necessary risks. He makes some other significant observations, namely, that uncommonly successful people always take responsibility for their life situation, shifting from the external to the internal.

EXAMPLE: A non-USP (uncommonly successful person) might think, *Pressure on my job makes me nervous,* but a USP in the same situation thinks, *Pressures on my job do not make me nervous. My thoughts about these pressures make me nervous.*

Dr. Kushel is exactly right in what he is saying. Let me point out that the more secure you are as an individual, the better you feel about yourself, the better the picture you have of yourself, the more likely you are to understand what Dr. Kushel is saying. And the more likely you are to believe that, at the least you can be happier, healthier, more prosperous, and more secure, and have more friends, greater peace of mind, better family relationships, and more hope. Now let's explore whether or not you can specifically set these eight things as goals.

HAPPINESS

Many people honestly believe they will be happy when they get into a home of their own; they will be happy when they get all of the little things that frequently convert a house to a home and have them neatly in place—but they won't. Then they'll be happy when they add the patio and the outdoor barbecue grill—but they won't. Then they'll be happy when they get the mortgage paid—but they won't. Then they will be happy when they get their second home down at the lake or up on the mountainside—but they won't. Then they will be happy when they win the trip to Hawaii—but they won't. Then they'll be happy when they get there for that dream trip—but they won't. The reason is simple: It makes no difference where you go, there you are. And it makes no difference what you have, there's always more to want.

> **"** *Happiness is not a when or a where; it can be a here and a now.* **"**

Until you are happy with who you are, you will never be happy because of what you have. I love what Dennis Prager said in a *Reader's Digest* article as he differentiated between pleasure and happiness: "Fun (pleasure) is what we experience during an act; happiness is what we experience after an act. It is a deeper, more abiding emotion." He says that going to an amusement park or ball game and watching a movie or television are fun activities. They help us relax, temporarily forget our problems, and maybe even laugh, but they do not bring happiness because their positive effects end when the fun ends. Again, until and unless we're happy with ourselves,

A goals program is a must 193

we are unlikely to be happy, period. Happiness is an attitude. Will Rogers wisely stated that "most people are about as happy as they make up their minds to be."

Mr. Prager also points out with unusual insight that "the way people cling to the belief that a fun-filled, pain-free life equals happiness actually diminishes their chances of ever attaining real happiness. If fun and pleasure equated with happiness, then pain must be equated with unhappiness, but in fact the opposite is true. More times than not, things that lead to happiness involve some pain." He's right on target and is eloquently stating the age-old truth that happiness is not pleasure. It is victory. And victory almost always involves at least temporary pain of some kind.

CAN YOU SET HAPPINESS AS A GOAL?

Remember, everyone also wants to be healthy, reasonably prosperous, and secure, and have friends, peace of mind, good family relationships, and hope.

NOTE: There are many things you can specifically do about all of these things, and each one of them has a direct bearing on happiness.

EXAMPLE: When your health (physical, mental, and spiritual) is good and your energy level is high (these are relative), by and large you are going to be a pretty happy camper. Follow the same procedure as you examine the other things all of us want, and you will reach the inescapable conclusion that you can do something about all of them and each one contributes to your happiness.

QUESTION: Suppose things don't work out as neatly as you have so carefully detailed: What happens to your happiness?

ANSWER: Success is not a destination: It is a journey. The happiest people I know are those who are busily working toward specific objectives. The most bored and miserable people I know are those who are drifting along with no worthwhile objectives in mind.

> **"** *Happiness is a by-product of who you are and what you do. And yes, you can set it as a specific goal.* **"**

In today's pleasure-oriented society there is very little happiness as evidenced by the excessive use of drugs and alcohol, as well as the prevalence of suicide, particularly among our young people. For example, alcohol, drugs, pornography, illicit sex, and gambling are all, for many people, pleasurable experiences. Yet, over a period of time, they become addictive and destroy any chance for happiness. Coleridge said, "Happiness can be built only on virtue and must, of necessity, have truth for its foundation."

WHAT MAKES US HAPPY?

I encourage you to notice as we discuss this issue that happiness is something you strive for on your own and it is not going to depend on what somebody else does to you or for you. As previously stated, others can provide you with pleasure, but you will never be happy until and unless you do things for other people.

It's true that all of us are happy—or happier—when our relationships with those we love or encounter on a regular basis are good. However, we do need to understand that nobody else can make us happy. Good relationships contribute to our pleasure and happiness, but we're the ones who play the key role in building good relationships.

When I make reference to the fact that everybody wants to be healthy, I'm speaking not of athletic fitness-type health but of a physical, mental, and spiritual health that enables us to use the resources God has given us. When you take care of your health, you are happier with yourself and, consequently, happier overall. When you eat properly, get a reasonable amount of sleep and rest, and are on an exercise program that fits your physical condition, you are on the right path. When you avoid drugs, tobacco, and alcohol, you work toward being happy and improve your health at the same time.

Your mental health involves the right mental attitude, forgiveness, gratitude, and lack of revenge, and it is affected by the input into your mind. Input influences your thinking and your happiness. As James Allen said, "We are what we think about."

Spiritual health is the third dimension, and for me and millions of others, once that spiritual health is reached, the chances for being happy are dramatically increased, as are the chances for peace of mind.

Research psychologist Lewis Andrews, after investing ten years investigating the connection between spirituality and mental health, says studies show that people who believe in one God and have very strong spiritual values are happier, healthier, and in most cases more intellectually involved than people who don't. Since spiritual health equates to mental and/or emotional health, what psychiatrist Max Lavine says also has considerable significance: "There cannot be emotional health in the absence of high moral standards and a sense of social responsibility."

THE LOVE OF MONEY

When we look at prosperity, I know there are some in religious orders who have taken the vows of poverty and others who have chosen professions of service. They will never have any real chance or desire for accumulating substantial wealth; however, they still want their needs met. It's also true that our concepts of prosperity vary.

I reference money again because in the real world we need a certain amount of it every day. It gives us more options, and properly handled, it can enable us to broaden our sphere of influence and service. This is especially true if we remember that the real measure of our wealth is how much we would be worth if we lost all our money.

Having said that, let me recognize that there are those who misquote the Bible and say that money is the root of all evil, which is not true. The Bible says, "The love of money is a root of all kinds of evil." The Bible talks a great deal more about success than it does about heaven. In addition, two-thirds of the parables that Christ Himself taught had to do with our physical and financial well-being. Realistically, the good Samaritan could not have paid the robbed and beaten stranger's bill at the inn had he not acquired a certain amount of money before the mugging took place.

NOTE: When a person has a value system based on the qualities listed in chapter 9, the chance of monetary prosperity having a negative impact on that person is virtually nil.

CONCLUSION: It is perfectly safe, even realistic, to make prosperity one of your goals.

Can you really have all eight of the things we're describing? Yes, I believe you can. This is evidenced by the fact that there are scores of people, including me, who do have all of these things.

RELATIONSHIPS ARE THE KEY

It's also exciting to know that if you're the right kind of person, you can build secure relationships because you're not going to violate the principles that would destroy the relationships. Remember, all people want an employer (or employee), friend, mate, child, or parent they can depend on to be consistent in actions and in love.

Certainly everyone wants to have friends, but as you've already discovered, when you go out in life looking for friends, they're going to be scarce. When you go out in life to be a friend, you will find them everywhere. You're not going to change anyone; however, when you change yourself and become the right kind of person, people gravitate to you.

They want a friend who is friendly, dependable, and loyal. A friend who will stand by them in times of need. Somebody once said that a fair-weather friend is someone who is always around when he needs you. A real friend is someone who is around when you need him and will never stand in your way except when you are falling. Since you are developing these winning qualities that attract friends from every direction, I feel confident you, even now (without having consciously set a goal to be a friend), are beginning to attract the kind of people you will be comfortable with and enjoy as friends.

The good family relationships we've talked about will come as a result of the qualities we've identified almost from page one in *Over the Top*. What husband or wife, parent or child, brother or sister, would not be able to get along with someone with the qualities we've identified? Setting the goal of positive family relationships will have consequences that far surpass the benefits you and your family reap. As I mentioned earlier, the stability of home life greatly affects our life in the outside world. Having the qualities and taking the steps we've outlined here will give you everything but a guarantee that family relationships will be good. I'm assuming the other members of the family are not alcoholics, drug addicts, or psychopaths—and even if they are, these qualities will improve your chances of building winning relationships with them.

Peace of mind starts with you and is not likely to happen until you set a goal to resolve completely the question of whose you are and where you are going to spend eternity. The reality is, if your past is forgiven, your present is going to be more secure and probably more prosperous, which means your future should be brighter and peace of mind a real probability. (If you have questions concerning this one, I'd be happy to send you information on how I resolved it for myself. Write to me at The Zig Ziglar Corporation, 3330 Earhart, Suite 204, Carrollton, Texas 75006.)

HOPE—THE KEY OBJECTIVE

If you look at all eight things all of us want, you will notice that hope is the last one I listed. You will see the reason for this when you answer these questions: How happy would I be if I had no hope? How healthy—physically, mentally, and emotionally—would I be if there were no hope? Just how prosperous would I be if there were no hope for my future? How secure would I be with no hope? How much peace of mind would I have with no hope? How many friends would I have and how would I get along with my family if I had no hope? I'd probably walk around looking like the picture on my driver's license, and that does not attract friends or endear me to my family.

Hope, according to the dictionary, is a feeling that what one desires will happen. It's expectation, anticipation, optimism; the ground for expecting something desired. Hope is to desire very much. It is yearning with anticipation. It is a positive expectancy. Hope is to place confidence in. It implies some expectation of obtaining the good desired or the possibility of possessing it. Martin Luther said that everything that is done in the world is done by hope. John Lubbock says, "It is certainly wrong to despair, and if despair is wrong, hope is right."

According to Grenville Kliser, "The hopeful man believes that the best is yet to be and paints in roseate colors the good times in prospect. He is buoyant, enthusiastic and confident when pessimism stalks abroad. He is an incorrigible optimist." (He is the kind of person who would take his last dollar and buy a money belt.)

S. Smiles says that "hope is like the sun, which as we journey toward it casts the shadow of our burden behind us." Johnson says that "where there is no hope there can be no endeavor."

Martin Buxbaum summed it up beautifully:

No matter what the difficulties, the trials, the disappointments, those who have risen to the top never lost hope. Hope gives us the promise of something good, despite the odds, something we can attain. Hope sets the mind in a positive vein, gives us something to look forward to and patience to wait. Hope is a heart-warming blend of desire, expectation, patience, and joy. It is an emotional medicine, indispensable to the soul.

The question is, Can you set hope as one of your goals? I believe you can if we carefully analyze it. Hope forms an acrostic for *h*onest *o*ptimism based on *p*ersonal *e*fforts.

H is for *honesty,* and when you honestly deal with all the factors we've discussed and then recognize these marvelous positive qualities you have, you will agree that you truly are a rare individual with unique abilities, which will enable you to go over the top.

O stands for *optimism,* which you will possess in abundance when you take these qualities and follow the plans and procedures we've identified.

P is for *personal,* which means you accept personal responsibility for your future.

E stands for *effort,* which will produce results because of your new picture of yourself.

Add it all up. Yes, you can put *hope* on your chart as one of the goals you can reach and, perhaps, have already reached.

We've already observed there is something we can specifically do about all eight of the most sought-after things in life. Now, as we did for happiness earlier in this chapter, let's put this in context with the other seven things everyone wants to be, do, or have. First, it's safe to say that happy people are hopeful people. And happy, hopeful people are in good shape to get all the good things in life, including health. Healthy people are more apt to be prosperous, which results in security, and when people are secure (financially and spiritually), they have peace of mind. True peace of mind leaves more time and energy for building relationships with friends and family, and people who have achieved any of the above have hope that the future will be as good or better than the present. To bring this full circle, it is also true that people who are the most grateful for what they have are invariably the happiest people.

Let's do a quick overview of this chapter. The four most common reasons people don't have a well-defined, balanced goals program are fear, poor self-image (picture of self), a lack of understanding of the benefits, and a lack of knowledge about EXACTLY how to develop a goals program. I addressed the issues of fear and poor self-image. In detailing how the eight things everyone wants can be goals, I explained the tremendous benefits you will gain by setting these goals for a balanced life.

DON'T FORGET THE MONEY GOAL

Extra! Extra! Extra! At this point I want to concentrate on financial goals because far too many people neglect this area and suffer the consequences late in life when they should be and could be enjoying the fruits of their labor. I have not invested much time in talking about the money goal, though I have referenced it several times. Even now, I do not want to make that goal more important than it really is, but I have a responsibility not to make it less important than it is.

Most of us have no need to be superrich, but I'd be comfortable in saying that all of us have great need not to be poor. Financial security is a desire, if not a goal, that most people have. Money is important because it gives us options, and if we do not set goals to have financial independence, the odds are that we will eventually be dependent on others.

The footsteps of old age creep up so softly that you don't hear them coming until they are upon you. Fred Smith comments that many people lamely say they will "cross that bridge when they get to it." He points out, however, that when you get to the point of needing the money, there will be no bridge—only a large hole. With that in mind, I strongly encourage you to work with someone who is skilled in financial management, if such a person is available, and set aside a certain percentage of your money for your future. You don't really have to earn that much. Just a portion of it regularly set aside in investments or savings can make a major financial difference when your work life is over. Remember, you are your number one responsibility, so pay yourself, your tithe, and your savings account first every payday. If you can live on 100 percent of your take-home pay, surely you can survive on 80 percent of it.

The Sunday, November 17, 1996, edition of the *Dallas Morning News* carried a story about Oseola McCarty from Hattiesburg, Mississippi, who recently funded a $150,000 scholarship for African-American students to attend Southern Mississippi University in Hattiesburg. Friends and acquaintances were stunned to learn that Ms. McCarty had given such a substantial sum of money. She had been forced to drop out of school at the age of eight to work as a laundress and take care of her grandmother, mother, and a sick aunt and had always lived in very humble circumstances.

Oseola McCarty's entire life has been devoted to working, caring for others, living frugally, and regularly saving part of everything she earned. When her aunt, who was her last living relative, died, she was left alone and continued to do what she had been doing since early childhood. At eighty-eight, Ms. McCarty felt time was creeping up on her, so she made the gift to the university. The completely unselfish gift (she asked for nothing in return) totally changed her life. She became a sudden celebrity and is being flown all over the country to appear on talk shows, do news interviews, and receive an honorary Doctor of Humane Letters Degree from Harvard University.

Despite all the attention she has received, Ms. McCarty still lives in the house that was left to her by an uncle in 1947. She still turns on the air conditioner only when company comes. She has a small color television now, in place of the tiny black-and-white set that got only one channel, but that hardly matters because she still does not watch television.

But the woman who comes to the door of the tiny house on the quiet street is different. In place of sneakers with the toes cut out, she wears gray pumps. Her iron-gray hair is covered with a small, neat wig. She is dressed not in the faded work smock she used to wear, but in a neat, colorful dress with little gold-colored buttons.

The main difference, however, to people who knew her before all this happened, is her voice. Before, as reporters filed one by one before her and television trucks lined her street, she was so painfully shy that it was hard to get her to say more than a few words at a time. "I'm braver now," she said. She almost chatters.

She is still quiet when she goes into a new city, as she stares up at the buildings, but that is because she is concentrating. "I want to see," she said. "I want to know." What she means is, she wants to remember.

Today Oseola McCarty's portrait hangs in the Administration Building at the University of Southern Mississippi, the first portrait of a black person to be displayed there.

The beautiful thing about this inspiring story is the fact that this humble lady, who lived at the poverty level all of her life, has inspired people from all walks of life to be more and do more. Her scholarships will enable deserving students to get an education, which will enable them to have a fuller, richer life. She is living proof that an unselfish, committed person can make a difference. And consider this: Oseola McCarty will get more true happiness and joy out of her life after her eighty-eighth birthday than most people will in a lifetime. She didn't, according to today's definition, live well, but she is finishing well and is a classic example of the statement, "You can have everything in life you want if you will just help enough other people get what they want."

NOTE: This inspiring story would never have taken place had Ms. McCarty not accepted financial responsibility for herself and planned for the future.

Your goals, to a very large degree, determine what you have

in life. Here's a basic format for setting your financial goals for retirement:

Goal: Retire financially secure at age ____
Benefits:
    Won't have to rely on Social Security
    Peace of mind
    Security
    Sense of accomplishment
    Have the means to help others
    Maintain current lifestyle
    Live independent of family members
    Increase dramatically my number of options
Obstacles:
    Lack of planning
    Lack of discipline in saving
    Giving in to instant gratification
    Apathy—procrastination
    Unplanned financial hardships
    Lack of knowledge
    Lack of time (starting too late)
Skills/Knowledge:
    Basics of compound interest
    Impact of inflation
    Basic personal investment philosophy
    Disciplined savings plan
People, etc.:
    Banker
    Financial Planner
    Family
    Friends
Plan of Action:
    1. Choose reputable financial planner
    2. Assess where I am currently
    3. Determine how much money is needed at retirement
    4. Determine future value of money, considering inflation

Establish specific savings goals and pay myself first

. Start setting aside money *now* to specific savings (use automatic bank draft if possible)

7. Use all stock dividends to buy more stock in the company

Date of Completion:

Retire in year 20XX

TEAM GOALS

This brings us to another significant point, namely, that goals are important not only for individuals but also for schools, families, businesses, athletic teams, communities, and nations. Goals work at all levels. D. W. Rutledge, the head football coach at Converse-Jordan High School, uses this goal-setting procedure, and three of the last four years his team has been the AAAAA state champions in Texas where high-school football is highly regarded. In 1996 they finished second. Dennis Parker went to Marshall, Texas, from Converse-Jordan and, using the same system, took his team to the play-offs for the first time since 1949. In 1990 they won the state championship.

At Tri-Cities Hospital, as a result of putting every department on a growth and goals program, remarkable things happened. Administrators, janitors, lunchroom workers, cart pushers, nurses, aides, and office personnel became a team because, as their training director, Dr. Bob Price, says, "Anybody who touches anybody in a hospital ultimately affects everybody, and the typical patient is touched by fourteen people every day."

A study by HCIA, Inc., and the Healthcare Provider Consulting Practice of William H. Mercer, Inc., in 1995 ranked Tri-Cities among the top one hundred hospitals in America. This study establishes a set of benchmarks for the hospital industry. To qualify, hospitals must reduce expenses per adjusted discharge by 16 percent, lower mortality by 20 percent, cut length of stay by 9 percent, and increase the return on assets by 58 percent, in comparison to the average U.S. hospital. Good things happened when the entire hospital got on the same page.

These exact procedures for teams and businesses also work for families. When we get the whole family involved in the goal-setting process, combined with the philosophy of *Over the Top,* the chances of having harmony, better communications, and prosperity in the family dramatically increase.

REMEMBER, ALL GOALS ARE NOT POSITIVE

Any goal or objective that is either illegal or immoral ultimately becomes extremely negative. Yet even these goals bear fruit, though eventually it turns out to be rotten. Professional thieves, bank robbers, and drug dealers develop carefully laid plans and follow them. Fortunately, our law enforcement people also set a goal, which is to catch, try, convict, and incarcerate them.

Other goals that are not positive are ones that are unrealistic or too big. For example, at age seventy it would be unrealistic for me to expect to make the PGA Tour or for most of us to set a goal to exceed Ross Perot's net worth.

When goals are unrealistically big, they are negative because unrealistic expectations are the seedbed of depression. A goal can be negative if it's set for the wrong reason. EXAMPLE: I want to own a new Lincoln because that jerk down the street has one, and if he can buy one, so can I! Or I want to go to State University because that's where my buddies are going, and together we can have a blast. The right reason would be that I'm majoring in engineering, and that school has the best engineering department in the state.

Yet another goal that can be negative is one that is set by someone else for you. Your parents, grandparents, professor, or minister might say, "You have such a great personality you should be a salesperson," or "You have such a love for children you should be a teacher." If that is not your goal and you go along in order to please the person you love and respect, you will ultimately be a frustrated individual.

A goal can be negative if it is outside your area of interest and/or natural aptitude. It is far easier to be successful in something you want to do and love doing.

A goal can also be negative if it depends on the wishes and/or performance of another person. EXAMPLE: You set a goal to marry a certain person. However, that individual might have no interest in you, so even following all the steps we're outlining won't help you reach that goal. In reality, this should not be a goal, but it's all right to have it as a desire.

MESSAGE: Set your goals carefully because when you work them through this process, you are more likely to accomplish them.

Chapters 11 and 12 reveal in minute detail EXACTLY how to formulate an in-depth balanced goals program. Tom Hartman and the other over-the-top people we identified fully grasped the information you are about to read. Their lives are proof positive that you, too, can become the winner you were born to be.

CHAPTER ELEVEN

A goals program: the key to a balanced success

All men dream, but not equally. Those men who dream by night in the dusty recesses of their minds wake in the morning to find it was but vanity, but those men who dream by day—these are dangerous men, for they dream with open eyes to make their dreams come true. T. E. Lawrence

I love to eat in cafeterias, and I especially like ones that are arranged so that I can view what's being offered before I get to the serving line. Several years ago The Redhead and I went into a new cafeteria, and I had the opportunity to carefully evaluate what was being offered. This enabled me to quickly move down the line, telling the people behind the counter to give me some of this and this and this. That's very important because regardless of how hungry you are, you cannot eat some of everything on the line.

THE CAFETERIA LINE OF LIFE

I wanted to choose foods that I felt would not only taste good but would also be good for me. In short, I had to pass up a lot of good food to get the best.

That's the first parallel between the cafeteria line of life and the cafeteria line for food. In life, we simply cannot be, do, and have everything in this big, beautiful world of ours. We need to choose, and the choices we make will ultimately determine how successful we are in the eight areas of life that I have repeatedly identified.

> **The choices we make will ultimately determine how successful we are.**

For example, about every five or ten years, at the beginning of the year, I engage in a little process that is meaningful to me. The last time I did this (which, incidentally, was 1988) I let my imagination dwell on anything and everything I wanted to do during the new year. Here's what I came up with:

1. Since the family unit is in serious difficulty, I wanted to conduct more family seminars.
2. I wanted to record a short, daily radio program combined with a daily newspaper column.
3. I wanted to play golf at least five days each week.
4. I wanted to become more active in taking alcohol advertising that depicts drinking as fun, glamorous, and essential to the good life off television.
5. I wanted to work in political campaigns to get more qualified people in public office.
6. I wanted to spend more time in the war against crime, pornography, and drugs.
7. I wanted to spend more time with my staff.
8. I wanted to write at least one book that year.
9. I wanted to learn how to speak Spanish.
10. I wanted to become socially involved with more of my neighbors.

11. I wanted to read and research a minimum of three, and preferably four, hours each day.
12. I wanted to spend at least an hour each day jogging and exercising.
13. I wanted to be more active in civic and social clubs.
14. I wanted to set a record on the treadmill for those of us who are over sixty years of age.
15. I wanted to tour Russia and China.
16. I wanted to eat Braum's French Chocolate Almond Ice Cream or some other dessert three times every day.

I tried to evaluate how much time would be required each week to do all of these things, and counting 7 hours of sleep per night, it came to a total of over 300 hours a week. Since there are only 168 hours in the week, I realized something very significant: I had to eliminate much of the good so I could choose the best, just as I did in the cafeteria line. That's what I'm encouraging you to do. Let's get back to the parallels between the cafeteria line of life and the cafeteria line for food.

EAT NOW, PAY LATER OR PAY NOW, EAT LATER

As I reached the end of the serving line, I reached into my pocket and pulled out my money, but the woman at the checking station smilingly told me that I did not pay until I got ready to leave the cafeteria. In mock surprise, I said, "You mean you're going to let me eat all of this food before I pay for it?" She acknowledged that yes, that was the way they did it.

That's the second parallel to life. In the cafeteria line, you eat and then you pay, but in life, you pay and then you eat. The student studies, prepares the homework, works hard, and is rewarded with the grades and recognition. The employee works one or two weeks before the pay is received. In short, you perform—then you receive the reward. The farmer plants the seed, does all the things necessary to bring the crop to maturity, then takes it to the marketplace, and only then does he or she receive the reward.

IMPORTANT: Since we can't be, do, and have everything on earth, let's look at another analogy that will help us understand why we need to take certain steps to avoid compromising by accepting the get by or even the good when the best (for us) is available.

Now just in case you think I'm neglecting the financial aspects of life at a time when you could be struggling financially, let me assure you that I understand the necessity of that cash flow. The next bit of research will get you REALLY excited!

A GOALS PROGRAM FOR MAXIMUM PERFORMANCE

David G. Jensen, Chief Administrative Officer, Crump Institute of Biological Imaging for the UCLA School of Medicine, surveyed the people who attend public seminars I conduct around the country. He divided them into two groups: those who set goals and developed a plan of action to reach them, and those who took no specific action to set their goals.

RESULTS: The goal setters earned an average of $7,401 each month. The nonaction group earned an average of $3,397 each month. Not surprisingly, the action group tended to be more enthusiastic, more satisfied with life and work, and happier in marriage, and their overall health was better. As Mr. Jensen stated, "These results also confirm the academic literature on goals that, over the past 20 years, has shown unequivocally that those who set goals perform better in a variety of tasks."

NOTE: At the beginning of this book I "tweaked" your interest and curiosity by telling you about one procedure that could double your income, improve family relationships, and make you happier and healthier. The procedure is goal setting and goal reaching, which is thoroughly covered in this chapter and the next.

In his cover letter to me, Mr. Jensen said, "Zig, although the statistics do not 'prove' that setting goals causes success in all aspects of life, I believe the combined analysis of all these pre-seminar questionnaires strongly supports what you have been professing for years."

> **❝** *It seems universally true that people who have direction in their lives go farther and faster and get more done in all areas of their lives.* **❞**

BECOMING A MEANINGFUL SPECIFIC

FACT: You will never realize more than a small fraction of your potential as a wandering generality. You must become a meaningful specific. Unfortunately, most people have only a vague idea of what they want, and very few people consistently act on vague ideas. The typical person goes to work every day because that's what he did yesterday. If that's the only reason for going to work today, he probably will be no more effective today than he was yesterday. The sad thing is, many people who have been with a company five years do not have five years' experience. They have one year's experience five times and no specific plans for making next year anything but a repeat performance.

Harry Emerson Fosdick said it best: "No steam or gas ever drives anything until it is confined. No Niagara is ever turned into light and power until it is tunneled. No life ever grows until it is focused, dedicated, disciplined."

Hockey superstar Wayne Gretzky brings it clearly into focus when he says, "You will miss 100 percent of the shots you never take."

Goals work for the individual, the family, a company, and a

nation. Goals involve a number of facets. We are making every effort to deal with all of them. A classic example of what happens with this approach is that of Ike Reighard, from Fayetteville, Georgia.

Ike was four years old when his family moved from Appalachia to inner-city Atlanta, Georgia. His parents had only completed their educations up to the fifth grade, so when Ike announced that he was going to college, his friends and even some members of his family ridiculed the idea, but Ike was determined to go, and he became the first member of his family to attend college. At the end of his freshman year, he had flunked out big time. Ike spent the next six years as a wandering generality with very little direction in his life. Most of that time he was a disc jockey at a low-powered radio station. He also labored loading and unloading trucks.

Then one day he picked up a copy of my first book, *See You at the Top*. For the first time in his life, Ike learned that he was a unique individual with remarkable ability, and a brand-new picture of himself was formed. The new Ike started working on one of the new concepts he learned: the importance of having goals. Julius Erving (Dr. J.) accurately states that "your goals determine what you're going to be."

Ike's first goal was to go back to college; however, his academic record was so miserable that Mercer University rejected him twice. After the second rejection, Dean Jean Hendrix bumped into him, and Ike poured out his heart to her and shed a few tears in the process. As a result, she permitted him to enroll conditionally. She required him to maintain a B average, or his academic career would be ended again.

A more confident, meaningfully specific, fear-free (well, almost) Ike Reighard had replaced the wandering generality, and he reentered the doors of academia with his goals clearly in mind. By going year-round and taking twenty hours per quarter, two years and three months later he graduated magna cum laude. His goals by then were even higher. That is one of the exciting benefits of having a goals program. As you accomplish your first objectives, new ones are born (remember the Gerry Arrowood story from chapter 5?), your confidence grows, your competence improves, you get more done, and you have more fun in the process.

Today, this child of a pulpwood cutter/stone and quarry worker is Dr. Ike Reighard, pastor of one of the largest and fastest-growing churches in the nation. It's located in Fayetteville, Georgia, just a few minutes from inner-city Atlanta where he grew up.

Actually, as Ike became successful in his own mind (that is where success always starts), his goals grew, and he changed from being a dreamer to a man who had dreams. That's important. When Alexander the Great had a vision (a dream)—and the vision had him—he conquered the world. When he lost the vision or dream, he couldn't conquer a liquor bottle. When David had a vision, he conquered Goliath; when he lost his vision, he couldn't conquer his own lust.

Another factor involved in Ike Reighard's success story is that with his change of direction and self-image, he adopted the day-before-vacation attitude and started treating every academic day in college with respect. This next analogy will help you put it in perspective in your own life.

DON'T BE OVERDRAWN

QUESTION: When you write a check, do you record the date, the amount, and to whom you wrote the check? The odds are astronomical that you answered yes because you clearly understand that if you write checks for more money than you have in the bank, the check will bounce and so will your reputation. In addition, you incur substantial charges for writing a bad check. There is even the possibility you could face criminal charges, and if the behavior is repeated, you could—and would—suffer financially by being denied business opportunities as well as the privilege of writing checks.

It's just good ethics and good common sense to record your checks so that you will be certain to write only good ones.

You've probably heard the statement, "Time is money," but you've never really taken it seriously. By that, I mean that you do not record carefully when you write a check on your time account or to whom you wrote it, the amount, and whether or not the purchase was a wise one.

THOUGHT: If you earn $30,000 a year for a forty-hour week and you work fifty weeks a year, you are being paid at the rate of $15 an hour.

Realistically, you would not begin each hour by placing fifteen one-dollar bills on your workstation and inviting your associates to come along and help themselves to those dollars at their discretion. The reality, however, is that for every four minutes someone squanders of your time, the person has just written a check on your time and taken one dollar of productivity and profit from you and your employer. Obviously, you would not turn your financial checkbook over to anyone and permit that person to write checks at will, so why should you turn your time checkbook over to someone else?

> **❝** *You can earn more money, but when time is spent, it is gone forever.* **❞**

I'm getting at something that is simple, and yet profound. Unless we keep a record of how we invest our time, it's easy to squander it or permit the wandering generalities of life to utilize our time in manners that are not good for them or for us. That's why I share proven procedures to help you become an effective time investor and not a time spender.

Psychologist Denis Waitley expresses it this way:

A goals program: the key to a balanced success 215

Time is an equal opportunity employer. Each human being has exactly the same number of hours and minutes every day. Rich people can't buy more time to spend it on another day. Even so, time is amazingly fair and forgiving. No matter how much time you've wasted in the past, you still have all of tomorrow. Success depends upon using it wisely by planning and setting priorities. The fact is, time is worth more than money and by killing time we are killing our own chances for success.

To go *Over the Top* and achieve success in our personal, family, and business lives, as well as the physical, mental, and spiritual aspects of life, we're going to need to use our time in the most effective way. That requires goal setting and goal reaching. The next story is further proof that goals are important and that they produce results.

YOU'RE FIRED

In 1963, after only one year on the job, a young assistant coach at the University of South Carolina was fired by the head coach, who told him that he was not cut out for coaching and advised him to find another profession. However, the young man was committed to coaching. He loved it and had set what, to most people, seemed an impossible goal: head football coach at the University of Notre Dame. In all probability, the man who had just fired him would have considered that goal not just out of reach but out of sight.

IMPORTANT POINT: Long before you go over the top, you have to become an over-the-top thinker. Dr. Robert Schuller said it well: "Some people say, 'I'll believe it when I see it.' I prefer to say, 'I'll see it when I believe it.'"

Fortunately, Ohio State and later William and Mary College gave the young man an opportunity, and he did such a great job that North Carolina State called him to be their head football coach. In four years, he built the best won-lost record that school had ever experienced.

A one-year trip to the pros preceded his call to the University of Arkansas where, over a dozen seasons, he built the best won-lost record in that school's history. In 1979, his Arkansas team was invited to face mighty Oklahoma in the Orange Bowl. The team enthusiastically accepted the invitation, but soon afterward his three top offensive players were caught with a woman in their room, and he dismissed them from the team. The loss of the players really created a dilemma, and the newspapers speculated that Arkansas should withdraw from the game because the team would certainly be no match for Oklahoma. However, the coach and his team were not quitters, and it never entered their minds to withdraw. He took inventory of the strengths of the team, they regrouped, and with a mighty team effort they soundly defeated the University of Oklahoma in one of the biggest upsets in Orange Bowl history.

SUCCESS BEGETS SUCCESS

In 1983, he left Arkansas and later accepted the challenge to rebuild the University of Minnesota team that had once been a real football power but had fallen on hard times. His efforts were successful, and within two years the team was in a bowl game. Before the game was played, however, he received and accepted a call to become the head coach at Notre Dame. The man I'm talking about is Lou Holtz.

There are a couple of factors that are very significant. First, the day he dismissed those three offensive players from his team at Arkansas is the day he really became the head coach at Notre Dame. The authorities at Notre Dame looked at him as a man who put principle and character development above a football game, and they decided the next time Notre Dame was seeking a football coach, they wanted Lou Holtz.

The second factor that is of interest to us is that when Lou Holtz accepted the head coaching job at Minnesota, the only provision or escape clause Lou wrote into the contract was that if Notre Dame called him to be their coach, he would be free to leave and accept that position, provided he had taken Minnesota to a bowl game.

Yes, commitment to reach your goal must be the first step toward reaching it. Here's why. When you make a commitment, whether it is to succeed in marriage, weight loss, or whatever, and the inevitable problems arise, you will look for a solution to the problems. Without a commitment you will take the easy way out and look for an escape from the problems. In either case, you can and probably will find exactly what you are looking for.

I can factually assure you that Lou Holtz has a complete goals program and not just the goal to coach at Notre Dame. The program he uses is the one you are now reading. His success as a coach and in all other areas of his life validates its effectiveness. The fact that 94 percent of his football players graduate indicates that it works for them as well.

By now I'm completely convinced you want your own goals program, so let's look at the fourth reason people don't have a goals program—they really do not know how to develop one.

DEVELOPING A GOALS PROGRAM

It takes time, but remember—lack of time is not our problem. It's lack of direction.

This procedure I'm going to recommend is tried and proven and, when followed, will give you an even better chance to accomplish a balanced success.

To be fair, we need to look at a standard bad news–good news example, and to conform to the formula, I'm going to start with the bad news first. Properly developing a goals program will take between ten and twenty hours. Goal setting is demanding, which is one of the reasons only 3 percent of us have a goals program (everyone has individual goals). This is also one reason the rewards for those who have a program are so great.

The thought of investing ten to twenty hours might be overwhelming, and you simply don't have time right now.

QUESTION: If you don't have time to invest in establishing a goals program, is it possible that you don't have time because you don't have a goals program? In all probability lack of time always has been and always will be the problem.

SOLUTION: Make the commitment to establish a goals program now and you will have more time in the future to do what you need to do and want to do.

STOP! Right now set aside one hour, and make the commitment to take step one before you turn out the lights tonight.

REMEMBER: (1) Change starts when you take the first step, and (2) without action there will be no progress.

The good news comes in two parts. First, if you take the steps I suggest, you will create for yourself an additional two to ten hours of productive time every week for the rest of your life (remember in an earlier chapter how you set your goals for the day before vacation).

The second bit of good news is that when you learn how to set one goal, whether it's a physical, mental, spiritual, social, family, career, or financial goal, you will know how to set them all. If you know the answer to 12×12, you can figure out the answer to $2,868 \times 4,731$ because you know the formula. And as you learn the formula for setting one goal, you will know the formula for setting all goals. It's also nice to know that a number of goals will involve several aspects of life and include goals within goals.

NOW FOR THE SPECIFICS

Step 1. On a Wild Idea Sheet let your imagination run wild, and print everything you want to be, do, or have. If you have a family, be sure to include them in this process. Estimated time, one hour.

Step 2. Wait twenty-four to forty-eight hours (during this time you will expand your list), and then answer *why?* for each item you have printed on your Wild Idea Sheet. If you can't articulate in one sentence why you want to be, do, or have it, eliminate it as a current goal.

NOTE: You now have a list that includes far too many things to work on every day. The next few pages will help you temporarily eliminate most of them so you can concentrate on those that are important right now.

> ## *Important: Until you commit your goals to paper you have intentions that are seeds without soil.*
>
> **Anonymous**

Step 3. Answer these five questions, all of which must have a yes answer:

1. Is it really my goal? (If you're a minor living at home, an employee or a team member, some of your goals will be set by others.)
2. Is it morally right and fair to everyone concerned?
3. Will reaching this goal take me closer to or farther from my major objective in life?
4. Can I emotionally commit myself to start and finish this goal?
5. Can I see myself reaching this goal?

NOTE: Answering the questions in steps 2 and 3 will be helpful in making decisions in all areas of life but especially in the financial area. (I challenge you, if you're having financial difficulties, to ask yourself the questions in those two steps every time you start to buy anything that costs over a dollar.)

Step 4. After each remaining goal, ask yourself these questions:

1. Will reaching this goal make me happier—healthier—more prosperous—win friends—give me peace of mind—make me more secure—improve family relationships—give me hope?
2. Most important, will reaching this goal contribute to a more balanced success?

Step 5. Divide the remaining goals into three categories: short-range (one month or less); intermediate (one month to one year); long-range (one year or more).

REMEMBER: (a) *Some* goals must be big (out of reach—not out of sight) because to grow, you've got to stretch. (b) *Some* goals must be long-range ones to keep you on track. Without long-range goals, daily frustrations begin to look like the whole oceanfront. If you have specific long-range goals, daily frustrations will look like pebbles on the beach of life. (c) *Some* goals must be small and daily to make certain that you become, and remain, a person with a dream instead of a dreamer. Daily goals make certain you become and remain a meaningful specific. (d) *Some* goals must be ongoing (education, healthy self-image). (e) *Some* goals (sales, educational, financial, weight loss) may require analysis and consultation. *Most* goals should be specific. Getting a promotion is not nearly as effective as becoming projects manager by January 1.

Step 6. Take the remaining goals you have listed on your Wild Idea Sheet and work each goal through the process, utilizing the examples we share on the next two pages.

TAKING INVENTORY

Most people, unfortunately, do not take inventory before they attempt to set their goals. For example, if you have a financial goal with a specific figure in mind that you want to reach by a certain date, you definitely have to know exactly

GENERAL GOALS PROCEDURE CHART

Goal #1	Goal #2

STEP #1 IDENTIFY YOUR GOALS

Original Goal 165 Lbs —34" Waist	Get A "Better" Education

STEP #2 MY BENEFITS FROM REACHING THIS GOAL

more energy — Less Illness Look and feel better Longer Life Span Better endurance more productivity Better Attitude + disposition more Creativity Better Example	Broaden + Increase opportunities Improve Self Image and increase relationships — Increase Income Improve Security + Knowledge Broaden Personal, business and Social Life + Contacts Improve discipline— Peace of mind Increase happiness—Confidence Enhance Sense of accomplishment

STEP #3 MAJOR OBSTACLES AND MOUNTAINS TO CLIMB TO REACH THIS GOAL

Lack of discipline bad weather — Irregular schedule Love for sweets — Lack of time Unhealthy eating habits Poor physical Condition	Lack of patience — physical exhaustion — Financial costs heavy family demands — Lack of confidence (out of school 15-20 years)

STEP #4 SKILLS OR KNOWLEDGE REQUIRED TO REACH THIS GOAL

dieting knowledge and techniques exercise and jogging procedures	Time management— positive attitude Patience — persistence — discipline better money management Effective study Procedures

STEP #5 INDIVIDUALS, GROUPS, COMPANIES AND ORGANIZATIONS TO WORK WITH TO REACH THIS GOAL

Dr. Ken Cooper, Dr. Randy Martin, program Chairman—Laurie Majors, The Red Head	Family — employer — academic counselor — financial consultant—mentor

STEP #6 PLAN OF ACTION TO REACH THIS GOAL

Make Commitment No bread or Sweet except on Sunday Jog 125 Minutes weekly Good breakfast — Only fruit or healthy snacks after Late Seminars Eat Well balanced diet Drink 8 glasses of water daily Eat slowly and only at the table	Make Commitment — Organize time Practice Self discipline (cut T.V. time) Secure family Support— Schedule significant family time Join Public Library — Listen to educational Inspirational Recordings while driving. Attend Seminars Reduce meaningless activities Schedule study time daily Shape up physically for increased energy

STEP #7 7/1 — 74   COMPLETION DATE None — On going goal

GENERAL GOALS PROCEDURE CHART

	Goal #1	Goal #2
STEP #1	**IDENTIFY YOUR GOALS**	
	Acquire a new customized mini-van (be specific)	Be a "successful" parent
STEP #2	**MY BENEFITS FROM REACHING THIS GOAL**	
	More dependable transportation Raise my sights and standards Improve job reliability Better attitude Increase travel opportunities Enhance social status Greater safety More comfort and fun	More happiness and peace of mind More stable marriage Better relationship with children, friends, neighbors and relatives Better career opportunities (if working parent) More old age security Enjoyment of potiential grandchildren Increase potential of children
STEP #3	**MAJOR OBSTACLES AND MOUNTAINS TO CLIMB TO REACH THIS GOAL**	
	Short of cash · Poor money management Present car has low trade-in value Income stabilized · Inflation · Mate disagrees Higher payments and insurance costs	Limited experience · Tight budget Heavy work load · Lack of patience Inadequate help or no help Alcoholic parent
STEP #4	**SKILLS OR KNOWLEDGE REQUIRED TO REACH THIS GOAL**	
	Money management · Automobile knowledge Dollar stretching techniques Information on how to buy and trade techniques	Mental, nutritional, spiritual and physical information Read books on common sense, diplomacy, communication skills, time management and organizational skills Discipline procedures Know something about being a "fixer"
STEP #5	**INDIVIDUALS, GROUPS, COMPANIES AND ORGANIZATIONS TO WORK WITH TO REACH THIS GOAL**	
	Family · Banker/Financier · Insurance agent · Employer Investment counselor · Part-time employer · Automobile dealer	Minister · Employer (if working) · Family physician · Mate (if any) Youth leaders · Educators · Parents-in-law · Neighbors Parent support groups
STEP #6	**PLAN OF ACTION TO REACH THIS GOAL**	
	Get financial statement Record expenditures for 30 days Skip vacation and deposit savings Follow ads and bargain hunt Establish and control budget Get family involved in *their* new vehicle Take family "window shopping" to see dream vehicle Deposit savings every week in interest-bearing accounts Take temporary and *limited* part-time job	Read books on positive parenting procedures Assign daily responsibilities Provide daily mental and spiritual input and direction Spend time daily talking, directing, teaching and encouraging Accept and love my kids unconditionally Give them daily doses of affection and approval Expect, teach and require them to do their best Discipline properly and consistently Admit when wrong and ask forgiveness
STEP #7	January 1, 1990 **COMPLETION DATE** Intangible	

A goals program: the key to a balanced success **223**

where you are before you can make plans for reaching that goal. In my own case I needed to lose some weight, but I needed to know exactly how much. That's the reason I went to the Aerobics Center founded by Dr. Ken Cooper.

When I get aboard an aircraft headed from Dallas to Orlando, Florida, the captain has to know that we're leaving from Dallas. If he thinks we're leaving from St. Louis, we've got problems! Yet, there are those who set financial, physical, or relationship goals without knowing where they are.

CLASSIC EXAMPLE: Countless numbers of husbands and wives labor under the illusion that they know exactly where they stand with their mates and children when, in reality, they don't have a clue. In my book *Courtship After Marriage,* there is a questionnaire to help couples understand where they are. Many of them have said it truly was an eye-opener and laid the foundation for improving and, in many cases, saving their relationships. That's what you need to do. Find out where you are: then and only then do you have a legitimate chance of moving from where you are to where you want to be.

NOTE: A goals program will include a wide range of individual goals, but the formula or process is the same for all of them whether the goal is physical, mental, spiritual, social, family, career, or financial.

I include four examples of the process you follow as you set each serious goal (pages 222 and 223).

You may invest considerable time (one to two hours) working some of your individual goals through the process only to discover that at this time it is not a goal you should pursue. That is infinitely better than working on a goal for months or years only to learn that the timing was wrong or the goal—for you—was wrong. For the moment eliminate that goal.

To recognize the importance of this point, you need to know that ten years after graduating from college, over 80 percent of the graduates earn their living in a field unrelated to their major field of study. As a practical matter, you should choose no more than four goals to concentrate on each day.

Review your remaining goals each week so that, when opportunity presents itself, you will seize that moment to make progress on that goal. For example, in my own life I'm generally collecting material for at least two new books, one new recorded series, and several different articles in addition to the family and personal goals I'm pursuing.

FACT: I can concentrate on only one major project at a time.

SOLUTION: When I pick up anything to read, I automatically pick up my pen to mark any item that fits any of these projects. Since I'm sensitive to each individual project, I can quickly and easily mark and file them for future concentrated attention. Over five years before writing *Over the Top* I started collecting information for it. Twelve months before my deadline I started giving it my concentrated attention.

On pages 226 and 227 you will find copies of sheets from our Performance Planner that I use every day to stay on track. There are a number of good systems available. To be most effective, you should commit yourself to use one of them every day.

(For more information about our Performance Planner, call us at 1-800-527-0306.)

By now, you may be asking, "Is it really worth the effort to work out a goals program? It looks like a lot of trouble to me." The answer is yes, a thousand times yes.

Please remember the eight things we initially discussed in chapter 3 (happy, healthy, reasonably prosperous, and secure, friends, peace of mind, good family relationships, and the hope that things will either continue as they are or get better), and answer these questions about them. First, have you specifically identified all of them as goals and written them down? Second, have you listed the benefits that will be yours? Third, have you identified the obstacles you have to overcome to achieve these objectives? Fourth, do you have the necessary skills and knowledge that will be required to reach them? Fifth, have you identified the individuals, groups, and organizations you need to work with? Sixth, have you developed a

MY GOALS FOR THIS WEEK:	MY DAILY GOALS ACTIVITY		
#1 I am current Phone calls & corresp.	2 hours 15 min. Phone calls - corresp.	Phone calls 45 minutes	3 hours phone calls, correspondence
#2 I weigh 165 lbs. and have a 34" waist	Ate sensibly Jogged	Ate sensibly No exercise	Ate sensibly Jogged 30 min.
#3 I finish revision R.P.K. March 1st	Nothing	Two hours Writing R.P.K.	Two hours writing R.P.K.
#4 I read and research 10 hours weekly	One hour	Ninety minutes	2 hours reading and research
NOTES, PROJECTS, REMINDERS & IDEAS	MY DAILY PRIORITY LIST		
	Breakfast - T.R.H.	Breakfast - T.R.H.	Family time
Check schedule for week and month	Update plans for week	9:35 Departure	Hit golf balls
	Review last week	Conduct Seminar	Call Dr.'s Campbell
	Studio recordings	Work R.P.K.	and Katterman
Get latest drug data - Dr. Tennant	Staff meetings	Christmas lights	8:25 to Pensacola
	Dinner meeting		
	Fred Smith		

	DATE		DATE		DATE	
Gather data - Info. Board Meeting	12-5	MONDAY	12-6	TUESDAY	12-7	WEDNESDAY
	TIME	SCHEDULE	TIME	SCHEDULE	TIME	SCHEDULE
Get publishing permission from authors & publishers	6:15	Arise-dress-breakfast T.R.H.	6:30	Arise - dress	6:45	Arise-dress
			7:00	Breakfast - T.R.H.	7:00	News
	7:35	To office	8:00	To office	7:15	Breakfast - T.R.H.
Verify travel schedule for week	8:00	Prayer and devotions Dr. Neil Gallagher	8:25	Details - Laurie M.	8:00	Relax - Newspaper
			8:35	To airport	8:30	Phone calls - corresp.
	9:00	Staff meeting	9:35	Flight cancelled	9:30	R.P.K.
Update and experiment with new Performance Planner	9:25	Details - Laurie Mager	9:40	Phone calls - reading	10:30	Reading - research
	9:45	3 short recordings	11:25	To Corpus Christi	11:10	Lunch - T.R.H.
	10:00	Phone calls and correspondence		worked R.P.K.		Keeper - Elizabeth
			12:35	Arrive Corpus	12:40	Phone calls - corresp.
Check Hay Group progress	11:30	Office Conference	1:30	Seminar (Lowe)	2:30	Hit golf balls
	11:50	To cafeteria	5:25	To hospital and visit	3:10	Jogging
	12:00	S.S. Lunch	6:15	To airport	3:40	R.P.K.
	1:30	To office	6:30	Dinner	4:00	Shower - pack
	1:40	Details - Laurie Mager	7:25	To Dallas (R.P.K.)	5:30	News - T.V.
	2:00	Home	8:35	Arrive Dallas	6:00	Dinner T.R.H.
	2:20	Phone calls and conv.	9:15	Visit Tom, Chachis, T.R.H.	7:15	To office - airport
	3:15	Work on pool - (clean)	10:10	Christmas lights	8:20	To Pensacola
	3:30	Jogging	10:40	To bed - read		Reading - R.P.K.
	4:00	Relax - T.R.H.	11:00	Lights out	10:30	Arrive Pensacola
	4:30	Reading - Research			11:30	Lights out
	5:30	News - T.R.H.				
	6:30	Dinner (Fred Smith)				
	9:00	Home				
	10:00	Rams and Bears				
	10:30	Bed - Reading				
	11:00	Lights out				

PHYSICAL ACTIVITY ▶	Jogged 30 min.	No Exercise	Jogged 30 min.
A BALANCED LIFE IS THE KEY TO TRUE SUCCESS AND HAPPINESS EACH DAY MARK EACH AREA WITH A + OR A − SIGN	PHYSICAL + FAMILY + MENTAL + CAREER + SPIRITUAL + SOCIAL + RECREATIONAL − FINANCIAL +	PHYSICAL + FAMILY + MENTAL + CAREER − SPIRITUAL − SOCIAL − RECREATIONAL − FINANCIAL +	PHYSICAL + FAMILY + MENTAL + CAREER − SPIRITUAL − SOCIAL − RECREATIONAL + FINANCIAL +

226   Over the Top

MAKE TODAY WORTH REMEMBERING

Phone calls and corresp.	Nothing	Nothing	Nothing
Two hours	Ate too much	Ate sensibly	Ate junk
Ate sensibly	No jogging	Jogged 30 min.	No jogging
Jogged 30 min.	Wrote R.P.K.	R.P.K. two hours	Nothing
Wrote R.P.K.	Two hours	Reading and research	Read two hours
One hour 10 min.	Read two hours	two hours	
Read one hour			

MY DAILY PRIORITY LIST

Check Hay Group progress report	Call Dr. Tennant	Prepare Sunday School lesson	Sunday School and church
1:00 p.m. speak	Check Performance Planner forms		
6:30 p.m. speak	Family time		

DATE 12-8 THURSDAY	DATE 12-9 FRIDAY	DATE 12-10 SATURDAY	DATE 12-11 SUNDAY
TIME SCHEDULE	TIME SCHEDULE	TIME SCHEDULE	TIME SCHEDULE
7:20 Arise - dress	3:30 Wake up - read	8:30 Arise - visit breakfast T.R.H.	7:00 Arise - shave, shower breakfast
7:30 Breakfast, paper	5:00 To bed		
8:20 Phone calls	7:30 Arise - dress	10:00 S.S. Lesson	8:45 To S.S. and church
9:00 Correspondence	7:45 To airport	12:00 Lunch and shopping	12:30 Lunch T.R.H.
10:00 R.P.K.	8:45 To Dallas, wrote R.P.K.	T.R.H.	2:00 Home - relax read paper - nap
11:10 Shave, dress	11:45 Arrive Dallas	2:30 R.P.K.	
11:30 Lunch	12:30 To office	4:30 Jogging	4:00 Visit the T.R.H. drink tea
12:20 To seminar	Lunch	5:00 Read	
1:20 Speak, sign books	2:00 Home - golf course	6:00 Dinner Tom - Chad his and T.R.H.	5:00 Shower
3:00 Newspaper intv.	4:00 Home - read		5:30 News
4:00 Jogging	5:00 Relax - news	8:00 Home - relax	6:00 Dinner T.R.H.
4:30 Shower	6:30 Dinner T.R.H.	9:00 Read - study	7:30 Relax - watch fire burn
5:30 Seminar	8:00 Visit Chad, Suze and grandchildren	10:00 To bed - read	
6:30 Speak, sign books		11:00 Lights out	9:00 T.V.
8:20 Dinner - nephew	9:30 Home - relax		10:00 News
9:40 Phone call	10:00 News		10:30 To bed - read
10:00 News	10:30 Reading		11:30 Lights out
10:30 Read	11:00 Lights out		
11:00 Lights out			

TIPS FOR A MORE PRODUCTICE WEEK:
1. EACH WEEKEND: SCHEDULE PROJECTS AND ACTIVITIES INTO YOUR CALENDAR FOR THE NEXT WEEK.
2. EACH EVENING OR EARLY IN THE MORNING: LIST YOUR HIGHEST PRIORITIES FOR THE DAY AND CROSS OFF WHEN COMPLETED.
3. EACH DAY: BE A "GOOD-FINDER"...LOOK FOR THE GOOD IN OTHERS AND GIVE SINCERE COMPLIMENTS.

Jogged 30 min.	No Exercise	Jogged 30 min.	Jogged 30 min.
PHYSICAL + FAMILY +	PHYSICAL + FAMILY +	PHYSICAL + FAMILY +	PHYSICAL − FAMILY +
MENTAL + CAREER +	MENTAL + CAREER +	MENTAL + CAREER +	MENTAL + CAREER −
SPIRITUAL + SOCIAL +	SPIRITUAL + SOCIAL −	SPIRITUAL + SOCIAL −	SPIRITUAL + SOCIAL +
RECREATIONAL − FINANCIAL +	RECREATIONAL + FINANCIAL −	RECREATIONAL + FINANCIAL −	RECREATIONAL + FINANCIAL −

A goals program: the key to a balanced success 227

specific plan of action? And seventh, have you set the completion date where that is possible?

BE SURE TO ASK THE QUESTION

Ask, Will what I could lose or have to give up in the process of reaching this goal be worth the end result of attaining this goal? As an example, after you have narrowed your list to the things you are specifically going to work on, ask yourself, Will reaching this goal make me happier, or will it only give me temporary pleasure? Will reaching this goal make me healthier? Will reaching this goal make me more prosperous? Will reaching this goal make me more secure? Will reaching this goal improve my family relationships? Will reaching this goal enable me to make more friends? Will reaching this goal give me peace of mind? Will reaching this goal give me a legitimate hope for the future?

Obviously, there will be some cases where all of these questions do not apply, and that is where common sense and judgment will enter the picture. For example, robbing a bank, embezzling funds, or dealing in drugs might temporarily make you more prosperous, but traditionally speaking, at the end of the road you will have fewer dollars than you would have had if you played it straight. That does not include what happens in all other areas of your life. Balance is the key. Sometimes decisions made on relatively small things can affect some things that are very significant.

For instance, you might really have a desire to take a weekend fishing trip. That would, in your opinion, make you very happy. On occasion you might really deserve to take that trip, especially if you take the same view that your mate deserves to take a trip somewhere for his or her pleasure. I'm speaking here primarily of family objectives, so you need to ask yourself, Will my pleasure cause undue hardship and sacrifice for my family? Would I be better off and would they be better off if we spent that time on that fishing trip together or camping or going to a nice retreat as a family or simply visiting friends or relatives down the road somewhere? The bottom line is that we cannot write a set of ironclad rules that apply to every occasion, but when you balance things according to the guidelines we have established and ask yourself, In the long run, will this enable me to achieve my long-range as well as my short-range objectives? you will find these guidelines to be applicable in virtually every case.

This process will enable you to save months or even years of time because it eliminates goals that are unrealistically big, are out of your field of interest, will throw your life out of balance, will cause you to give up far more than you will gain, and depend on luck as a factor in reaching that goal.

As you reduce the list through this process, you will still have perhaps ten to fifteen specific objectives in mind. You need to choose four of them you can specifically work on each day. Keep the remaining list handy for easy reference, and work on goals as time permits. As you reach each of the four goals you have chosen for immediate action, you move another goal from the larger list to your immediate action list to work on each day.

In my own life I always pray for guidance as I choose my goals. God doesn't always reveal to me exactly what He wants me to do, but if I set goals that are not right for me and are not pleasing to Him, He won't give me any peace in the matter. That's the reason I love the acrostic for GOALS: *g*odly *ob*jectives *a*ssure *l*asting *s*uccess.

WINNING IS A FOCUSED GOALS PROGRAM

I want to conclude this chapter with a story that clearly represents the principles, procedures, and visualization process we've discussed throughout the book.

One of the most exciting letters I've ever received was from Andrew Gardener, an assistant vice president with Merrill Lynch. Andy pointed out that Merrill Lynch has a very large number of $100,000 income earners who come from all walks of life. All ages, creeds, colors, and many religious backgrounds are represented. Some are introverts; some are extroverts. They are male and female, tall and short, stocky and slender. Some are specialists in product and service while others serve as general practitioners. Yet all of them have one thing in common: They all set specific production goals and constantly monitor their progress. They all know exactly where they stand on a daily, week-to-date, month-to-date, and year-to-date basis.

FACT: Knowing exactly where you are on your goals at any given moment gives you added confidence and helps you maintain the right mental attitude.

Andy was working with Merrill Lynch in Atlanta and struggling. His manager, P. Parks Duncan, called him into his office, had an encouraging talk with him, and told him he believed Andy could make the Executive Club. Being in this club is an honor recognizing the success, professionalism, and integrity of new stockbrokers. He showed Andy the blueprint for their yet-to-be-finished new offices a half mile away and told him that if he made the club, he would give Andy his own private office (that's incentive motivation).

After his talk with his manager about the new office, Andy skipped lunch, walked the half mile over to where the new office was being built, and rode the construction elevator to the sixth floor. Other than a main frame, only scaffolding, mixing machines, ladders, tools, dust, and piles of wood were there.

Andy found the spot where his new private office was going to be, looked out the window, and as he said, he liked the view. He turned around, faced the open space, and crouched down as if sitting. In his mind's eye he saw the sales assistant at her desk beyond the interior window answering the phone, "Good afternoon, this is Mr. Gardener's office." That was eight months before the new office was actually finished (that was classic visualization). He could see himself in that office, which meant he could see himself making the Executive Club.

Up to that point, Andy said he wasn't on target to make Anybody's Club, if there had been one, much less the Executive Club! "But what I had now," as Andy says, to go along with his PMA (positive mental attitude), "was a visualization of my success." He reinforced this picture by repeating the process many times (self-talk), first on a weekly basis and then daily. He had a specific definable goal with a deadline—December 21, 1984, which he broke down into monthly, weekly, and daily goals.

Through November, he had made good progress and had more than doubled his average daily production without compromising Charles E. Merrill's golden rule: "The interests of our customers must come first." However, he was still far short of making the Executive Club, and he knew that to qualify, his December production would have to be 300 percent greater than his new daily production.

At that point some acquaintances suggested he give up on the Executive Club goal, work through a good December, and plan for a great '85. Andy said that seemed awfully tempting at times, especially when three big "sure things" fell through.

MAJOR POINT: Giving up always seems logical for those who are filled with self-doubt and have not made the commitment.

Fortunately, as a committed over the topper, Andy did not have that problem. Not only did he have a vision—the vision had him. Here's the way he expressed it: "But, Zig, I had no choice. You see, as I continued to go over to 3500 Piedmont to see my office, the construction began to catch up with my visualization. So, increasingly, quitting became impossible. By continuing to pump in order to find enough people to help them achieve their desires, and by establishing my daily goals and visualizing a dream, I made the Executive Club on December 21, 1984."

Since then, Andy's progress has been even more remarkable (success begets success). He made the club again in '85 and '86 and then agreed to manage an associate office in Houston, which he did for two and a half years. He then moved to the Houston Galleria office where he now serves as an assistant vice president in Merrill Lynch's Private Client Group. He made the Executive Club again in 1990 and then was named to the President's Club in 1991. He now manages over $60 million in investment portfolios.

Now I quote from his letter verbatim:

Zig, my business had been progressing well, but I knew I needed a turbocharge. And boy did the June "Born to Win" provide it [that's our high-intensity, three-day, personal development seminar in Dallas, which teaches these over-the-top principles in a creative environment]. June turned into my biggest month—ever—by over 80 percent. July turned into my second biggest month, and August outpaced July, almost overtaking June. Until those three life-changing days I was on target to make the President's Club again, no small feat in itself. But since my success following "Born to Win," my new stretch goal is to be named a "Win Smith Fellow," which is among Merrill Lynch's most coveted awards.

The good news is that 1992 was truly a banner year because Andy reached his goal and became a "Win Smith Fellow." And not so incidentally, Andrew's best years by far took place during the serious recession of late 1990, 1991, and 1992. One more time—it's not what happens "out there." It's what happens in your mind.

Yes, a goals program, carefully followed, will produce wonderful results and more than just a little employment security. Now let's go to the next chapter and learn how to reach those goals.

CHAPTER TWELVE

Reaching your goals

The man who succeeds has a program. He fixes his course and adheres to it. He lays his plans and executes them. He goes straight to his goal. He knows where he wants to go and he knows that he's going to get there. He loves what he's doing and loves the journey that is taking him to the object of his desires. He is bubbling over with enthusiasm and he is filled with zeal. This is the man who succeeds. Anonymous

When your goals are properly set (and if you have followed the suggestions here, your goals are properly set), you've taken the first—and by far the most important—step in reaching your goals, but there are some very specific steps you must take to reach your goals.

THE SPECIFIC STEPS TO REACHING YOUR GOALS

1. Make the commitment that you are going to reach the goal

Author Fred Smith says,

233

Commitment is essential for victory in an individual's life. Committed lives have meaning, accomplishment, purpose, and excitement. On the other hand, tentative living is never satisfying. Tentative generally becomes negative, and negative becomes critical or even cynical. Tentative lives are never victorious. Have you ever read a biography or a history story related to someone who lived tentatively and became a hero?

The goal-setting process you have just gone through is designed to help you eliminate frivolous goals or goals that at this time are not important. At this point if the goal is still in your Performance Planner or goals planner of your choice, I'm assuming that you have already made that commitment. That's the first—and most important—step necessary to reach your goal.

2. Commit yourself to daily detailed accountability

The reason becomes obvious when you understand that if it can't be measured, it can't be managed. If it can be done, it can be measured, and if it can be done, it can probably be done better. Most of us suffer a fairly serious reality gap between what we tell others we do and what we really do. In short, we kid ourselves, and this negatively affects our performance, puts ceilings on our potential, and unnecessarily limits our future. For this reason, the first thing you must do after committing yourself to reach a goal is commit yourself to being accountable to yourself to reach the goal (this is the don't-kid-yourself approach).

Former heavyweight boxing champion Joe Frazier put it this way:

You can map out a fight plan, but when the action starts, it may not go the way you planned, and you're down to your reflexes—which means your training. That's where your roadwork shows. If you cheated on that in the dark of the morning, well, you're getting found out now under the bright lights.

MESSAGE: Over-the-top people perform in the same responsible manner in the dark as they do under the bright lights.

Your accountability action step now is to take the four goals you identified in chapter 11, which you will work on each day. Line and label a blank sheet of paper to make your own Personal Performance record sheets and print your goals on them. With your goals firmly in place and your strong commitment to reach your goals, take these worksheets with you to give you a running record of your daily activities. (Remember, time is generally wasted, lost, stolen, misplaced, or forgotten in minutes, not hours.) After the end of your day, list the six most important things you must do the next day and the order of their importance. (Both activities take a total of ten to fifteen minutes.) REMEMBER: You were more productive the day before vacation because of the planning the night before.

WARNING: It takes an enormous amount of discipline to do this, but I guarantee you that if you do this every day, your performance in all areas of your life will improve and you will experience a freedom that only disciplined accountability can bring. That's over-the-top living. You should also plan to invest about thirty minutes once each week to keep your goals current and to plan for the next week. This next example is another classic one about an all-time great who teaches us that the results fully justify our efforts.

> *Success is the sum of small efforts—*
> *repeated day in and day out.*
> **Robert Collier**

Small daily goals to reach big, long-range ones. In the world of athletics, virtually every record will eventually be broken. However, there's one record the experts unanimously agree not only will never be broken but will never be approached. I speak of the eighteen wins Byron Nelson accumulated on the PGA (Professional Golfers Association) Tour in

1945, eleven of them consecutively. That year, Byron entered thirty-one tournaments and, in addition to the eighteen wins, finished second seven times. The worst he finished that year was a tie for ninth place. That's incredible!

The question is, How did he accomplish these objectives, aside from being such a phenomenal golfer? He started many years earlier, but 1944 really set the stage. That year he won eight tournaments and was the leading money winner on the tour. It was the prelude for what Byron believes was the main reason for his phenomenal success in 1945. For years he'd had a dream of owning a ranch. He and his wife, Louise, had grown up and lived through the depression, and they didn't want to borrow money for the ranch—they wanted to pay cash for it. He had to make enough money from golf to do that. His success in 1944 made him realize that he could achieve that dream within a few years. All he had to do was continue to play well enough to keep winning—or at least finishing in the top ten.

He says the second reason he did so well in '45 had to do with something he did in '44 when he won nearly $38,000 (that's the equivalent of $453,790.65 today, and when you factor in the size of today's purses, his winnings would have been about $7,000,000). During 1944, Byron kept a record of the rounds and recorded whether he chipped badly, drove badly, or putted terribly. At the end of the year, he went back over his books like a businessman taking inventory. In the process he found two things that were repeated too often during the year, and they were poor chipping and careless shots. He made up his mind that for all of 1945 he would try very hard to avoid a careless shot.

He says his game had gotten so good and so dependable that "there were times when I actually would get bored playing." He'd hit it in the fairway and then on the green, make birdie or par, and go to the next hole. However, having the extra incentive of buying and paying cash for the ranch made things a lot more interesting. Each drive, each iron shot, each chip, each putt, was aimed at the goal of getting that ranch, and each round meant another cow, and each tournament win meant a few more acres, and another big step toward realizing his dream.

"Finally," he says, "I had one other incentive. I wanted to establish some records that would stand for a long time. I wanted to have the lowest scoring average and though I had won eight tournaments in 1944, I knew that the way some of these boys played that number wouldn't stand up very long. I also wanted the record for the lowest score for an entire tournament. At the time it was 264. I also wanted to be the leading money winner again."

Now, let's analyze what Byron Nelson has just said. First, he had a dream of owning a debt-free ranch—that was his big long-range goal. His game plan was to earn the money through golf. The plan of action included specific record keeping so he would know exactly where he stood. That's called daily disciplined accountability. His objective was intense concentration that he achieved by realizing that every putt, every chip, every fairway iron or drive, could mean buying another cow or another acre of ground. In other words, he was very specific in his objectives.

SUMMATION: He wanted to hit every shot well (specific short-range goal), buy a ranch (family long-range goal), have the lowest scoring average (career—big goal), be the leading money winner (financial goal), and set the record for lowest tournament score (all big career goals). It's safe to say that none of us will reach the goals Byron Nelson did, but it's even safer to say that the principles and procedures he followed will also work for us.

This is just a small sample of the exciting story told in Byron Nelson's book *How I Played the Game.*

3. Break your goal into small pieces

My first book, *See You at the Top,* has 384 pages. After completing the research, I wrote the book in ten months. That boils down to writing an average of 1.26 pages per day.

> **You build a successful career, regardless of your field of endeavor, by the dozens of little things you do on and off the job.**

You raise positive kids in a negative world by giving daily injections of time, love, and attention to your children. You build a beautiful marriage by the daily applications of kindness, consideration, respect, faithfulness, thoughtfulness, and attentiveness to your mate. You build a successful career, regardless of your field of endeavor, by the dozens of little things you do on and off the job. MAJOR POINT: You reach those significant goals by breaking them into small segments.

4. Get in shape physically, mentally, and spiritually

We are physical, mental, and spiritual and we need to deal with all of these natures. Everybody recognizes the importance of sound mental health and good physical condition. *Over the Top* deals with your mental health from beginning to end, and I deal with physical health in several different areas. Your spiritual health is even more important (you are going to be dead much longer than you're going to be alive!), but for some strange reason many people do not recognize the connection between spiritual health and peace of mind. Mary Crowley said, "There comes a time in everyone's life when we need help that goes beyond what any person can render." That's when spiritual strength is necessary. That's where God enters the picture. He's written an entire Book so we can share His wisdom and learn of His love and of His power.

I am expressing more than just an opinion when I reference our spiritual needs. The *Dallas Morning News* of February 12, 1996, published a report on a study done by Patrick Fagan of the Heritage Foundation. The study revealed that regularly attending worship services reduces suicide, drug and alcohol abuse, crime, out-of-wedlock births, and divorce. These people, whether they attend church, synagogue, temple, or mosque, are far happier and healthier, have a lower rate of depression, higher self-esteem, longer, happier marriages and, for the women (men were not mentioned), better sex. The study also revealed that regular worship attendance helps inner-city youth escape poverty, and the family income of those who regularly attend worship services is $37,021; for those who do not attend it is $24,361. (That is an extra $1,100 per month for the family. Not bad, since admission is free!)

Perhaps most significant is the fact that virtually all of the African-American men in prison today either never attended worship services or stopped going by the time they were ten years old. The study further revealed that pregnancy among African-American and Spanish-American teenagers is rare for those who regularly attend worship services (Caucasians were not included in the study). NOTE: I did not say that those who do not attend worship services get pregnant or go to prison. I did say that regular attendance at a worship service dramatically reduce the chances of pregnancy or prison. Also, poor African-Americans and Hispanics who attend church are definitely more optimistic about their future, have better relationships with parents, have more serious goals, see racism as less of an obstacle, and view the world as a place in which they can achieve. Yes, the spiritual side of life is significant in our quest for the better life.

In the event you elect to start attending regular worship services, let me assure you that in most cases you won't be alone in that decision. A 1996 study revealed that on a typical weekend more people are in the worship service of their choice than attend all the major league baseball games, plus all the NFL games, plus all the NBA games all year long. In short, more than 105 million people on a typical weekend are in a worship service.

MORE GOOD NEWS: There is no admission charge; there will be very few people high on drugs or alcohol; most of them are courteous and friendly and will represent the kind of people you would like to have as neighbors.

In addition, despite what some cynics might say about hypocrites, here's a scenario Chuck Colson proposes for you or any cynic: It's midnight. Your car has broken down in a dimly lit, crime-infested area of the city. No service station is in sight. You realize you can't sit there, so you start walking. A block later you spot four rather large young men on the other side of the street who abruptly turn and head toward you. Seriously speaking, wouldn't you breathe considerably easier if you knew the young men had just gotten out of a Bible study? Enough said.

5. Make your liabilities your assets

History records that many people with handicaps overcame them and made them their greatest assets. The classic example is Demosthenes, the Greek orator who stuttered so badly he lost his inheritance in a public debate. He overcame that handicap so completely that Adlai Stevenson said of him, "When Cicero finished an oration, the people would say, 'How well he spoke.' When Demosthenes finished speaking, the people would say, 'Let us march.' "

Necessity is the mother of invention. On September 21, 1993, while speaking to over thirteen thousand people in Denver, Colorado, I noticed a gentleman almost flat on his back in a reclining wheelchair who was getting tremendous delight from what he was hearing. The smile on his face was broad; he frequently broke out in laughter, and on a number of occasions, to the best of his ability, he applauded vigorously. When my speech was over, I stopped by to chat with him because I've seldom, if ever, seen anyone with as much joy and pure delight on his face. I commented on his enthusiasm and said I had to meet the man who was so "handicapped," and yet who obviously was far less handicapped than many of the able-bodied people who were there. When he talked about the freedom he has, I was astonished. Here's why.

Walter W. "Sunny" Weingarten at age seven survived the

third-worst polio epidemic of the twentieth century. He was paralyzed from the chest down, and for the next twenty-five years of his life he required the use of an iron lung weighing over 650 pounds. He used it eighteen hours each day and slept in the same bedroom every night for over twenty-five years. He was a prisoner of the life-support system that made his life possible.

Although polio was largely eliminated with the introduction of the Salk and Sabin vaccines in the late fifties and the manufacture of the iron lung came to an end, Sunny Weingarten became increasingly aware of the need for a much more portable, high-tech iron lung.

It has often been said that necessity is the mother of invention, and in this case that is certainly true. In 1975, Sunny Weingarten designed the first Porta-Lung™ prototype and began traveling all over the United States. Now we get the picture, don't we? For over twenty-five years that iron lung dictated where he could and couldn't go. Now, he's outside and can laugh and applaud and enjoy life much, much more. Things really are relative, aren't they?

His Porta-Lung™ invention is even more effective than the iron lung because, with the use of a separate, portable pressure unit, it provides higher pressure levels at variable inspiration/expiration ratios. In 1984, because of persuasion by several pulmonary physicians in the Boston, Massachusetts, area, several handmade prototype Porta-Lungs™ were made for persons with muscular dystrophy (a disease that causes various neuromuscular disorders) that had progressed to the upper body and affected the respiratory muscles. By developing a production model for children and young adults, Sunny Weingarten has made Porta-Lungs™ available to people in twenty-seven different states and seven foreign countries.

Sunny Weingarten, a committed Christian, is definitely a passionate, over-the-top person who is in the process of finishing well. Ironic, isn't it, that when he solved a major portion of his own problem he also solved the problems of many other people. He turned his liability into an asset for himself and countless others. His physical freedom increased substantially when he developed the Porta-Lung™, but far more than physical freedom is involved. His joy and happiness because of the contribution he is making to many other people give him an entirely different kind of freedom. His sense of self-worth catapulted upward and is enabling him to live a much richer and fuller life. I have an idea we will hear a lot more about him.

6. Learn to respond to disappointment

It's not what happens to you but what you make of what happens to you that will ultimately determine your success in all areas of life. EXAMPLE: As the football season wound down in 1986, the University of Notre Dame and Penn State were playing. Penn State was undefeated, and Notre Dame, under Lou Holtz, the new head coach, was in the first year of a rebuilding program. Time was running out, and Penn State was ahead. With just a few seconds left on the clock, Notre Dame was in possession of the ball and started a drive downfield. The tight end from Notre Dame broke clear in the end zone, and the quarterback hit him with a perfect pass, right in the hands. The tight end dropped the ball; Penn State won the game and later went on to win the national championship.

Ten of the eleven men on the Notre Dame team did everything that was asked of them, and the eleventh one tried awfully hard. The dropped ball, however, is typical of what can happen to us in life. I tell this story because in your life there are going to be occasions when you're going to do everything you're supposed to do, and somebody else is going to drop the ball. How you handle the dropped balls of life will determine, to a large degree, your success in reaching your goals. The young man mentioned earlier was able to handle that dropped ball quite well and used it as a learning experience when he later played in the NFL (National Football League).

7. Discipline yourself

There will be times when you will become discouraged and lose heart. There will be some days when you simply will not feel like getting up and going to your job or pursuing your goals. When that happens, character and commitment take over.

> *It was character that got us out of bed, commitment that moved us into action, and discipline that enabled us to follow through.*

There have been numerous occasions when all of us did not feel like doing what we needed to do, but because we had made a commitment to do the job, we dragged ourselves out of bed and went to the assignment. Interestingly enough, after we became engrossed in what we were doing, we soon forgot all about not feeling well and performed admirably.

After we took those steps, we felt like doing the job. The point is that motivation follows action and not vice versa.

> *Remember: When you discipline yourself to do the things you need to do when you need to do them, the day will come when you can do the things you want to do when you want to do them.*

8. Change direction, not decisions

To reach your goals, you need to understand that when setbacks and disappointments do occur, as my late brother, speaker Judge Ziglar, said, you do not change your decision to go for that goal—you simply change your direction in order to get there. That's very important because we have no control over many things that occur. We can't control the flow of traffic, market changes, the rate of inflation, the interest rate, the stock market, and a host of other things, but we can keep our own commitments to ourselves and our loved ones to pursue our objectives.

9. Get all the help you can: share give-up goals freely and go-up goals carefully

Here's what I mean: If you are going to give up smoking, drinking, taking illegal drugs, eating too much, swearing, and/or abusing other people, you can and should share these goals with just about everybody. You will discover that most people will encourage you when you share these goals with them. They will give you their emotional support and convince you that yes, you can do it. One of the reasons Alcoholics Anonymous, Overeaters Anonymous, Gamblers Anonymous, Narcotics Anonymous, Sex Addicts Anonymous, Nicotine Anonymous, and other such organizations are so effective is that the other people in the groups are so encouraging and supportive.

> **"** *The people with whom you share your goals will play a major part in whether or not you reach the goals.* **"**

If your goal is a go-up goal, you need to be very careful with whom you share it. This is especially true if it's a big one. If you plan on being the starting quarterback, writing a book, being the number one salesperson, or finishing first in your class, you need to share that goal only with those who, by their nature or their relationship with you, will be inclined to be encouragers. If you're married, it's ideal if your mate is the one with whom you can share. If your mate will not be supportive, I really encourage you to carefully consider the entire message of *Over the Top* and put "building a winning and loving relationship with my mate" high on your list of goals.

There's nothing more discouraging than to share a goal about which you're excited and enthusiastic with someone who should be supportive only to have him or her dump cold water on the project! That doesn't mean the person can't ask questions, because oftentimes another person can ask questions that will lead you to more carefully think things through. The questions essentially should be thought-provoking along the lines of, "How do you propose to reach this objective?" instead of negatively directed like, "What on earth makes you think *you* can do that?"

10. Become a team player

Joe Paterno, the head coach at Penn State University, is one of the most successful and best known football coaches in the country. His players do not wear their names on their jerseys, and Penn State is one of the few schools in the country that take this approach. Paterno wants his players to become completely unselfish, work together, and think in terms of playing as a team.

As you might recall, they won the 1986 national championship by beating the Miami Hurricanes and Heisman trophy winner Vinny Testaverde, Miami's outstanding quarterback. Penn State has beaten Boston College when Boston had Heisman trophy winner Doug Flutie. The Penn State players beat the University of Georgia when Georgia had Herschel Walker as the Heisman trophy winner, and they beat the University of Southern California and Heisman trophy winner Marcus Allen.

In other words, Penn State—the team—beat the other teams that had such outstanding individuals. Now please do not read anything into what I'm saying that is not there. I'm not even mildly hinting that these fine teams, with their outstanding coaches and outstanding Heisman trophy winners, were not team oriented. They obviously were and are. All I'm saying is that Paterno and Penn State have perhaps taken it one short step farther.

Now just in case you're thinking in terms of, "Yes, but what about the individual benefits of the Penn State players?" let me point out that at the present time there are only two colleges in America that have sent more players to the National Football League than Penn State. It's obvious that when you have individual skills that you utilize for the team's best interests, the team benefits and you benefit personally.

Incidentally, when a Penn State player scores a touchdown, he wins a fast trip to the bench if he hotdogs it in the end zone. Paterno has coached the players to quietly hand the ball to the nearest official, run back to the huddle, and congratulate the team on the touchdown they scored. That's class. That's teamwork. That's the over-the-top way—and it's completely realistic. In life when anyone accomplishes major objectives, you can know that a "team" helped him. In other words, when you see a turtle on a fence post, you can know he didn't get there by himself.

Speaking of being a team player, if one of your goals is to break a destructive habit like smoking, it's ideal if you can form a partnership with another person who has also decided to quit smoking. Make a commitment to call each other every evening, and discuss how you handled the day. Inquire specifically of the other person if he or she, too, abstained from smoking that day. The fact that you know the call is coming will oftentimes be the deterrent you need not to light up that day. Yes, a team effort is very helpful in reaching your goals.

11. Paint a positive picture

Do you play to win—or not to lose? Because negative pictures are so destructive, let's take one more look at what happens when we paint them.

I'm sure many of you remember the tragedy that took place in San Francisco in 1981 when the San Francisco 49ers beat the Dallas Cowboys in the NFC championship game. Yes, I recognize there are some of you folks with your own bias and prejudices who do not consider that loss a tragedy, but the reality is, it truly was a tragedy. The 49ers had slaughtered the Dallas Cowboys 45–14 in the regular season.

After the San Francisco debacle, the Dallas Cowboys did a 180-degree turnaround, marched through the play-offs, and were in the big game at Candlestick Park in San Francisco. Here's the scene: two minutes to play; the Cowboys are leading. Joe Montana and the 49ers get the ball at their own end of the field and start their relentless march downfield against our prevent defense. They tear off chunks in megayard bites until they get close to the end zone. On the final play of the drive Dwight Clark, not realizing that Joe Montana is trying to throw the ball out of the end zone, jumps twenty-eight feet up in the air (well, almost!) and makes the catch to win the game for San Francisco.

The next day in Dallas, Tex Schramm, the president of the Cowboys at that time, was asked by a member of the media, "What happened, Tex?" Tex's answer not only explained the loss, but it told us much about life itself. Schramm said that the Cowboys went out there determined not to lose the game. The San Francisco 49ers went out there determined to win the game. Their picture was winning; the picture in the Cowboys' minds was not to lose. There's a dramatic difference. Over-the-top people win because they play to win, plan to win, prepare to win, and therefore can legitimately expect to win.

12. Paint that picture in your mind of what you want to be, do, or have

A tragic fact of life, as I've indicated earlier, is that most people flow with the tide and permit their minds to dwell on the negative because negative news, negative people, and a negative environment are so much in evidence. Because of this input, it's easy to drift into the habit of imagining bad things instead of good things. The mind works to complete whatever picture we paint, so it is important that we learn to paint the picture of what we want instead of the picture of what we don't want, as the following examples illustrate.

If you want to reach your goals, you must see yourself as already being there. You must paint that picture in your mind of what you want to be, do, or have. As an over-the-top person, you must see yourself receiving that diploma, living in the home of your dreams, enjoying a beautiful relationship with your mate and/or children. You must see yourself getting that desired position, writing the book, making the speech, being a better golfer, achieving your ideal weight, winning the race, or whatever your objective is. You must vividly dream or imagine this in living color—and claim those victories with passion.

To make these dreams come to life, you need to apply the claiming the qualities formula detailed in chapter 9 to these specific objectives *after* you have followed the general procedure for thirty days. (You've got to be before you can do.) This process not only gives you a better, more realistic picture of

> 66 *Most Americans honestly believe America is the most powerful nation on earth, but actually, the most powerful nation is Imagi-nation.* 99

yourself, but gives you a broader picture of life, the world around you, and a bigger, better, more specific role you can play in the world. This procedure worked and is working for me, and it will work for you.

I dreamed over forty years ago that I would be traveling the world, making speeches to every conceivable kind of group. I literally saw myself in front of vast audiences making those talks. I made thousands of talks in my mind before I ever made one in front of an audience. I jokingly tell my audiences today that it's too bad we could not have recorded just one of those speeches that I made in my mind. If we had, I'm convinced we would have sold millions of copies. I say this because the speeches in my imagination were absolute perfection. I never laid an egg or made a mistake; the audiences always responded enthusiastically, applauded wildly, laughed uproariously at my jokes, and gave me prolonged standing ovations. In my mind I had the audiences rolling in the aisles or sitting with open-mouthed astonishment that a mere mortal could utter such incredible words of wisdom!

13. Your dreams can come true

This step could be—probably is—the most important step in the entire process of goal setting—goal reaching. You are using your mind—your imagination—positively to get what you want instead of what you don't want. CAUTION: Be careful what you dream about, because if you dream it boldly and vividly and follow the steps suggested—combined with the other principles of *Over the Top*—my friend, your dream could well become a reality. Every significant dream I've ever dreamed (with one major exception and not including those I've dreamed in the last three years) has already come to pass, and I'm convinced the dreams (goals) that haven't been reached yet will be reached because I'm following the same procedures I followed to reach the other ones.

Obviously, attitude plays a vital part in reaching your goals. It's got to be right. Motivation is critical, so I deal with attitude in great detail, but I emphasize again that you must deal with the total person. You can't separate or eliminate the importance of self-image, a good relationship with others, a commitment, a firm foundation, and all the other factors we discuss throughout this book.

I firmly believe that if you look at the total concept I portray from hello to good-bye, you will discover that I cover what you need to know and do to get what you want. Remember, countless letters, phone calls, and personal testimonials certify that many people are getting more out of life because these concepts have worked for them.

When you're down, whether the down trip is a temporary visit or a long-term stay can make a dramatic difference in your health, wealth, and happiness. When you're emotionally down, you are under a shadow and things get distorted; little nicks become serious injuries. A slight, misunderstood word becomes a gross insult; a short step backward turns into a catastrophe. The problem becomes distorted out of all proportion and, for that reason, we need to get out of the doldrums as quickly as possible.

In the next chapter we're going to look at some specific steps we can take to maintain an up attitude, because negative thinking, worry, and undue concern, as an unknown writer said, will pull tomorrow's cloud over today's sunshine.

CHAPTER THIRTEEN

Getting up—and staying up— when you've been knocked down

Forgiveness is the key that unlocks the door of resentment and the handcuffs of hate. It is a power that breaks the chains of bitterness and the shackles of selfishness.   William Arthur Ward

I t is safe to say that in a lifetime, all of us have what we consider to be more than our share of ups and downs. In that sense, life truly is a roller coaster. Sometimes things happen to us that are genuine accidents; sometimes we sabotage ourselves and are our own worst enemies. On occasion people or life itself deals us a series of body blows that devastate us.

251

LIFE IS A ROLLER COASTER

The following story is true. If you find it hard to believe, you can look it up in the 1982 *Encyclopedia Brittanica Yearbook* under "Unusual Events of the Year."

The story is about one day in the life of Bryan Heiss, who lives in Provo, Utah. It seems his day began with a leak in the ceiling of his apartment. The water was splashing in his face, so he jumped out of bed and called his landlord to see what could be done about the problem. When he stood, he splashed in the water that was gathering on the carpet, so his landlord told him to go rent a water vacuum in a hurry.

Bryan tore down the stairs to get in his car to go rent the water vacuum, but he discovered that all four of his tires were flat. He went back upstairs, reached for the phone, and was shocked so severely it nearly knocked him down. He called for a friend and asked him to take him to get help.

When he got back downstairs, Bryan found that someone had stolen his car. He knew it didn't have much gas. So he and his friend walked a few blocks, found the car, and pushed it to a service station, where they bought gas and put air in the tires.

Bryan later returned home and went upstairs to get dressed for an ROTC graduation ceremony that night. He donned his uniform and tried to get out of the house, but the water had caused the door to swell in its frame, and he had to scream until someone could come and kick the door down from the outside.

When he finally sat down in his car, he sat on his bayonet, which he had carelessly left in the driver's seat. Bryan was taken immediately to the hospital for some *very strategic* surgery.

Friends took him home, and when he opened the door, he saw that falling plaster had toppled the cage of his prized pet canaries, killing all of them. As he ran across the wet carpet, he slipped and fell and injured his back. Once again, he was taken to the hospital.

By this time a newspaper reporter had caught up with

Bryan and asked, "Mr. Heiss, how can you explain all of this happening to one person in a single day?" He answered, "It looked like God was trying to kill me, *but He kept missing!*"

None of us will have that many things happen to us in one day, but we all have our moments.

This chapter is essential because life's twists and turns—and the feelings that result—distract us from reaching our goals. In order of significance, let's deal with the stumped toe incidents of life, the blahs of life, and the truly serious life-changing events that challenge all of us on occasion.

First, let's look at the stumped toes. These simple incidents, in the total scheme of things, mean little—if anything—to our lives if (and half of life is IF) we deal with them when they happen. I'm referring to a one-incident-type problem (fender bender, accident, misunderstanding, hurt feelings, etc.) where damages were slight and costs were small. I encourage you to take the advice of speaker and writer Clebe McClary, the American hero who was so grievously wounded in Vietnam. Clebe uses the FIDO approach that literally means to *Forget It* and *Drive On*.

For some people, FIDO is easier said than done, but you have reached the point in your life—and in this philosophy—where you don't sweat the small stuff, so with patience and practice you can handle it. Incidentally, if you have a chance to hear or hire this former marine from Pawley's Island, South Carolina, do so—he's a very funny and inspiring speaker.

RECOVERING FROM THE BLAHS

Sometimes little irritations come our way that are not earth-shattering or life-changing, but they cause a momentary stop in our progress. Sometimes we permit the little incidents to linger entirely too long and give us problems far beyond their significance. Let's say that you are caught in one of these situations, and at the moment you're not depressed, but you're not exactly on Cloud 87, either. As a result, you know that you are not as friendly or as productive as you would like to be, so you want to snap out of it. What do you do?

Step number one, acknowledge that you're in a funky mood; you've got the blahs.

Step number two, recognize that your momentary switch from positive thinking to stinkin' thinkin' is neither permanent nor even life-threatening so it won't be fatal. It's eventually going to end, so instead of waiting for a change in circumstances to bring an end to the blahs, make a conscious decision to end them! Which means you have once again accepted responsibility for improving your circumstances. Okay, now what?

THE LAST DEPOSIT

It's smart to leave every encounter on a positive note. For instance, when you're leaving the house in the morning, it's much nicer to ask your spouse to pick up the dry cleaning first and save the "I love you" for last. Think about it. If you said, "I love you," then said, "Please pick up the dry cleaning," your spouse might feel manipulated. And suppose you died in a car

---

" *The last deposit in your mind is the first one you will withdraw.* "

---

crash right after you left? Your spouse would always remember your last words were, "Please pick up the dry cleaning," instead of, "I love you." Yes, last impressions are important.

I use this example because it is simple and clear. However, it is devastating to those who have had the misfortune of not being able to change their last words. This is true not just in regard to those you make the last impression on but also for you when someone else or something else (radio, TV, newspaper) makes the last impression on you.

If a person gave you that blah or down feeling, change the deposit by going to another person to get a quick fix. Call one of your friends or acquaintances who is an upbeat person and chat a couple of minutes. You might start by asking what is the most exciting thing or happening at the moment. The beauty of this approach is that both you and your friend will be better off as a result of the call.

If the offender was a TV, radio, audio, or video program, don't just turn it off; change the deposit—switch channels, stations, or tapes until you hear something positive. Remember, our minds dwell on that last deposit until the imagination builds it bigger and bigger, and it's much better to have a big positive than a big negative. My favorite method of achieving a big positive is to watch a Gaither Family gospel video for a few minutes just before I go to sleep. The joy of the performers combined with the hope the songs espouse produces restful sleep and sweet dreams.

Here is an effective method of dealing with an incident-induced case of stinkin' thinkin': Clearly understand that since you did survive and the initial pain and shock are over, it's got to get better from here on out. I think you'll agree that laughing at your difficulties is more effective than crying about them. Not only that, but with a change of attitude you'll start looking for the solution to the problem or circumstances that put you in that stinkin' thinkin' mood.

All of this says that your blah attitude is something you can control, and it is your opportunity and responsibility to do exactly that.

HANG IT ON A TREE

The man in this story had a definite plan for dealing with his blahs, according to Robert R. Updegraff in his little book *Be Thankful for Your Troubles* (The Updegraff Press, 2564 Cherosen Rd., Louisville, KY 40205). He tells us about one man in a highly challenging job who seemed to always be in a good frame of mind when he got home, regardless of how challenging the day had been. When queried about how he did it, the man said, "I have a little Copper Beech tree in the yard by the front door and I call it my 'private trouble tree.' Every night when I come home I mentally hang all the day's troubles on that tree and I say to myself, 'Hang there for the night, I'll pick you up when I start for work in the morning.'

"The funny thing about it," he continued, "is that half the time when I leave the house the next morning I discover that most of what I thought were troubles when I hung them up had blown away during the night. Even the ones that are still hanging there aren't half as heavy or worrisome as they seemed when I came home the night before."

Scientifically speaking, it's been validated that the overwhelming majority of our problems are in our minds and never really happen to us in life. According to Mr. Updegraff, for many years the *Boston Globe* carried on its editorial page this wise observation: "I am an old man and have had many troubles, but most of them never happened. Uncle Dudley."

I love the way Mr. Updegraff concludes his thoughts:

Be thankful for the troubles of your job. They provide about half your income because if it were not for the things that go wrong, the difficult people you have to deal with, and the problems and unpleasantness of your working day, someone could be found to handle your job for half of what you are being paid. It takes intelligence, resourcefulness, patience, tact, and courage to meet the troubles of any day. That is why you hold your present job and it may be the reason you aren't holding down an even bigger one. If all of us would start to look for more troubles and learn to handle them cheerfully and with good judgment as opportunities rather than irritations, we would find ourselves getting ahead at a surprising rate. It is a fact that there are plenty of big jobs waiting for men and women who aren't afraid of the troubles connected with them.

WHAT ABOUT THE BIG PROBLEMS?

These procedures will work for a slight case of stinkin' thinkin', but if you have a chronic case brought on by a major setback or a series of frustrations in your personal, family, or business life, you will obviously need to take stronger action. The cure won't be instantaneous, but it can and will happen if you make it happen. Keep reading.

HANDLING SERIOUS CIRCUMSTANCES

Even as you read these words you still might not be all that gung ho about your future because of reversals and lack of progress in the past, so let's address that issue. Let's say that at this moment you're genuinely discouraged or downcast; you don't know which way to turn; you're frustrated and at the end of your rope. What do you do?

Acknowledge where you are

I encourage you to take a piece of paper and write down exactly how you feel. Do not deny it. A major problem in our society today is that over 90 percent of the people who have problems, including alcohol or drug abuse, bad temper, irresponsibility, and a host of other things, will not admit in a month of Sundays that they have the problems—they're in denial (and I'm not talking about the river in Egypt, but I will say that if you stay in it, you will surely drown). So your first step is to write it down and say, "Here is where I am."

> You cannot solve a problem until you acknowledge that you have one and accept responsibility for solving it.

You cannot solve a problem until you acknowledge that you have one and accept responsibility for solving it. Get rip-roarin', snortin' mad about it, and if humanly possible, blame somebody, some place, or even an institution (like your school, hospital, or the government) for the difficulty. You read it right—blame somebody else. That somebody else might be a parent, a mate, a brother, a sister, or an associate.

Take action

Pick up a pen and some paper, and vent all your feelings of anger and frustration against the person or institution who wronged you. It might take two pages or ten pages to really express yourself. Write that letter, and lower the boom on that person or institution. Now, put the letter aside for a couple of hours, then carefully reread it, make certain you've covered all the bases, and if you left anything out, write a P.S. or even two or three or four P.S.'s. Empty your system of all the anger, hurt, and bitterness.

Address each issue

One more time, read the letter very carefully to make certain everything is covered, and then walk outside and page by page address each issue and say, "You did that to me. It was wrong. You shouldn't have done it, but I just want you to know I forgive you for it." Do that on every single incident, and then burn the pages one by one. When all the pages are burned, you will probably feel much better.

WARNING: For some of you, what I have just encouraged you to do is an absolute impossibility. The hurts are too many and too deep, and they did too much damage—or at any rate, that is your feeling, and feelings are what we are dealing with. If that is your feeling or perception, whether the incidents were that serious or the other person or persons were that guilty will make little difference. Your feelings will be exactly the same, and we must deal with the feelings. In the case of rape, brutality, or incest, you will probably need counseling to steer you through the pain and into the channel of forgiveness. I encourage you to get that help because you must—repeat *must*—forgive that person. This forgiveness is a must regardless of the offense because the commandment to forgive does not include any exceptions. The next story explains the benefits of forgiveness.

POWER AND PEACE IN FORGIVENESS

Several years ago in a conference I heard one of the most moving testimonials related to the peace and power that go with forgiveness that I've ever heard. A strong man, very successful in business, was telling about his experiences as a child with his father. Soon after his birth, his father went off to war, and the first four years of his life he seldom saw his dad. In the meantime, his mother and grandmother were his primary caregivers. When Dad returned home, he very quickly observed that "those women had ruined his son," and he was "going to make a man out of him."

His dad was a strict and harsh disciplinarian who took a traveling job that kept him away most of the week. He generally returned on Friday evening, and at that time his wife gave him a list of all the grievous sins and wrongdoings the child had committed during the week. Corporal punishment was usually the end result. Needless to say, it was not a happy experience for the little boy when his dad got home.

Once, as a six-year-old on his way home from school, he was accosted by a big bully who proceeded to beat him up. He ran home crying, and his dad told him that as long as he was acting like a girl he would dress him like one. He put a dress on the little boy and sent him back to face the bully.

As the strong, successful businessman sat there with tears streaming down his cheeks, he said that was one of the reasons he has had some emotional difficulties in his life, including becoming an alcoholic. However, he said he realized through working the Twelve Steps of Alcoholics Anonymous that his dad did not treat him that way because he hated him;

he treated him that way because he loved him. That was the way his dad had been raised as a child, and that was the only way he knew how to deal with problems of that nature. He pointed out that once he understood why his dad did what he did, he was able to forgive him and get on with his life.

Many of you who read these words may have been mistreated or abused. Forgive the person who abused you. You might well rationalize that the person doesn't deserve forgiveness. I encourage you to leave that up to God; let Him be the decider of who deserves and who does not deserve forgiveness.

> *He who cannot forgive others destroys the bridge over which he himself must pass.*
>
> **Anonymous**

Whether you feel that individual deserves forgiveness or not, you deserve to forgive him or her because, until you do, that person who abused or mistreated you is going to be in control of your life. FACT: That person has negatively influenced your past. Surely you are not going to permit him or her to harm your present and build ceilings on your future. And remember this:

MOUNTAIN CLIMBERS DON'T CARRY BRICKS

Just as mountain climbers don't add bricks to their backpacks, through forgiveness you will have removed the bricks of anger, hate, and resentment. Your load will be so much lighter you can move forward and upward much faster. You also have the benefit of recognizing that through the process of forgiving you will have made friends with the past and will be able to focus on the present. This gives you the freedom to grow and become the person you are capable of becoming, ensures a brighter future, and moves you in the direction of finishing well.

THINK ABOUT IT THIS WAY

If you had a broken leg, you would not hesitate to seek professional help, but there are still many people living under the illusion that our emotions or our mind-sets are things we should be able to take care of and heal ourselves.

CONSIDER THIS: There are three times as many people under the care of physicians for mental and emotional reasons as there are for physical reasons, so yours is not an isolated case. I encourage you to seek professional counseling, preferably from a counselor whose counseling is based on biblical principles.

The reason is simple: You get information out of books, magazines, and newspapers, and from the television set and radio. You get knowledge out of good books, encyclopedias, and educational institutions, but until you add the spiritual dimension, you're going to miss the insights, wisdom, and common sense that are critical to the healing process.

Realistically, we know that knowledge is not the answer to everything. If it were, every Ph.D. in America would be rich, happy, and well balanced, and we know that is not the case. If knowledge alone were the answer, every grade-school or high-school dropout would be broke and miserable, and we know that is not the case, either. My own mother with a fifth-grade education is a classic example of a person who did not have much book learning, but she had enough wisdom to raise six children who were too young to work when her husband died in the heart of the depression.

Wisdom is simply the correct use of knowledge to make the right decision. I encourage you—get the counseling from a person who has wisdom as well as knowledge. I will even be bold and suggest (this probably should have been my first suggestion) that you can go right to the top for the help you need.

CONSIDER THIS: If you had access to the most brilliant counselor in town at no charge, wouldn't you immediately go to that counselor and solicit advice and guidance on how to maintain the right outlook on life?

Actually, you do have the services of the most capable counselor in town at your disposal. The charge is zero; He's available twenty-four hours a day; and He has plenty of time to listen and give advice. If you get tired of talking, you can read His Book. Bible reading is a tremendous confidence builder. It's exciting to know that 365 different times in the Bible you are told to "fear not." Fear of something (especially the past and encountering someone you need to forgive) is a positive-thinking destroyer. There is one "fear not" for every day in the year except leap year—and surely, you can get through that day. Just in case you can't, God is always open for business, even on that extra day.

FORGIVENESS IS CRITICAL

WARNING: Forgiveness is tough, dangerous, and exciting: tough because of our human nature; dangerous because it forces us to take responsibility for our future; exciting because it frees us to become our best selves.

When you forgive others and then accept responsibility for your future, you will have a heavy burden lifted from your shoulders. With the weight removed you will immediately have a brand-new attitude and outlook on life. Then you can move upward and onward infinitely faster, and you will be happier, healthier, and have considerably more fun in life.

As long as there is bitterness, resentment, or anger toward another person, you might not deliberately wish the person ill luck, but you wouldn't exactly cry or lose any sleep over unfortunate things happening in that person's life. It's safe to say that if anything good happens in the person's life, your resentment is kindled anew. Whether you admit it or not, that is just another way of saying you want to extract a measure of revenge for what that person has done to you.

Hans Selye, the great stress authority, says that revenge is the most destructive of all the human emotions, and gratitude is the healthiest of all the human emotions. This process we're talking about eliminates revenge. The most important thing you can do for yourself is to forgive the other person.

I want to emphasize that it is desirable but not necessary to let the other person know that you have forgiven him or her. In some cases it could involve danger or extraordinary difficulty. You do not, therefore, need to go see that person. The pain may have been brought on by a bitter divorce involving a third party. For you to go see that person or even to write a letter might create problems within the existing marriage. That is something you must not do because it could bring additional problems for all parties concerned. If circumstances are favorable, however, there are benefits in letting that person know that all is forgiven. If it's impractical to see him or her in person, a letter or phone call works well unless there is a remote chance either anger or passion could be aroused.

He thinks you are the bad guy

You will possibly be surprised at the response you get. Let me caution you that the other person might be amazed that you felt it necessary to forgive him because he might feel you are the bad guy. Over a period of years, to protect his own peace of mind, he may have rationalized you right into the bad guy role. If that's the case, it is his problem, but remember, you have forgiven him—and that's the important step.

As a practical matter, until you do forgive him, he is your enemy, and you are at war. The problem with war between individuals is that almost always there are two losers. The beauty of making peace with that person is that now there is an excellent chance of having two winners. GUARANTEE: True forgiveness on your part will make you the winner.

Forgive yourself

Forgiving yourself might sound relatively simple, but in many cases it is very difficult, even if you are innocent of any wrongdoing. I want to emphasize that if you have difficulty forgiving yourself, you should seek biblical-based counseling so that you might do so. Until you do, your picture of yourself is not as accurate or good as it needs to be to go over the top.

I'm convinced, based on numerous letters, phone calls, and personal encounters with many, many people, that the procedures I'm describing will be effective in hard-line, even advanced cases of stinkin' thinkin'. However, I am not talking about clinical depression, which is a far more serious matter and will require the help of a skilled physician.

Forgiving others and yourself is frequently a process and not an event. There may be a number of things you need to sort out and work through. Patience and prayer can be your greatest assets, but I encourage you to do whatever it takes. The rewards fully justify the time and effort.

Much of the process I'm covering involves considerable pain, so let's listen as John Leddo helps us put pain in perspective.

THERE'S PAIN IN GROWTH

Psychologist John Leddo from Leesburg, Virginia, points out that when we try to grow, we must confront pain, which can be a powerful obstacle to growth. He says this pain can manifest itself in many ugly ways—fear, resistance to change, facing a truth about ourselves we don't particularly like. Often the pain is powerful enough to deter us from growth, and we suffer what he believes to be a heinous wave of pain. Heinous because it is a subtle pain that robs the life from us, brings on stagnation, and sends us through life on cruise control.

Dr. Leddo observes that pain is temporary, but growth is permanent. With marvelous insight he points out that God could take away the pain of the moment, but the price would be to deprive us of the growth that lasts forever—and no loving parent would do such a thing.

He points out that many times a child desperately wants

something or wants to do something that would be destructive or dangerous for the child to have or do. The wise parent knows the child is hurting and is in pain because that parent loves the child enough to say no. The parent also knows that giving in to that child would relieve the pain, but what about the long-term consequences? All of us know what happens to children whose parents never say no. They grow up spoiled, expecting the world to give them everything on a silver platter. Think of the tragedy involved when parents give in and it's not in the child's long-range best interest.

Then Dr. Leddo points out we need to thank God for helping us to grow by permitting some pain to take place in our lives because the result of growing pains is growth. And growth is necessary for progress. It's safe to say that pain is never pleasant, but it is frequently profitable.

A major source of pain in our lives can be wrapped up in one word—*relationships*. As a rule of thumb, if you are getting along well with the important people in your life (mate, parents, children, siblings, employer, employees, etc.), you are probably a reasonably happy person. If you're not getting along well with these people who are important to you—well, that's an entirely different ball game. Fortunately, even as you read these words, you are getting along better and better with the person who holds the key to building winning relationships—you.

HELP FOR THOSE WITH SERIOUS MOOD SWINGS

Dr. Leland M. Heller gives some strong endorsements to the concept that optimism, motivation, and positive thinking have a scientifically valid place in health care. In his book *Life at the Border,* Dr. Heller deals primarily with what most physicians call the *borderline personality disorder*. He believes it is much more positive and beneficial to people who are afflicted to refer to them as simply borderline or victims of the borderline disorder.

He points out that between 4 and 8 percent of the population is afflicted with this disorder, and he describes it as one of the major preventable causes of child abuse, divorce, substance abuse, and impulsive, violent crimes. He says the borderline disorder is basically a form of epilepsy in the brain's limbic system. Victims have abnormal neurological examinations, brain waves, memory, and sleep cycles. Borderline disorder is clearly a medical problem. The limbic system is malfunctioning.

It is also an emotional problem. Borderlines have no self-esteem, no effective psychological defenses, and they have spent a lifetime with crippling mood swings (extreme optimism and pessimism), horribly painful dysphoria, and frequent bouts of psychosis that have distorted their understanding of life and people. It is not their fault. They didn't cause it, and they have been powerless to stop it. Without the proper medication, they had essentially no chance to recover, even with counseling.

Dr. Heller says that between seven and twenty million Americans suffer from this incredibly painful illness, and virtually no one wants to help them. He then makes a startling and exciting statement in his book when he says,

In my opinion, it is unlikely a borderline will ever achieve mental wellness without reading positive books. They are as important as Prozac. They teach you how to be a successful person. While even five minutes a day would be of enormous help, I recommend at least 15 minutes every morning and five to 15 minutes before you go to bed at night. Try reading at lunch—the more you read, the better and the faster you'll recover.

He then says,

Motivational tapes are a must. Your car and tape player can be the best school in the world. This is a secret most successful people already know. You can let great ideas enter your

mind without any effort and the more you listen the healthier you become. Listen to tapes while getting dressed, cleaning the house, doing dishes, cooking, etc. You need to get the right information to change the way you think and feel.

The next part is obviously the part I like best:

Zig Ziglar has a magic effect on many borderlines. Zig is not only funny and motivational, but he describes values and attitudes that improve one's chances for a happy, successful life. Untreated borderlines have shifting values due to their illness. Zig Ziglar gives a set of values borderlines (and the rest of us) can believe in and live by. You may disagree with some things—not everyone agrees on everything (especially the religion)—but you will likely find few areas of disagreement. I greatly admire the work he does and what his tapes have done for my patients.

Needless to say, it's gratifying to get this kind of an endorsement from the scientific community. IMPORTANT: I'm not suggesting that motivational books and recordings are the answer for borderlines. They will help, but if you are or even think you may be a borderline, you start with a skilled physician and listen to him or her. I also encourage you to read Dr. Heller's book, *Life at the Border.*

BEEN KNOCKED DOWN? TRY THIS

Remember how your favorite teacher made you feel like you were the most important student in the class, and the impact it had on your grades, versus the one who didn't want to be bothered with you? The same thing holds true in business. The employee who feels that the employer likes him is far more likely to do a better job.

The people around us can largely sense how we feel about them, but some people are good at masking their feelings so it's helpful to remove all doubt from a positive perspective and let people know when they are appreciated. Bob Hope was recently asked why he did not retire and go fishing. His response was classic: "Fish don't applaud." And all of us want and need applause. Someone said that when you applaud someone else, both of you feel better.

One of the most moving examples of what I'm talking about occurred several years ago during one of the "Born to Win" classes we teach in Dallas. One company sent four couples to attend the seminar. At the seminar I speak every day, but most of the time is spent around small tables in groups of eight people. Each time anyone does anything, the other seven people write a little note on our special pad called "I like _____ because . . ." (This helps them remember to look for the good.) They put the person's name in the blank and give some specific, observable behavior as to why they like the person. The four couples were very much impressed with the potential benefit from following this procedure.

After the first day, they went to one of Dallas's finest, most expensive restaurants. They hit the jackpot as far as a waiter is concerned. He had been there over twenty years and had been a waiter for over twenty-five years. He was superb and professional in every way. He was there when he was needed, but he did not join the party. He was friendly but not familiar. When a need arose, he would miraculously appear, fill the need, and graciously withdraw so the couples could enjoy one another's company. He was really good and contributed to their enjoyment of the meal.

THE BEST THINGS IN LIFE AREN'T THINGS

When they got ready to leave, each person wrote the waiter an "I like _____ because . . ." and left a 25 percent tip. In that particular restaurant that represented a substantial amount of money. They walked out the door and had gone about a hundred or more feet when they heard the voice of the waiter calling, "Wait a minute, folks. Wait a minute!"

He came running up to them, waving those eight slips of paper in his hand. When he drew abreast, he said, "You know, I've been a waiter over twenty-five years," and then he broke down and wept for a few seconds before he regained his composure. When he did, he said, "In all those years this is the most beautiful experience I've ever had. I will never forget tonight." With that he turned and walked back into the restaurant. He never said a word about the tip.

The waiter was highly motivated and deeply moved by the experience. QUESTION: Wouldn't you have loved being at the next table that waiter served? Don't you know they got the best service that anyone has ever gotten in the history of the restaurant business? He was motivated, and as a direct result of a simple action that took no more than a minute or two of each person's time, his effectiveness and enjoyment of life went up substantially.

Yes, the waiter's benefits were considerable, but as great as his benefits were, the benefits each one of the eight diners received were substantially greater. I wish you could have been in class the next day when those four couples walked in. They were higher than kites! Figuratively speaking, we had to pull them down off the ceiling to get them in the door! They were so moved by the experience that they bought a case of the "I like _____ because . . ." pads and said they were going to saturate the world with them.

ENCOURAGERS ARE WINNERS AND PRODUCERS

Unfortunately, many people seldom, if ever, get that word of encouragement that all of us so badly need. Encouragement is needed in the home, school, church, business, government, and all of society. Probably every member of your family, all of your friends, and every one of your associates and acquaintances feel, and some would even tell you, that they don't get enough praise and recognition.

A word of concern, encouragement, and appreciation will

do wonders for just about anybody. The impact might not be as dramatic as it was in the waiter's life, but you never know when a kind word will make you a catalyst in someone's life.

THE TABLES CAN TURN

I know of at least one occasion when the person who was waited on got the tip! Sometimes a simple compliment can produce outstanding results. Larry Lippert, who taught at Balyki High School in Bath, Illinois, tells this story: One of the students' assignments for his class that teaches these over-the-top concepts is to say or do something nice for a member of the family. Jon told Mr. Lippert that he could not do that because he did not live at home. Mr. Lippert asked Jon if he ever went home, and Jon replied that he did eat the evening meal there on Sunday night, so Mr. Lippert challenged him to take advantage of that opportunity.

Monday morning Jon ran into Mr. Lippert's classroom waving a ten-dollar bill and shouting, "It worked!" Jon had told his mother, "Thank you for supper. It was the best fried chicken I've ever eaten."

Jon said the tears started streaming down his mother's face, and she jumped up and ran out of the room. She came back, walked up behind Jon, and started hugging him. Jon felt her slip something into his shirt pocket—it was a ten-dollar bill.

QUESTION: Who do you think got the most out of the compliment, Jon or his mother? P.S. Children, including yours, can be taught to be courteous and thoughtful.

Mr. Lippert carefully explained to Jon that good things would happen if he continued to give honest and sincere compliments but that he would not get ten dollars every time he said something nice. That's sound advice, and I will elaborate on it by adding that sincere compliments, freely given, demand nothing in return. However, let me caution you to be careful in what you say. Never say anything to anyone personally that you would not say behind the person's back. That's flattery, and flattery ultimately is negative and destructive. Yes, encouraging someone can do a lot for the person, but it does infinitely more for the encourager.

STRANGLERS VS. WRANGLERS

Author Ted Engstrom sums it up beautifully and gives us additional insights and advantages to being good-finders and encouragers in his story on Wranglers and Stranglers:

Years ago there was a group of brilliant young men at the University of Wisconsin, who seemed to have amazing creative literary talent. They were would-be poets, novelists, and essayists. They were extraordinary in their ability to put the English language to its best use. These promising young men met regularly to read and critique each other's work. And critique it they did!

These men were merciless with one another. They dissected the most minute literary expression into a hundred pieces. They were heartless, tough, even mean in their criticism. The sessions became such arenas of literary criticism that the members of this exclusive club called themselves the Stranglers.

Not to be outdone, the women of literary talent in the university were determined to start a comparable club of their own. They called themselves the Wranglers. They, too, read their works to one another. But there was one great difference. The criticism was much softer, more positive, more encouraging. Sometimes, there was almost no criticism at all. Every effort, even the most feeble one, was encouraged.

Twenty years later an alumnus of the university was doing an exhaustive study of his classmates' careers when he noticed a vast difference in the literary accomplishments of the Stranglers as opposed to the Wranglers. Of all the bright young men in the Stranglers, not one had made a significant literary accomplishment of any kind. From the Wranglers had come six or more successful writers, some of national renown such as Marjorie Kinnan Rawlings, who wrote The Yearling.

Talent between the two? Probably the same. Level of education? Not much difference. But the Stranglers strangled and choked out hope, while the Wranglers wrangled and pulled the best out of one another. The Stranglers promoted an atmosphere of contention and self-doubt. The Wranglers highlighted the best, not the worst.

Again, when we see ourselves in the proper perspective and have the confidence to be honest in our evaluations, we can eliminate the setting of double standards, have a better sense of humor, and laugh at ourselves when we see identifications like these submitted by an unknown author.

Use the Same Measuring Stick

When the other person blows up, he's nasty. When we do it, it's righteous indignation.

When he's set in his ways, he's obstinate. When you are, you're just being firm.

When he doesn't like your friends, he's prejudiced. When you don't like his, you're simply showing good judgment of human nature.

When he tries to be accommodating, he's polishing the apple. When you do it, you're using tact.

When he takes time to do things, he's dead slow. When you take ages, you're deliberate.

When he sees flaws, he's picky. When you do, you're discriminating.

When he reads the riot act, he's vicious and insensitive. When you do it, you're just being honest for his own good.

These little quips certainly point out double standards, and since we've been talking about making the last deposit into our minds a positive one, keep reading to find out what can happen when you measure up to your own standards. Before you get started, I want you to really think about two extremely important points from this chapter. The first is that when you accept yourself and learn to get along with yourself it's easy to get along with most other people. The second major premise is that when life knocks you down, the best way to get back up is to help someone else get up.

YOU DON'T NEED CREDENTIALS

One of the most delightful letters I've ever received was from clinical psychologist Jocelyn K. Fuller, Ph.D., who first bought into our concepts at a sales seminar. Since our sales training and all of our other training programs are built on the over-the-top principles, she quickly related to the concepts. She applied the philosophy we've been talking about to her life and made the following observation:

> I have found that when I care about other people and sincerely try to help them get what they want out of life, my life becomes much richer. As my attitude changed, I found that I began to attract people who were positive in contrast to people who were negative. This facilitated the beginning of the development of an exciting network of wonderful friends and business associates.

She also stated,

> I have found that I no longer need my long list of academic credentials to validate my existence or to prove that I am a worthwhile person. Although these credentials are helpful in my business endeavors, it is nice to realize that I am separate from them and that I am a worthwhile person in and of myself.

She continued,

> I have become much more interested in the business world and have developed many creative ideas as to how to integrate my psychology background into the business world.

This results in a much more profitable situation than a normal psychological practice and at the same time will help a vastly larger number of people.

I strongly encourage you to reread what Dr. Fuller had to say and to underline it several times. She summed up a tremendous amount of the philosophy of this book in a very few words. That's exciting!

CHAPTER FOURTEEN

Commitment + Courage + Discipline = Freedom

Ambition—fueled by compassion, wisdom, and integrity—is a powerful force for good that will turn the wheels of industry and open the door of opportunity for you and countless thousands of other people. Fueled by greed and a lust for power, ambition is a destructive force that ultimately does irreparable damage to the individual in its grasp and to the people within its reach.   Zig Ziglar

How important is commitment? Sam Walton, in his book *Made in America,* gave as his number one rule for building a business,

Commit to your business. I think I overcame every single one of my personal shortcomings by the sheer passion I brought to my work.

John Maxwell declared,

> *Commitment keeps me going when things get tough. It is the driving force that empowers me to do great things. My conviction keeps others going when things get tough. People around us are motivated by emotion, our conviction, that tangible sense of morale. People do not follow a leader because of character; they follow a leader because of conviction.*

People do not do a thing because it's right; they do a thing because they feel it's right. When we act on our conviction, others are drawn to us. Without conviction we may communicate truths, but we'll develop no new leaders, which must always be a major objective. It's true—before any great accomplishment is achieved, it's believed in the heart and mind.

THOSE NEW YEAR'S RESOLUTIONS

On January 7, 1992, I drove past the Plano Recreation Center where I formerly did my exercise and weight lifting (I had to ease up on the weight lifting because I was bulking up and a lot of folks thought I was on steroids). I drove past because there were no parking places. The next day I managed to squeeze into a parking space. However, when I went inside to the Nautilus room, there was a line behind every machine. You cannot get a good workout if you have to wait from five to fifteen minutes between each repetition, so I went to the front desk and asked the young man what was going on. He smiled and told me not to give it a thought. "Wait about three weeks and everything will be back to normal because these are the 'New Year's Resolution' people."

In most cases, according to Fred Smith, a New Year's resolution is little more than a New Year's confession: "I confess, I've got to lose some weight." "I confess, I've got to get better organized and spend more time with my family." "I confess, I've got to go back to school and complete my education." The list is endless, and most people keep resolutions as long as there is no trouble, time, or work involved and they happen to remember them.

Having said that, let me emphasize that the resolution is the most important part of the goal-setting process because it is the first step. You need to repeat that resolution many times, especially to someone such as a mate, employer, or close friend who will hold you accountable. When you've made the resolution enough times, the day will come when you will verbally stomp your foot and say, "I'm going to do it!" You've made the decision, and that is a mammoth leap forward.

Now you realize you must have a plan of action. This is true whether you've resolved to get more education, lose weight, quit smoking, get better organized, build a house, or whatever. When the plan is in place, then and only then do you make a commitment. No responsible person will make a commitment until he or she has a plan of action that gives a reasonable chance of fulfilling that commitment. Please understand that if you are pursuing a long-range goal, encouragement is the key to reaching that goal. You get this encouragement, as well as ongoing training and education, from seminar leaders, friends, associates, employers, and others. Reading inspiring material and listening to motivational tapes daily will provide the encouragement all of us need.

Over a period of time we become convinced that we can reach the objectives we have set when we make that commitment. In a nutshell, a resolution—repeated regularly and reinforced with encouragement and training—becomes a commitment, and commitment is the direct path to accomplishment and ultimately freedom.

NOTE: Carefully reread that last paragraph, combine it with the rest of this chapter, and you have an excellent formula to help you fulfill your commitment and give it "one more shot" when things are tough.

COMMITMENT

Commitment is the factor that will make the difference in your own life and permit you to make a difference in the lives of other people. A firm commitment also enables you to dig deeper and bring out the extra or hidden physical, mental, and spiritual resources that are available to you.

We are also now at the point where we are free to admit that we don't have all the answers and haven't had all the experiences. This intriguing combination of confidence (that you are a capable, unique person) and humility (you recognize that you don't know it all) gives you some exciting options. For example, this attitude frees you to call a brainstorming session with friends, family, and associates and ask them to toss in ideas that might be of value to you. This is also a good time to isolate yourself for some quiet thinking and praying time. This time alone could produce some invaluable ideas that might be the missing pieces to some of the puzzles of your life.

The point in the entire matter of commitment is that once you have made that commitment, you call on all of your resources instead of just throwing in the towel. It's when you've done all that you can do that your real value to yourself, your family, your company, and your country really kicks in. Without commitment, the "I'll do what I have to do and nothing more" individual takes the easy way out and calls it quits.

I say to you that if you'll put the qualities of conviction, commitment, and courage on the front burner, almost regardless of how few or how many birthdays you have had, you might well be just getting started.

Why is commitment so essential to climbing over the top? Consider our two greatest presidents. EXAMPLE: George Washington won only two battles in the Revolutionary War. But he won the last battle, and that is the one that counts. The British drove Washington down through Long Island and into Brooklyn. They drove him across the East River and all the way up Manhattan Island. They drove him to White Plains and then on to Hackensack. They drove him from Hackensack to Brandywine. They drove him on and on, defeating him time after time. But a few days later at Yorktown, British General Cornwallis surrendered, handing over his sword, as was the gallant custom in those days. He said to Washington, "Sir, I salute you, not only as a great leader of men, but as an indomitable Christian gentleman who wouldn't give up" (*Leadership:* The Economics Press, Fairfield, N.J.). With commitment, as long as there is hope, you just won't quit.

Abraham Lincoln, our other truly great president, would have, in today's terminology, been branded a "loser." In baseball terms he was hitting .200 since he lost twelve of the fifteen most significant battles of his life. The last victory, however, was the big one; he was elected president and was the key to freeing the slaves and preserving the union.

IT TAKES ENERGY TO KEEP COMMITMENTS

Over-the-top people need lots of energy, and that energy level, in most cases, can be traced directly to the care we (that's you) give our bodies. Couple that with the fact that, in most cases, by following sound health procedures, we feel better now and for a lifetime. As a matter of fact, the way we take care of our health is a classic example of the difference between pleasure and happiness.

I'll have to admit that from a pure pleasure point of view, no one enjoys eating rich desserts or having some fat mixed into the diet more than I do. I'll also admit that there are many occasions when I would rather relax than work out or take a vigorous walk, and that's when I'm faced with a choice.

Am I willing to give up some of the energy I have as a direct result of the discipline I have imposed upon myself for over twenty years? Am I willing to take a chance on my body deteriorating more rapidly and taking my mind with it? Am I willing to give up the dreams I have in my personal, family, and business lives while encouraging people from all walks of life to be, do, and have more of what life has to offer?

When I examine it in a very realistic manner, my conclusion is absolutely clear. I just flat feel so good that I would not consider making the swap! To be candid, I'm quite happy to be able to wear clothes I could not have forced my way into when I was twenty-five years old! I'm very happy being a companion to my wife and being with my children and grandchildren. I'm happy to be able to follow busy travel, speaking, and writing schedules that require an incredible amount of energy. My point is clear: Not only do I get considerable pleasure from this discipline, but in the long run I am getting even more happiness. Yes, we do have a choice as to what we can do with our health, and the choice we make is critical. Sometimes it's awfully tough to follow through, but this next example will give you some solid reasons for doing exactly that.

THE CHOICE IS YOURS

When I was in the process of shaping up by jogging and eating properly, I labored under the erroneous belief that I had to run every day and that I had to do it early in the morning. That was tough on me because I preferred to start my day a little more slowly, but I'd made an unbreakable commitment that I was going to get in shape and lose weight.

Then there was that day. I flew to Seattle, Washington, made a talk, caught a plane, and flew back home that evening. By the time I drove home and got ready for bed, it was exactly 4:00 A.M. My clock was already set to awaken me at 5:30 A.M. so I could do my running. As I sat there looking at that clock, I realized I would get only ninety minutes of sleep and began wrestling with the decision of whether or not I really wanted to get up that early.

There were some basic things I knew at that point. First, I knew that I would be dog-tired and would not be very effective from a productivity point of view for the rest of the day.

However, as I wrestled with the decision, I recognized that I'd made a commitment that, come what may, at 5:30 A.M. I was going to get up and do my running.

To be candid, fear entered the picture. I was afraid that if I made an exception and slept in because I was tired and sleepy, it would be easier to make an exception the next time, and I knew that the exception often becomes the rule. The commitment goes out the window. The goals would never be reached, and I would become just another statistic in the world of "what might have been." As those thoughts entered my mind, I reached for the clock, checked the setting for 5:30 A.M., lay down, and went to sleep.

It's true that when that clock sounded off I did not feel like getting up, but it's also true that my passion to keep my commitment rolled me out of bed. I did not enjoy the run, I had a fairly unproductive day, and overall I did not feel my usual perky self. Having said that, I suppose my next statement will surprise you. I consider that one of the most important choices I've ever made. I kept my commitment, and keeping the commitment that time made it easier to do it the next time, the next, and the next.

EXCEPTIONS ARE DANGEROUS TO YOUR HEALTH AND FUTURE

The basic truth is, exceptions are the most dangerous things that we have to deal with in our lives. They get us off track, and once the exception is made, it's easier to make exceptions the second time, then the third, and so on. It's also true that I was in bed that evening by 8:00 P.M., and the next morning at 5:30 A.M. I rose with exuberance, did my running, and felt better than I'd felt in a long time.

We're all familiar with exceptions. We go on a sensible low-fat diet, and after a few days, we decide it wouldn't be too bad to have just one order of french fries, so we make that exception. The only problem is that a couple of days later we make

> **Exceptions are the most dangerous things that we have to deal with in our lives. They get us off track.**

that exception again, and you know the rest of the story.

How many alcoholics have thought they could make that exception and have taken just one drink with tragic results? I can't tell you the number of smokers who have put the cigarettes down for a year or two, and for whatever reason they're tempted, make that one exception, and bang! They're puffing away full-time. Watch those exceptions! Make that motivation daily! Make certain you have great input. Surround yourself with the right kinds of people. Read good books. Review your goals and objectives regularly so that you can be constantly reminded of the benefits that come your way with setting your goals and keeping your commitments.

Exceptions in all areas of life can be disastrous. Many times a happy marriage is destroyed because the husband or wife is tempted, makes that one exception, and commits adultery. A person who has behaved in a law-abiding manner all of his life gets into financial difficulty, makes that one exception, steals or embezzles money, and gets away with it. The next time he becomes even bolder, and a habit is established, again with disastrous results.

As a final note on this thinking, need I remind you of the people you have encountered (and perhaps you have experienced it yourself) who got on a particular program of study, growth, or weight loss and were making substantial progress. They made that exception and a year later had completely abandoned a program that was producing real results.

The person probably fell victim to the exception syndrome that is the major—but not the only—reason many people abandon winning habits and procedures and go back to old customs and habits.

WHEN YOU "SLIP"

When you do make that exception and break a commitment for bettering your life, what do you do? First, accept the fact that you made an exception, which was a mistake, but not a disaster. Understand that it is a choice you made and not something that happened to you.

Also understand that you probably made that slip when you were experiencing a "down time," such as anxiety, depression, or boredom. You could also have made that slip as a result of a happy event, such as a social function where everyone was laughing, joking, and nibbling on goodies.

Now what? Forgive yourself, back away, renew your commitment immediately, and get back on the program. That would include getting back into the self-talk process you've already started as a result of *Over the Top.* Start with a confession: "I admit I slipped, which is unlike me. This is one bump on the road to reaching my objective. I now commit myself to get back on the right path because I know I am a winner."

YOU CAN BUILD ON COURAGE

QUESTION: What is the most important single quality an individual must possess to be successful and go over the top? ANSWER: I honestly don't know because if you had only one quality, you'd fall short in accomplishing anything significant in life. However, I do believe that courage is a must if you're going to extract from life even a fraction of what life has to offer. The kind of courage, however, is very important because integrity makes incredible demands—and courage enables you to meet the demands.

Sidney Harris said it well:

I'm tired of hearing about men with the courage of their convictions. Nero and Caligula and Attila and Hitler had the courage of their convictions. No one had the courage to examine their convictions or to change them, which is the true test of character.

Courage with the right convictions, built on integrity and wrapped in confidence, will upgrade your performance and increase the productivity of those around you. That builds employment security and gives you an infinitely better chance for success in all areas of life.

Conviction always precedes serious commitment. A person of conviction becomes so wrapped up in what he or she needs to do that it moves into the must-do category. People who are convicted with a mission are more convincing when they share those convictions with others.

It is my personal conviction, as a result of what you have learned in *Over the Top,* that you are convicted to do something about your own life, as far as improving it is concerned. In this process you have also realized that one of the best ways to do that is to persuade friends, family, and associates to join you in these concepts that will also enrich their lives. By this very process, you, therefore, ensure a greater and more stable country and economy, which gives you substantial benefits as well.

It takes courage to make commitments at any age. Just in case you're thinking you wish you had acquired this information when you were younger, or you want to keep it in mind to use later in life, let me assure you that the timing is perfect. You are *exactly* the right age. Keep reading. The last chapter—almost regardless of your age—will convince you that now is the time and it's your turn.

TIME AND TIMING

For a number of years, people have considered age sixty-five to be the time to go out to pasture. Many prestigious universities, religious denominations, Fortune 500 companies, the military, airlines, and countless numbers of organizations automatically retire their people at age sixty or sixty-five. Let's explore whether or not age is really the issue.

When Bismarck was chancellor of Germany in the 1870s, he observed that virtually all of his powerful enemies were men who were sixty-five years old or older. He persuaded the German legislature to pass legislation making sixty-five the mandatory age for retirement. It had nothing whatever to do with a decline in their mental faculties or a drop-off in productivity—and certainly had nothing to do with senility. It had to do with their wisdom, experience, power, organization, and everything you can name in a positive vein that generated fear and respect for them in Bismarck's mind. For some strange reason other countries in Europe followed suit, and the policy was eventually adopted in America.

> *You're not old until you have lost all of your marvels.*
>
> **Anonymous**

What an absolute tragedy to encourage people to quit when they are at the very peak of their intellect, wisdom, contacts, power, experience, organization, and networks that they have built over a period of a lifetime! Could that be the reason that the only time the Bible mentions retirement it is as a punishment?

Douglas MacArthur said it magnificently well in his farewell address to the cadets at West Point:

Whatever your years there is in every being's heart the love of wonder, the undaunted challenge of events, and an unfailing childlike feel for "what next" on the job and in the game of life. You're as young as your faith, as old as your doubts; as young as your self-confidence, as old as your fear; as young as your hope, as old as your despair. In the central place of your heart, there is a recording chamber. So long as it receives messages of beauty, hope, cheer, and courage, so long are you young.

THIS I BELIEVE

None of us are guaranteed even five more minutes of life, but I firmly believe that in my case I'm at least five—maybe ten, could be fifteen—years away from hitting my peak. I honestly believe my career is in front of me rather than behind me. The word *retirement* is not in my vocabulary. I'm having more fun than ever, and my mail indicates that my effectiveness is greater, so why should I quit doing something I love to do and believe is making a difference in the lives of others?

The question is, Am I being realistic? I hope so, and I obviously believe I am. From a health standpoint, my blood pressure is lower than it was at age forty-five (126/64); my cholesterol level is lower (158) and my resting heart rate (51) is lower than it was at that time. One reason I believe my future is in front of me is that when I was seventy I stayed on the treadmill nearly three minutes longer than when I was forty-five years old, overweight, and out of shape. I truly feel like a "recycled teenager." If I never conceive of another idea, I now have more on the drawing board than I can possibly get done in the next five years.

I am shifting my schedule somewhat because I'm reducing the number of speaking engagements I accept by nearly 50 percent, beginning in 1997. I'm doing that primarily because I'm now writing a daily newspaper column that is syndicated by Creators Syndicate of Los Angeles, and my optimism tells me that a daily radio program is inevitable. That's been a "burr under my saddle" for several years, and it's time to make it happen. I believe the benefits of a ninety-second encouraging message people could hear on their way to work and on their way back home would make a difference in their lives. In addition, I have five books that I plan to write.

I'm certainly grateful that I'm blessed with the health that I have at age seventy. I believe a portion of that health can be attributed to decisions I made twenty-five years ago, when I started eating sensibly and exercising regularly.

HAVING BIRTHDAYS WITHOUT GETTING OLD

Psychiatrist Smiley Blanton says that in his years of practice he has never met a senile person, regardless of age, who developed and maintained a healthy, lively interest in other people. That sounded pretty strong to me, and wishing to validate it from yet another source, I called Dr. Les Carter at Minirth Meier New Life Clinics because of the clinic's reputation and because of my relationship with the doctors there. I made a statement to Dr. Carter and asked its validity. I said, "Alzheimer's is a disease, but senility, in most cases, is the result of a long series of poor choices." Dr. Carter assured me that, when stated in that way, it was correct.

Other studies indicate that if we will do three things—(1) eat sensibly and exercise regularly; (2) continue to learn, grow, and develop mentally; and (3) maintain an interest in other people—our chances of becoming senile are slim.

It is my conviction that we can have lots of birthdays without getting old. As previously stated, it has to do with the choices we make and the attitudes we maintain. About two years ago I was on a radio talk show, and a woman called in with an advanced case of the "blahs." She said she was fifty-three years old, she had never done anything with her life, and now "it was too late." Here's the way the dialogue went from that point:

ZIG (in my best southern drawl): Ma'am, how old did you say you are?

Commitment + Courage + Discipline = Freedom **287**

DISTRESSED WOMAN: I'm fifty-three, and it's too late for me.

ZIG: Ma'am, at fifty-three you are just a spring chicken. As a matter of fact, does your mama know where you are?

The woman (no longer distressed) started laughing, and we had a productive and beneficial visit. It's amazing what a little humor and an attitude adjustment will do for you!

> *Remember: It's never too late to make the most of what you are.*

I would like to suggest that we consider the athletic terms and business terms I discussed earlier as they relate to momentum and the way it affects our mental, physical, and spiritual lives. At the moment, your momentum might be downhill, but just as in the baseball analogy we can apply "stoppers." I believe stoppers are at least "slow-downers" on the descent into the deterioration of our health. In the example with the fifty-three-year-old woman, I injected one stopper, and that's humor. I again encourage you to find a copy of *Anguished English* and/or *More Anguished English* by Richard Lederer, and I challenge you not to laugh out loud as you read some of those real-life situations.

NOW IS THE TIME—FOR YOU

Regardless of your age, the time is now for you to make a move to being an even greater you. FOR EXAMPLE: At age ninety-six, George Burns signed a five-year deal with Las Vegas's Riviera Hotel instead of one for ten years because he wasn't sure the resort would last ten years. "They wanted to make it ten years," he said, "but what's the hurry? If they're still around after five years, we'll talk." Of course, there were those two Methuselahs in the world of athletics;

pitcher Nolan Ryan retired at age forty-six, and boxer George Foreman is still fighting championship fights at age forty-seven.

Just in case you're more than fifty-three years of age, let me point out that research conclusively proves—and my long-life experience validates the point—that almost regardless of your age and physical condition at the moment, there's still a good chance that you can make up some lost ground. Studies on people eighty and ninety years old who used wheelchairs revealed that when they got on an exercise program and started lifting light weights, many of them literally climbed out of those wheelchairs and resumed far more active lives.

This is not to say it's easy, because in most cases it's not, but the rewards are enormous and it definitely can be done. I encourage you to remember that you did not get in the shape you're in overnight and you're not going to correct it overnight, either. To paraphrase an earlier statement, health is not what you acquire "overnight"— it's something you achieve "over time."

Author Gail Sheehy says that people with positive outlooks are far more likely to extend their "second adulthoods" (don't you love that phrase?) into healthy and satisfying later lives. But she also says the decision to renew ourselves after age sixty-five requires a real investment of faith, risk, and physical discipline. However, "experts in gerontology make a clear distinction between passive aging and successful aging." She states,

Successful aging is actually a career choice, a conscious commitment to continuing self-education and the development of a whole set of strategies. If we don't constantly rebuild the body, it becomes rickety and weak. If we don't keep "growing" the brain by challenging it, life becomes dull and draining.

These are certainly words of wisdom that will enable you not only to live well but also to finish well.

Commitment + Courage + Discipline = Freedom   **289**

I can with considerable conviction say that with your new picture, your attitude, and your goals, amazing things can happen—as a matter of fact, are happening—right now in your mind, which is where everything starts.

QUESTION: What are the benefits that come to the committed, disciplined, courageous individual? Let's see.

FREEDOM AND OPPORTUNITY

*F*reedom is a word you hear a great deal about, and yet it is truly one of the most misunderstood of all words as far as its meanings and implications are concerned. For example, many of today's songs utter the refrain, "I want to be free." Unfortunately, in too many cases, people are singing about being free to say what they want to say and do what they want to do, regardless of the consequences to themselves or anyone else. Does that constitute real freedom?

> *When you exercise your freedom to express yourself at the lowest level, you ultimately condemn yourself to live at that level.*

Freedom, according to the dictionary, means "exemption from power or control by another." It is liberty, independence, and the capacity to exercise choice, free will.

You're free in our society to indulge in smoking and drinking and, as a practical matter, illegal drugs and virtually every immoral behavior. The choice is yours, but that choice all too often becomes a habit and then an addiction, which means that at that point you've given up your freedom and have chosen slavery.

Pythagoras said, "No man is free who cannot command himself."

Gandhi said, "It is my certain conviction that no man loses his freedom except through his own weakness."

Kingsley said, "There are two freedoms—the false, where a man is free to do what he likes; the true, where a man is free to do what he ought."

The Bible says, "And you shall know the truth, and the truth shall make you free."

Will Durant, the noted historian, said, "Have we too much freedom? Have we so long ridiculed authority in the family, discipline in education, rules in art, decency in conduct, and law in the state that our liberation has brought us close to chaos in the family and the schools, in morals, arts, ideas, and government? We forgot to make ourselves intelligent when we made ourselves free."

James Howard, the president of Honinteg International, which, incidentally, is derived from the words *honesty* and *integrity,* identifies some additional freedoms that come our way with this over-the-top approach to life: freedom from "bad attitudes, confusion, low productivity, poor motivation, blaming others, selfishness, not enough time, dishonesty, fear, distrust, poor self-image, lack of direction, lack of teamwork, and lack of pride," and "freedom to do the right things right."

Now having identified freedom, I believe that with the development of the qualities (which you're in the process of doing), you have the freedom that is real—the freedom to be your best self.

IS THIS REAL FREEDOM?

I have talked a great deal about ethics, morals, values, and the qualities that enable a person to be successful in every department of life, but a major benefit that comes from developing these qualities is freedom itself.

How much freedom does a person who cheats on income tax, shoplifts, or steals from an employer really have? Think of the fear dishonest people live in—fear that the law will discover them, that they will be arrested, perhaps serve time in prison, embarrass themselves, deny their family their presence and financial support, not to mention the moral and spiritual guidance and direction they should be providing. The freedom to steal, when exercised, literally entraps people, and they lose the freedom they claim as their own. Even if they are not caught, they're still in bondage.

A friend of mine who is a mathematical genius and a marketing expert wanted to buy his mother-in-law a small business. Fortunately, he is able to look at a set of books and determine their validity. Needless to say, he wanted to buy a profitable business. He examined the books of over twenty small companies, and in 100 percent of the cases, because the books looked suspicious, he asked each owner a question: Do you have another set of books? One hundred percent of them answered in the affirmative.

Interestingly enough, some of them had stolen only a minimal amount of money in the grand scheme of things—$2,000, $5,000, $10,000. But think of what that cost them each time a disgruntled employee left who was in the know. The employer lived in fear that his secret would be out. Each time the telephone rang at the business or at home, he was always wondering if someone was checking up on him from a tax perspective. When he filed his tax returns and was audited, can't you imagine the trauma he underwent? That's not freedom.

FREEDOM TO BE HAPPY

Loyalty is one of the qualities I've identified as being present in the people who are genuinely successful. Let's look at loyalty in family life. In all the years I've been beating the bushes, including several thousand nights on the road and roughly five million miles of flying, I've seen men and women from every walk of life in virtually every situation known to man. In my lifetime, I have never encountered a genuinely happy man or woman who was not completely loyal to his or her mate.

Freedom by some is perceived as refusing to be committed

to one relationship, but is that real freedom? I've seen numbers of people half drunk or under the influence laughing, in many cases far too loudly, and apparently having a good time with individuals other than their spouses as they tried to mask or drown their feelings of guilt and fear.

When they got home and had to face their spouses, when they picked up their children and told them how much they loved them and how much they missed them, what were their real feelings? QUESTION: How many happy hypocrites do you know?

What about those late night telephone calls, which in 99 percent of the cases are routine, and yet many times they cause the guilty party to jump for fear it's about that rendezvous last week? When a letter comes personally addressed to the home or business and the mate sees it, how many fears are raised in the mind of the guilty party because questions are raised in the mind of the innocent mate? Is that freedom?

> **❝ The truth is, fear and immorality are two of the greatest inhibitors of performance. ❞**

Living a double life never permits you the freedom of being your best in either one of the lives you are living. Unless you have the freedom to be your best, you are not really free. In this day of AIDS, there's also another genuine fear. Faithfulness to your mate eliminates the possibility of AIDS in the overwhelming majority of cases.

Dr. J. Allan Petersen expressed it more eloquently and compellingly than anyone I've ever heard in his publication *Better Families:*

> *Lying to anyone has a strange effect of turning that person into an enemy, so when we lie to ourselves we become our own worst enemy.*

Commitment + Courage + Discipline = Freedom **293**

In the tender intimacy of love we find deep pleasure in opening our hearts to another in telling the truth. But when we feel the necessity of lying to the one we love—the one who trusts us implicitly—we're trapped in a double bind. The boomerang comes back.

This is the predicament of the unfaithful husband who still loves his wife. When he comes back, he wants to restore the closeness with her, but he can't tell her what he has done, so he lies again. The lie protects him from her anger and rejection. At the same time it robs him of the tender intimacy he longs for. He can't open his heart to her—every thought must be monitored, every word weighed. Fear grips him lest a lapse of memory betray him. He is indeed his own worst enemy.

When God said, "Do not commit adultery," He knew exactly what He was doing. Adultery ends in humiliation, heartache, and revenge. From the hundreds I've counseled, I know this to be true.

Please understand that the last thing I want to do is hang a guilt trip on you. *Over the Top* is written to prepare you for a better future and is in no way intended as a club to hit you with your past. At this point, I encourage you to completely abandon the what-if game: "What if I had done this, not done that, said this, or said that?" That is counterproductive. You can't saw sawdust.

MERITED OR UNMERITED?

Having said that, I'd like to emphasize that some guilt (merited guilt) is healthy and necessary for your own well-being and the good of mankind. There is a vast difference between merited and unmerited guilt.

Unmerited guilt occurs when a person manipulates you into feeling responsible for causing physical, mental, emotional, or spiritual problems, but in reality you are innocent. You have done nothing wrong, and if you find yourself feeling guilty about something you had nothing to do with, tell yourself (out loud) that you are not to blame.

On the other hand, not to feel and respond to merited or deserved guilt would ultimately lead us into an uncivilized society. Apologizing and asking forgiveness would be things of the past, fidelity in marriage would be history, crimes of all kinds would decimate our society, and civilization would no longer exist.

> *There's harmony and inner peace to be found in following a moral compass that points in the same direction, regardless of fashion or trend.*
>
> Ted Koppel

Society must have a moral compass to direct our lives, and merited guilt is a marvelous guidepost to live by. Merited guilt occurs when you intentionally take any action that harms another person physically, mentally, emotionally, or spiritually. The greater the harm, the greater the feeling of guilt. Fortunately, this guilt can be neutralized or even eliminated with a change of heart, the sincere asking of forgiveness, and restitution to the extent of your ability to do so. The next story is about someone who neutralized her guilt and is now making restitution because she longed for freedom.

LOCK ME UP; I WANT TO BE FREE

For twenty-three years, Katherine Power was a fugitive. She had driven the getaway car in a bank robbery that ended in the death of policeman Walter Schroeder. Extreme depression and the realization that she could not, would not, get better without taking responsibility for her part in the heinous crime led her to surrender.

Commitment + Courage + Discipline = Freedom **295**

Physically, she surrendered to the FBI; emotionally, she surrendered to survive. The self-imposed prison she had been living in, the one she personally constructed out of fear and merited guilt (she denied a wife the companionship and support of her husband and nine children the love of their father), was much worse than the physical building she would ultimately occupy.

Serenity, relief, and hope etched Katherine Power's face when the judge handed down her sentence of eight to twelve years. She was smiling the smile of someone who has been set free after years of unfathomable torture and solitary confinement. Confession is good for the soul.

This next example is not as serious as the last one, but it is still an example of merited guilt. When Gil Hodges was managing the Washington Senators (now the Texas Rangers), he got word that four members of his team had broken curfew. Gil was a no-nonsense, strict disciplinarian kind of guy. He called the whole team together, gave them a piece of his mind, and told them he knew about the curfew being broken and he knew exactly who it was. He said, "However, this time I'm going to let you off the hook. I'm not going to embarrass you by identifying you. What I want you to do is, each one of you put one hundred dollars, which is the fine, on my desk." That evening when Gil stopped by his desk he found seven hundred dollars.

We know when we're guilty even if no one else does. Katherine Power would agree that the saying, "You're as sick as your secrets," has a lot of validity. If you have been living with merited guilt, set yourself free and begin building on a new foundation today.

THE FOUNDATIONAL VALUES

I am talking, as I have been from the first chapter, about values. Why? Foundational values are the base upon which we must build if we're going to be winners in every phase of life. Having them will not guarantee your success in every department, but not having them will guarantee your failure in your quest for some—if not most—of the eight things we've identified that everyone wants.

CONSIDER THIS: In the 1770s, 3 million Americans produced Thomas Jefferson, Alexander Hamilton, George Washington, Benjamin Franklin, John Adams, and James Monroe, among others. In 1997, 266 million Americans produced _____? You fill in the blank. I can't think of one equal to any of our Founding Fathers.

Why is that? According to the Thomas Jefferson Research Institute, in the 1770s over 90 percent of our educational thrust was of an ethical, moral, religious nature. By 1926, the percentage was down to 6 percent, and by 1951, the percentage was so low it could not even be measured. That means that people generally do what they are taught to do and expected to do. That's the reason I've emphasized the importance of ethical values.

Values determine behavior; behavior determines reputation, and according to Laurel Cutter, vice chairman of FCB Leber-Katz Partners, New York City, the only sustainable competitive advantage of any business is its reputation. Just another way of saying the good people really do win.

How important are values? Jim Breck, former chairman of Johnson & Johnson, is a legendary advocate arguing that J & J's credo (foundational values) was responsible for the company's rapid action in taking Tylenol off the market after a poisoning scare. To prove his point, he commissioned a study of the financial performance of U.S. companies that have had a written values statement for at least a generation. The net income of those twenty companies increased by a factor of 23 during a period when the gross national product dropped by a factor of 2½.

It's a fact. The good guys and ladies win. In 1987, Rockdale High School in Conyers, Georgia, coached by Cleveland Stroud, won the state basketball championship. When the season and tournament were over, Coach Stroud discovered that he had used an ineligible player for forty-five seconds. Although that player had zero impact on the outcome of the

Commitment + Courage + Discipline = Freedom **297**

game, Coach Stroud and the team turned the trophy back in. Many people would say—and did say—that they had really won it and should have kept it, but here's one of the ironies of life. Had they kept the trophy, deep down they would have known they had not won it and were not really the state champions. Since they returned the trophy, in their hearts they knew they really did win and were more than champions. That's freedom and the over-the-top way of life.

> **"** *Integrity gives you real freedom because you have nothing to fear, since you have nothing to hide. You will do the right thing, so you will have no guilt.* **"**

In the quest for freedom, many people overlook the fact that only with courage, discipline, and integrity can they obtain genuine freedom. When you remove fear and guilt, your trip over the top will be easier and faster.

Franklin Roosevelt said, "To stand upon the ramparts and die for our principles is heroic, but to sally forth to battle and win for our principles is something more than heroic." Realistically-might add it is more than heroic because it guarantees our freedom.

When you work hard, do an excellent job, and give it your best shot, then—and only then—are you truly free to relax and enjoy the fruits and rewards of your labor. That's freedom.

THE FREEDOM OF DISCIPLINE

The sailor has freedom of the seas only when he has become a slave to the compass. Until he is obedient to the compass, he must stay within sight of the shore. Once he is obedient, he can go anywhere a sailing vessel will take him. When you take the train off the tracks, it's free, but it can't go anywhere. Take the steering wheel out of the automobile and it's under the direction and control of no one, but it can't move. Man is very much the same way. Freedom—real freedom—comes only when discipline, undergirded by moral absolutes, becomes a way of life.

DISCIPLINE MAKES A DIFFERENCE

Discipline is one of those qualities that gives us an enormous amount of freedom. Rhonda Harrington Kelly, in her book *Divine Discipline,* points out that discipline of self is not caught, it is taught. You become both the teacher and the student. For example, we are heading in freedom's direction when we discipline ourselves to delay some of the pleasures of life at the moment so we can enjoy financial security later. Genuine happiness and freedom from fear go with knowing we've provided for our own financial retirement and the education of our children. There's happiness in knowing we can contribute to worthwhile causes and be a support to our parents if they need it—that's freedom. That's real freedom.

> *Discipline is the habit of taking consistent action until one can perform with unconscious competence. Discipline weighs ounces but regret weighs tons.*
> **Jhoon Rhee**

In her book *All That Was Ever Ours,* Elisabeth Elliot points out that while freedom and discipline have come to be re-

Commitment + Courage + Discipline = Freedom **299**

garded as mutually exclusive, freedom, in fact, is the final reward of self-discipline.

> *When I discipline myself to eat properly, live morally, exercise regularly, grow mentally and spiritually, and not put any drugs or alcohol in my body, I have given myself the freedom to be at my very best, perform at my best, and reap all the rewards that go along with it.*

Now, I believe you will agree that you've made some serious progress and come a long way since page one when we started this exciting journey to go over the top. If you've followed me carefully throughout these pages, embraced the ideas, taken the steps suggested, and made the commitment to continue to grow in your life, you're in the process of acquiring a full measure of that most beautiful and priceless of all our desires, and that is the legitimate hope (which is identified in chapter 10) of being your best self, which will be a major factor in finishing well.

CHAPTER FIFTEEN

Finishing well

After the cheers have died and the stadium is empty, after the headlines have been written and after you are back in the quiet of your own room and the Super Bowl ring has been placed on the dresser and all the pomp and fanfare have faded, the enduring things that are left are: The dedication to excellence; the dedication to victory; and the dedication to doing with our lives the very best we can to make the world a better place in which to live. Vince Lombardi

I want to emphasize that I am not trying to persuade you to make an effort to be the best in the world at what you do. That could be terribly frustrating and self-defeating because only one person can be the best at any given thing. The purpose of *Over the Top* is to persuade you to make the commitment to be the best you can be and convince you that if you will recognize, confess, and continue to develop what you have, what you can do is awesome. The prophet of long ago was right when he said you really are God's most amazing creation.

301

DO YOUR BEST

When you make the commitment to be the best *you* can be, you will have contentment, happiness, and peace of mind that will enable you to approach life in a more effective manner. When you reach the point where you know who you are and whose you are, you will have nothing to prove. This gives you the freedom to give life your best shot and to be at peace with yourself and with the results. You will know that you're doing the best you can with what you have and that you're following the moral, ethical absolutes we have invoked. You will be comfortable with the knowledge that you are doing all that you, God, or any man can possibly ask of you. That's not only success—it's living over the top, and it means you will finish well.

THINK ON THESE THINGS

I hope you will ponder these final thoughts carefully. I believe your first reading of the principles and procedures covered in *Over the Top* has lifted you to higher ground. From this vantage point you will get insights during the second reading that you may have missed earlier.

My experience, combined with countless letters from others, persuades me that a second, third, or even fourth reading of significant information is far more beneficial than the first reading, especially in the creation of new ideas. Consecutive readings produce connecting links and bring philosophical ideas into harmony with their practical daily application. This approach will pull out your ability and talent and help you plan your future.

YOUR MISSION STATEMENT

As you undoubtedly recall, early on I talked about the importance of having a mission statement. I identified our company's mission statement and acknowledged that it was a little grandiose. However, because one person can impact so many others, I felt that it was a mission statement that defined what we were about and that it was attainable.

I suspect you've identified your own mission by now, whether you've put it in statement form or not. I believe that you now have a good handle on real success and that you understand what it is to go over the top. I also believe that you feel the necessity of a plan of action and the importance of a mission statement of your own. Perhaps you've done everything but verbalize that mission statement and now it's just a question of committing it to paper and fine-tuning it so that it says exactly what you want it to say. To assist in finalizing the last bit, let me encourage you to go back to the end of chapter 1 and reread my definition of the top. This should and probably will give you some ideas to start jotting down for your own mission statement. Start *now* and you can almost assuredly have many of them in place by the time you finish your second reading of *Over the Top*. This is especially true if you will work the goals program we detailed in earlier chapters.

Having said that, let me also acknowledge that millions of people have difficulty articulating their feelings. If you fit in that category, don't feel frustrated—and don't quit. It took me several months and much staff brainstorming to develop our mission statement. Give it your best shot and remember that millions of people lived well *and* finished well before the term *mission statement* became part of our vocabulary. However, they did have a mission, and the mission had them.

To give you another example of the importance of having a mission and a mission statement, let's look at Providence St. Mel, a school located in Chicago's bleakest, most crime-ridden neighborhood. Their mission statement, undergirded by the strong, loving leadership of Paul Adams, is proof positive that one committed difference maker can produce hundreds, even thousands, of other difference makers.

The school was once a Catholic school, but since 1979 it's

been a private school whose mission statement and the implementation of many of the same principles we've covered throughout *Over the Top* explain why in the last fifteen years 100 percent of the graduates have been accepted at colleges all over America. As college graduates, many of them have become professors, businesspeople, bank officials, doctors, teachers, and police officers.

Today, green grass and other signs of vibrant life are growing on the campus at Providence St. Mel. There are no gangs, drugs, gambling, stealing, fighting, graffiti, weird haircuts, or radios. Mr. Adams's motto—"The price of living is giving"—combined with the school's mission statement—"We believe in the creation of inspired lives produced by the miracle of hard work . . . so we work, plan, build, and dream in that order . . . and with God's help, we will find a way or make one"—says it all. The good news from this school is that Paul Adams and many of his teachers, students, and former students are on their way to finishing well.

YOU CAN'T GO BY YOURSELF

As we conclude *Over the Top*, I want to share one more step that will enable you to live well—and finish well. TAKE SOMEONE WITH YOU. This can be a colleague, family member, employee, neighbor, small child, or anyone who wants more out of life via the learning process.

You might be a millionaire, CEO, or Ph.D., but interestingly enough, a small child, a shut-in, a person who is vision-impaired, or an adult who is illiterate could enable you to reach new heights in a unique and exciting way. Read *Over the Top* to that person on a regular basis. The age of the child or the comprehension of your listener will dictate the speed at which you read and the frequency of your pauses. Two things will happen: First, you'll be thrilled about how much the listener will learn; second, you'll be amazed at how much more clearly you understand and, consequently, apply the message of *Over the Top* to your life.

The positive feelings you get by helping a person from whom you expect nothing in return will benefit you in every phase of your life and could well be the boost that takes you *Over the Top.*

QUESTION: What could you possibly do that would produce more rewards than teaching a child or an illiterate adult the lessons of life? Jan McBarron-Liberatore, the nurse who became an M.D., finds teaching people who are illiterate how to read the most gratifying experience of her life. She's doing well and is on her way to finishing well.

DID HE FINISH WELL?

In the summer of 1993, Fred Smith, Jr., from Tyler, Texas, called his dad and suggested they take a trip to London to visit old bookstores, museums, cathedrals, and other historical landmarks in England. The trip was also designed to allow father and son an opportunity to spend exclusive time together and do some serious talking.

On arriving home, Fred Smith, Sr., related to me in glowing terms how marvelous the experience was. He was particularly intrigued that his son wanted to know many of the intimate details of his long-standing relationships with some of the truly outstanding men and women in America.

After his son had listened to the details of many of these experiences, Fred, Sr., noticed that Butch, as he calls his son, always asked, "Did he finish well?" In other words, where was this person at the end of life? Had he established lifelong friendships and finished life on a high note? That's certainly an important question, and a clear indicator of whether or not a person finished well.

LIVING WELL AND FINISHING WELL

It's always dangerous to try to pinpoint just a few qualities that are the most important, but since our major objective in life is to live well and "finish well," there are three factors that bear special consideration.

First is compassion, which has love as its foundation. The two greatest commandments given in the Bible are, "Love the Lord your God with all your heart, with all your soul, with all your mind, and with all your strength," and "Love your neighbor as yourself." All the other commandments are built on these two. Only when we have compassion built on love for others can we fully comprehend the concept of, "You can have everything in life you want if you'll just help enough other people get what they want."

The second foundation stone for finishing well is faith. Faith gives us confidence. We need to have faith in ourselves, our friends, our job or profession, our country and, most important, God.

The third foundation stone for finishing well is courage. Regardless of how much love and compassion you have, or how much confidence you have through your faith, if you do not have the courage to take action, nothing significant is going to happen. Fortunately, with love and faith, courage is the natural by-product that will enable you to look back and say, "I'm glad I did," instead of, "I wish I had."

Take these three foundation stones, and because you do genuinely care for others, your faith and confidence will give you the courage to take action. With that combination, your creativity will go into overdrive, and you will develop the necessary ideas and methods. Put all of these together and not only will you finish well, but you will live well in the process. You'll have a magnificent chance at getting many of the things that money will buy and all of the things money won't buy.

One of the best "finishing well" stories I've ever heard took place in the 1968 Olympics in Mexico City. John Stephen

Aquara from Tanzania was running in the marathon. Not long after the race started he fell and suffered serious injury to both his knee and his ankle. After receiving some medical attention, still bleeding and with both knee and ankle bandaged, he got back on the trail and started limping, hobbling, skipping, moving as best he could toward the finish line. Two hours after all the other marathon runners had finished, he painfully crossed the finish line and then took the victory lap around the stadium.

A reporter asked him why he had continued to run when he knew there was no chance that he would win a medal. John Stephen Aquara answered, "My country didn't send me seven thousand miles to enter the race. They sent me here to finish the race."

That's quite a message. It was a tremendous display of courage and commitment, as well as acceptance of responsibility. He endured much pain and agony and yet, in the process of finishing, he maintained his dignity and honor. His people had sent him, at considerable cost, to participate in a worldwide event. He finished under the most difficult circumstances imaginable, which means he finished well.

ONE FORMULA FOR FINISHING WELL

Eartha White was the granddaughter of a slave. She was successful in all areas of life and finished well. Paraphrasing John Wesley, Eartha White said, "Every day all of us should do all we can, where we are, with what we have." That's good advice, and it will help you to finish well.

The classic example of applying her advice and finishing well yourself while helping others do the same is in the twelve-step philosophy of Alcoholics Anonymous utilized by countless other programs dealing with people who have become addicted to everything from drugs and pornography to sex, television, gambling, and food. Scores of people have applied the AA philosophy that exemplifies the belief that "you can have everything in life you want if you will just help enough other people get what they want."

In order to remain sober, which is the goal of every person who participates in the AA twelve-step program, it's absolutely essential that members be available for other members and potential members who call for help when they're dealing with the craving for alcohol. Twelve-step calls, when answered, virtually guarantee the volunteer's continued sobriety. Each time a member of AA answers that call for help and sits with, talks to, works with, and encourages the other person to refrain from taking a drink, the helping member is strongly strengthened and has a much better chance to remain sober himself.

Incidentally, if a newly sober person is asked for help by a member or potential member who needs encouragement to stay away from taking just "one" drink, he is strongly encouraged to take someone with him who has worked through all twelve steps of the program. The AA philosophy that individuals share their experience, strength, and hope with other alcoholics strongly indicates that the longer a person has been sober, the more experience, strength, and hope that person will have to share with others.

At AA sessions, which take place under every imaginable circumstance, a lot of caring, talking, and listening are involved. Much sleep is lost, but countless lives and families are saved. Among the ironies is the fact that you often find a high-school dropout effectively helping an alcoholic college professor or physician. You also see the millionaire CEO desperately calling a weekly wage earner for help at a critical moment. Does it work? I'm grateful to be able to say that it does. Experience in my own family (no, not me) as well as millions of other families clearly proves its effectiveness.

The strong and wise admit they're weak and unhesitatingly call for help when they confront a situation where their sobriety is in danger. They know, often from painful experience, that they face a life-and-death proposition, because that is literally the case with the alcoholic. By following this process, one day at a time, they conquer their Goliath of a problem.

Interestingly enough, when a member of AA is called out at six o'clock in the evening and literally sits up all night to keep the acquaintance or friend from taking that one drink, something spiritual happens. Even though the all-night experience should drain all their physical energy, over and over, as one member told me the day before I wrote these words, the helper seems to have an unusual amount of energy the next day. That ties right back to the first step where the alcoholic is forced to acknowledge that he or she has a problem that is beyond human solution and needs help from a higher power— God, as they "understand" Him. This also validates the point made earlier that when you do something nice—or, in this case, critically important—your brain is flooded with seratonin and other energizers. By practicing this philosophy, many members of AA and other twelve-step programs are finishing well because they're helping others to finish well.

MAJOR POINT: All of us are frequently put in positions to help others. When we do, our own chances of finishing well increase. Keep reading and you will see how Dr. Norman Vincent Peale's life exemplified this point.

WORLD RENOWNED AND HUMBLE

M any men qualify under one word or the other but *world renowned* and *humble* are seldom used to describe one man. *Godly, gentle, modest, generous, compassionate, dignified,* and *respectable* also describe the character of the late Dr. Norman Vincent Peale. I know this to be true, first, because as I mentioned earlier, I studied and applied his philosophies to my life with great success and, second, because I had the privilege of knowing him personally.

Many times Dr. Peale and I shared the platform. I knew the public and the private man. He truly was what he appeared to be—and then some. His enormous success and popularity never turned his head or caused him to lose his sense of awe and gratitude. The people he inspired and took over the top by way of his books, cassette recordings, and publications such as *Guideposts* number in the millions.

There is more to the story. A few pages back, I said, "You can't go (over the top) by yourself." Dr. Peale had his wife, Ruth Stafford Peale, as his loving supporting companion, friend, adviser, protector, and business partner. She also was an effective, creative writer, and together they provided workable, commonsense solutions to the problems many of us encounter in our daily lives. It is safe to say that Dr. Peale finished well and that Ruth Stafford Peale is finishing well.

FROM A TIN-ROOFED SHACK TO A MANSION

Surely a dedicated woman, completely committed to preparing her children for the best future possible, is a force to be reckoned with. Gertrude Johnson Williams was such a woman, and even though she was a guest in the White House on more than one occasion, most Americans do not know her name or story. Her son, John, said of her, "By means we can only imagine she completed third grade. She was then driven—by poverty, by need, by want—into the fields and kitchens of the Mississippi Valley. But she always lived in a valley on the other side of oppression. Her body was in the fields and kitchens, but her mind was in another sphere in the first-class section." [What a powerful picture of visualization!]

"She was a short and forceful woman, not quite five feet tall, with the family bow legs, a big smile, and a will of steel. She walked straight up, her head held high, a woman of stature and quality. She had known pain and discouragement and fear. Out of all of this came a special kind of dignity—the dignity of a person who'd seen a lot and survived and wasn't afraid of the future." [What a marvelous role model!]

Gertrude Johnson Williams was a woman of commitment and a leader in her home, church, and community. Despite the poverty and prejudice that surrounded her, she lived with the firm hope and belief that something far better lay in the future for her and her children. Her formal education was limited, but her common sense, wisdom, and desire were unlimited, so she made plans for a better future.

Her plans included moving to Chicago, where opportunities for jobs and education were much better. Those plans were temporarily stalled because she did not have enough money to buy train tickets. During this delay, her son, John, finished the eighth grade. Since there were no high schools for blacks in Arkansas City, Arkansas, she made a far-reaching decision. She made John go back through the eighth grade, despite his objections, chagrin, and embarrassment. She did that because she knew he needed to be busy and learning, and she did not want him to get comfortable and accustomed to doing menial jobs.

For the next year she was a driven woman, accepting every opportunity as a domestic in homes and as a cook and scrubwoman for work crews to earn money for those precious train tickets. When John wasn't in school, he, too, contributed countless hours of labor doing whatever he could to earn money. One year later they were on their way to Chicago with high hopes, big dreams, and a temporary home with relatives until they could get on their feet.

They had some tough times, including the embarrassment of being on welfare for two years, but things did work out. Gertrude Johnson Williams finished well and indirectly took scores of others with her. Son John Johnson did all right, too. You can read all about it in his fabulous autobiography, *Succeeding Against the Odds,* but here are some highlights. He was born in a tin-roofed, shotgun house on a muddy street in Arkansas City, Arkansas, but he now lives in a high-rise on Chicago's Gold Coast. He has been listed as one of the four hundred wealthiest people in America and has been a guest of every president since Dwight D. Eisenhower. He has met with heads of state from nations all over the world, and he has made major contributions to the social, religious, business, political, and educational communities. He is the founder and owner of the largest black-owned publishing company in the world (Johnson Publishing Company), *Ebony* magazine, two cosmetics companies, and numerous other business entities. It's safe to say that like his mother, he, too, will finish well, and I speak of infinitely more than business and finance.

NINETY-ONE DIFFERENCE-MAKING WORDS

The most moving statement I've ever read concerning gratitude, finishing well, and the impact one person can have on another is in these words by Helen Keller.

> *I learned a great many new words that day. I do not remember what they all were, but I do know that mother, father, sister, teacher were among them—words that were to make the world blossom for me "like Aaron's rod, with flowers."*

> *It would have been difficult to find a happier child than I was as I lay in my bed at the close of that eventful day and lived over the joys it had brought me, and for the first time longed for a new day to come.*

She was writing about the day Anne Sullivan came into her life. In just ninety-one words, Helen Keller eloquently expressed the joy and hope Anne Sullivan gave her and that she in turn gave countless others. Because she found hope and lived her life to share it with others, Helen Keller finished exceptionally well.

YOU, TOO, CAN FINISH WELL

It's true that the "icing on the cake" is the good night's sleep after having a productive day. It's the sunset as we kiss the day good-bye and welcome the coolness of the evening. Finishing well or, in some cases, finishing at all is the crowning achievement of life. By now I hope you're persuaded that if you're the right kind of person doing the right thing with the right motives and the right game plan, you not only will live well but also will finish well.

I close this book, with the exception of the final three paragraphs and the self-talk instructions, in the same way I closed the first chapter. I do this because I believe that when you read "THE TOP" again you will perceive it differently from the way you did the first time.

This second presentation of "THE TOP" sets the stage for the last three paragraphs, which are written to give you that final assurance that you really are an over-the-top person.

THE TOP
You are at the top when . . .

1. You clearly understand that failure is an event, not a person; that yesterday ended last night, and today is *your* brand-new day.
2. You have made friends with your past, are focused on the present, and optimistic about your future.
3. You know that success (a win) doesn't make you, and failure (a loss) doesn't break you.
4. You are filled with faith, hope, and love; and live without anger, greed, guilt, envy, or thoughts of revenge.
5. You are mature enough to delay gratification and shift your focus from your *rights* to your *responsibilities.*
6. You know that failure to stand for what is morally right is the prelude to being the victim of what is criminally wrong.
7. You are secure in who you are, so you are at peace with God and in fellowship with man.
8. You have made friends of your adversaries, and have gained the love and respect of those who know you best.
9. You understand that others can give you pleasure, but genuine happiness comes when you do things *for* others.
10. You are pleasant to the grouch, courteous to the rude, and generous to the needy.

11. You love the unlovable, give hope to the hopeless, friendship to the friendless, and encouragement to the discouraged.
12. You can look back in forgiveness, forward in hope, down in compassion, and up with gratitude.
13. You know that "he who would be the greatest among you must become the servant of all."
14. You recognize, confess, develop, and use your God-given physical, mental, and spiritual abilities to the glory of God and for the benefit of mankind.
15. You stand in front of the Creator of the universe and He says to you, "Well done, thou good and faithful servant."

I hope you agree that our major objective has been accomplished, namely, that I have shared with you a philosophy that will enable you to get more of the things money will buy and all the things money won't buy. My mission has been to move some of you from survival to stability, more of you from stability to success, and all of you from success to significance. The psalmist stated my objective far more eloquently when he said, "Mark the blameless man, and observe the upright; / For the future of that man is peace" (Ps. 37:37). I'm sure you will agree that all of us want that happy, peaceful ending—we want to finish well.

As I finish my message on finishing well I wish it were possible for us to be face-to-face so I could ask you the same question the young minister in the hills of East Tennessee asked little Ben Hooper (who did not know his earthly father). That dramatic question was, "Whose boy are you?"

If we were together, I would look you right in the eye and ask you, "Whose boy are you?" or "Whose girl are you?" Then I, too, would smile with joy in my heart and say the same thing the young minister said, "Oh, I know whose child you are! Why, the family resemblance is unmistakable! You are a child of God." (You can choose to be one as we're clearly told in John 1:12.) Assuming you make that choice, which I encourage you to do, then

I could say to you, "That's quite an inheritance you've got there. Now go, and see to it that you live up to it," because if you do I will see you, and yes, I do mean YOU, not just at the top. I will see you OVER THE TOP!

NOTE: If you would like an 8″ × 12″ reproduction of "The Top" suitable for framing, send a *stamped* (to cover two ounces), self-addressed envelope OR two dollars to The Zig Ziglar Corporation, 3330 Earhart, Carrollton, Texas 75006-5026.

NOTE: Photocopy the remaining pages and keep them in your Performance Planner or briefcase for easy ready reference. Send us a self-addressed, stamped envelope, and we will mail you a folding, plastic, pocket-sized self-talk card with the qualities you need to claim to have a balanced success.

CLAIMING THE QUALITIES

Step #1: For *thirty days* first thing in the morning, last thing at night, by yourself, in front of a mirror, stand up straight, square your shoulders, look yourself in the eye, and quietly, but with conviction, say in the first-person present tense:

"I, _____, am a person of integrity with a good, positive, "Gosh!" attitude and specific goals. I have a high energy level, am enthusiastic, and take pride in my appearance and what I do. I have a sense of humor, lots of faith, wisdom, and the vision, empathy, and courage to use my talents effectively. I have character and am knowledgeable. My convictions are strong, and I have a healthy self-image, a passion for what is right, and a solid hope for the future.

"I am an honest, sincere, hardworking person. I am tough but fair and sensitive. I'm disciplined, motivated, and focused. I am a good listener and patient, but take decisive action. I am bold, authoritative, and confident, yet humble. I am an encourager, a good-finder, an excellent communicator, and I am developing winning habits. I am loving, caring, gentle, and kind, and I am a student, a teacher, and a self-starter. I am obedient, loyal, responsible, dependable, and prompt. I have a servant's heart and self-control. I am ambitious, cheerful, courteous, respectful, compassionate, and a team player. I am personable, optimistic, and organized. I am consistent, considerate, generous, and resourceful. I am intelligent, competent, persistent, and creative. I am health-conscious, balanced, and sober. I am flexible, punctual, thrifty, and diligent.

"I am a giving, forgiving, personable, friendly, unselfish, mannerly, neat, obedient good-finder who does my best at whatever I do. I am also a versatile, curious, mature, action-oriented person who responds to life's challenges, and I have a strong desire to succeed in all areas of life.

"I am a prudent, honorable person, and I run my life with integrity and discernment. I am truly grateful for the opportunity life has given me. These are the qualities of the winner I was born to be, and I am fully committed to develop these marvelous qualities with which I have been entrusted. I know that by doing this I will be happier, healthier, more prosperous, and more secure. I will also have more peace of mind, more friends, better family relationships, and more hope for a better future. Tonight I'm going to sleep wonderfully well. I will dream powerful, positive dreams. I will awaken energized and refreshed, and tomorrow's going to be magnificent!"

Repeat the process the next morning and close by saying, "These are the qualities of the winner I was born to be. Today is the first day of the rest of my life, and it is wonderful."

STEP #2: After thirty days add this step: Choose your strongest quality and the one you feel needs the most work. EXAMPLE: Strongest—honest; needs most work—organized. On a separate 3″ × 5″ card, print: "I, _____, am a completely honest person, and every day I am getting better and better organized."

Do this first thing in the morning and last thing at night for one week, then repeat the process with the second-strongest quality and the second one that needs work. Do this until you've completed the entire list. This process will change your life for the better.

NOTE: Keep this handy and use it regularly for the rest of your life!

STEP #3: Concentrate on the qualities that more specifically apply to each area of life, and focus on them while understanding that many of them will overlap and some of them apply regardless of your objective.

"To build better relationships with my family and fellowman, I, _____, am a sincere, patient, giving and forgiving, cheerful, friendly, personable, mature, flexible, understanding, courteous, respectful, compassionate, considerate, sensitivie individual with integrity and a good sense of humor. I am also neat, clean, and sober, a good listener and a good-finder. I am a loving, caring, gentle, kind, loyal, compassionate, faithful, mannerly, unselfish person who is affectionate and generous with my family and have great affection for my fellowman.

These are the qualities that enable me to build permanent winning relationships with my fellowman and loving, lifetime relationships with my family."

To succeed in whatever your field of endeavor and move into executive or leadership positions:

"I, _____, am a consistent, creative, committed, emotionally intelligent, competent, respectful, humble, mature person. I am a disciplined, dependable, creative, courteous, hardworking good listener who is also a good-finder, using wisdom, good judgment, and patience in dealing with people and problems. I have a positive attitude, high energy level, self-control, and good communications skills. I am focused and tough on myself and fair with others. I am bold, authoritative, and confident, and I take decisive action. I have complete integrity, a great sense of humor, and a thirst for knowledge. I am action oriented and run my day by the clock and my life with a vision. I keep my life in balance and am on a daily personal growth program in my physical, mental, and spiritual lives, so I will live well and finish well. I have integrity, a passion for what I do, intense faith, a servant's heart, and a strong desire to work for the benefit of my family and my associates. These are the qualities that are enabling me to become the leader I was born to be.

"To improve my health, increase my energy level, and enable me to be more so I can do more and have more, I, _____, am a highly motivated, disciplined, mature individual with great self-control who is health-conscious and committed to a lifestyle that will improve my health, increase my energy, and help ensure a high quality of life all of my life. I eat healthy, well-balanced meals in appropriate proportions, exercise sensibly on a regular basis, and get an adequate amount of sleep. I abstain from alcohol, tobacco, and drugs and protect my mind from negative or degrading input. I seek and enjoy the company of people who share my outlook and values because I know that my associates will encourage me in my commitments."

MESSAGE: Recognize your unique qualities, then specifically apply these qualities to your objectives, whether you wish to lose weight, get a better education, increase your net worth, move up the corporate ladder, or achieve another worthwhile goal.

FINALLY: Turn back to pages vii–viii and check the twelve objectives I identified for you plus the procedure that can increase your income, improve your family relationships, and make you happier and healthier. Mark ones you feel you have accomplished and start again on page 1.

GUARANTEE: If you will read *more* slowly and mark *more* carefully the things that inspire you, you will get far *more* from the second reading than you did the first reading. *And* if you read it to a child, a person who cannot see, or a functionally illiterate person, you will get *dramatically* more from *Over the Top* your second or subsequent time through.

"Failure is a word I don't accept—and neither should you. *Over the Top* by Zig Ziglar is filled with inspiration and motivation for those who want to succeed in the way that the title suggests."

—John H. Johnson
Publisher, Chairman, and CEO
Johnson Publishing Company, Inc.

"I am convinced if you apply the proven principles outlined in *Over the Top* you will soon be soaring over the top. By combining real-life stories and recent research into a practical step-by-step system, Zig's new book is a complete guide to your total growth. Zig's commitment to uncovering the scientific facts will convince you that these valid principles work. All it takes is just one good idea to make a difference. This book is filled with hundreds of great ideas."

—David G. Jensen, M.Sc.
Chief Administrative Officer
Crump Institute for Biological Imaging
UCLA School of Medicine

"Zig Ziglar is the best! His book truly turned my life around from a depressed housewife to a successful sales and motivational speaker. With this book you will learn how to make your life everything you ever wanted it to be in all areas—family, professional, spiritual."

—Pam Lontos
Lontos Sales & Motivation, Inc.

"A host of adjectives come to mind in reading this fascinating book: challenging, informative, scriptural, ethical, motivational, forthright, captivating—and on and on. Above all, here is a practical message that inspires the reader to constantly reach for the higher and better. How I wish that Zig Ziglar had written this book at the beginning of my career, but I am happy to accept it now even as I begin to wind down a bit. In fact, now I am ready to rewind—and go over the top!"

—Ted W. Engstrom
President Emeritus, World Vision

"*Over the Top* achieves a remarkable goal: dealing effectively with all aspects of a person's life—physical, mental, spiritual, personal, and financial. Based on my expertise in the physiological and medical aspects of the human condition, I enthusiastically endorse *Over the Top*."

—Leland M. Heller, M.D.

"I think *Over the Top* is one of the best overall guides on how to live a successful and happy life. Zig has a knack of summarizing diverse psychological principles into a single framework for everyday living. Zig's formulas for building positive attitudes, a healthy self-image, and solid character crystallize countless years of psychological thinking. Anyone who follows Zig's teaching will undoubtedly lead a much richer and happier life."

—John Leddo, Ph.D.
Psychologist and President
Innovative Thinkers, Inc.

"Ziglar expertly mixes the physiologic needs of the body with the desires of the ambitious mind. This book provides the means of not only achievement but greatness."

—Forest Tennant, M.D.
Research Center for Dependency
Disorders and Chronic Pain

"*Over the Top* is Ziglar at his very best. Written in his trademark, conversational style, it is meant to be read and read again—to be highlighted, dog-eared, and used. Rather than a 'success manual,' it is better described as a manual for successful living. The powerful, fifteen-point definition of 'the top' is worth the price of the book."

—Pamela Johnson, Writer

"Once again Zig Ziglar has touched the mind, heart, and soul of the reader. His unique skill in integrating spirituality with sound psychological practice has provided us with an extraordinarily clear and trustworthy map of life."

—Robert E. Wubbolding, Ed.D.
Director, Center for Reality Therapy

"Zig Ziglar's newest book *Over the Top* should be added to the required reading list in every high school and college in America! This enlightening, encouraging work presents the answers for the future success of our youth. The real keys to success and a disciplined life include physical, mental, and spiritual structure that must be the building blocks of our character. I read at least a book a week, and this latest book will be one that I will read over and over."

—Clebe McClary
Author of *Living Proof*